Transformative

EDITED BY
Linda L. Layne

TRANSFORMATIVE
MOTHERHOOD

ON GIVING AND

GETTING IN A

CONSUMER CULTURE

New York University Press

New York and London

NEW YORK UNIVERSITY PRESS
New York and London

Library of Congress Cataloging-in-Publication Data
Transformative motherhood : on giving and getting in a
consumer culture / edited by Linda L. Layne.
p.   cm.
Includes bibliographical references and index.
ISBN 0-8147-5155-5 (pbk. : alk. paper)
ISBN 0-8147-5154-7 (cloth : alk. paper)
1. Motherhood—United States. 2. Surrogate motherhood—
United States. 3. Open adoption—United States. 4. Foster
parents—United States. 5. Parents of handicapped children—
United States. 6. Fetal death—United States. 7. Infants—
United States—Death.   I. Layne, Linda L.
HQ759 .T74 1999
306.874'3'0973—dc21   99-6661
                              CIP

10 9 8 7 6 5 4 3 2 1

For Fletcher and Jasper, my children

and for Tina and Dan, for their gift

CONTENTS

Contents

ACKNOWLEDGMENTS

The essays in this volume were first presented in 1997 on the panel "The Child as Gift: Transformative Mothering in a Consumer Culture" at the American Anthropological Association's annual meeting in Washington, D.C. I owe special thanks to Danielle Wozniak, my co-organizer, for providing the impetus I needed to organize the panel and for all her help in seeing it through. Thanks also go, not only from me, but from all the contributors, to my assistant Kathie Vumbacco. Her help has been invaluable. I am grateful to Eric Zinner, Daisy Hernández, and Despina Papazoglou Gimbel from New York University Press for their editorial assistance. Working with them has been a pleasure from start to finish. I am obliged to Rayna Rapp for her always insightful and gracious commentary, and I am grateful to the other contributors for their good-natured cooperation and stimulating intellectual exchange.

FOREWORD

Rayna Rapp

The essays collected in *Transformative Motherhood: On Giving and Getting in a Consumer Culture* constitute a gift of their own: each provides thoughtful analysis of the valorization of a nonnormative, problematic, unsettling, and culturally fraught form of family making in the contemporary United States. Can the rhetoric of gifts exchanged in kinship relations transform the cultural oppositions set up between matter and spirit, love and money, social solidarity and market contract in current U.S. consumer culture? Each of the essays you are about to read puts this question to empirical test. My job is somewhat different: in order to contextualize these questions, I want to suggest that we first return to a primary and ancestral source, Marcel Mauss's book *The Gift*, mining it for theoretical inspiration.

Mauss conceived of his essay, published in 1925, as at once an ambitious positivist research program and a political polemic. Anthropologists heard the first message loudly and clearly: no fieldworker would henceforth ever again leave home without a tool kit that included attention to the total social inventory of exchanges, wherever she might land. Investigating the *hau* (or spirit) of the gift became the route toward understanding the why (or social function) of the gift.[1] This investigation assumed a central place in the development of anthropology's modernist mission. In providing an empirical methodology, *The Gift* enjoined us to study the totality of prestations. We would then be able to account for who benefits and who is burdened by the whole range of exchanges: "*The Gift* was like an injunction to record the entire credit structure of a community" (Douglas 1990:x).

Yet the second lesson of *The Gift*—its political critique—also needs recalling: as Mary Douglas so precisely puts it in her foreword to the

1990 edition of the book, *The Gift* is a highly original and creative intervention into a battle long raging across la Manche (or as the resolute British would have it, the English Channel). Mauss was aiming his canons directly against English utilitarianism. Aligning himself with Durkheim (who was, of course, aligning himself with Tocqueville, who was aligning himself with Rousseau . . . it's French elephants all the way down), Mauss objected to liberalism/utilitarianism on at least three theoretical grounds, as outlined by Douglas: The first was its diminished, impoverished concept of the person as an independent individual, rather than an embedded social being. The second was its neglect of the impact of the mode of production ("business culture") that accompanied changing social relationships. Third, utilitarianism embodied a negative concept of liberty, brought about through the marketplace, with a consequent failure to appreciate the morally positive significance of political participation.

The Gift insisted that social solidarity was achieved through continuous, spirit-laden exchange. Total prestations characterized the voyagers of the Trobriands, royal Polynesians, and potlatches of American Indians on the Northwest Coast, as well as Hindu, Greek, and Roman law; they formed the underground wellspring of archaic civilizations. Such morally imbued and totalizing exchanges were not, however, limited to bygone eras or the study of comparative civilization. They were still a necessary counterpart to the invisible hand of the market in the era of utilitarian contractual capitalism. Why else struggle for workers' pensions, except that they proved that society owed its laborers far more for their contributions than employers' wages could ever provide? It is the gift as permanent and circulating object of reciprocity, one that can never, of course, be repaid, that Mauss placed into theoretical struggle against contractual utility. And social solidarity, even in its most subaltern and embattled forms, is not to be taken lightly. The solidarity produced through prestation may be transformative and coercive; let us not be romantics. But surely, it is also constitutive. "Gifts make slaves as whips make dogs," the Inuit tell us.[2]

We are elevated when we give, demoted when we receive, enrolled in a permanent and diffuse cycle of social debt. This is surely nowhere more true than in the production and circulation of people, as Mauss's long-term debtors, from Lévi-Strauss to Gayle Rubin and beyond, have taught us. What might attention to such diffuse solidarity help us understand when we approach nonnormative or problematic family making—the production, circulation, and integration of anomalous progeny and the embattled, diffuse solidarity that attends them—in contemporary U.S. culture?

Let us begin with Gail Landsman's ethnographic puzzle: Does God give special kids to special parents? Many well-meaning friends and relations of disabled newborns seem to think so, describing the atypical child as a special gift. This rhetoric of gifting preserves their own claim on normality, as Gail Landsman tells us: the speakers are merely average in their parenting abilities and responsibilities, while the parents of disabled newborns are "special," elevated, more worthy of praise. But for many mothers of disabled infants, this bromide of distanced compassion will only get you so far: the hard work of mothering an extremely labor-intensive child who falls outside the biocultural penumbra of normality produces something valuable. But this gift is fully produced, not lightly awarded, it is achieved, not ascribed. It is earned day by day, as mothers of disabled children come to understand their offspring not so much as gifts but as givers: impaired, imperfect, damaged goods, unsatisfactory merchandise on the commodity exchange of conventional kid culture, these children bring and teach a lesson of unconditional love. Elevated from inferior product to lifelong giver, disabled children give their mothers the gift of their own self-knowledge. They are not special moms, soaked in treacle, tethered by medical adhesive tape to ventilators and physical therapists. In achieving unconditional love from and for a disabled child, such mothers reclaim their own ordinariness. "I have the perfect children," a mother of two disabled boys in Landsman's study tells us. "They're not physically perfect, but they're . . . perfectly mine." Loving a disabled child restores two gifts, the child's elevated personhood and the mother's ordinary, that is, normal, worth. Accepting such a gift, despite the judgments of commodity culture, is an achievement of endless work.

Yet as Gail Landsman tells us in conversation with Linda Layne's essay "'True Gifts from God': Motherhood, Sacrifice, and Enrichment in the Case of Pregnancy Loss," if some mothers give endlessly, others can't seem to give enough. When misfortune strikes and a pregnancy fails or a newborn dies, parents (especially mothers) speak a rich litany of the thwarted desire to give and to receive. Gifts are invented in at least six registers: the baby is a gift from God; and/or the baby is the parents' gift to God; and/or the baby's life and death bring moral uplift, surely a gift; and/or the baby brings gifts to the parents; and/or the gift of social support through bereavement obligates parents to repay their network with more solidarity; and finally, beyond bereavement, the public acknowledgment of loss is a gift of attention in a culture that conventionally valorizes happy endings, silencing anomalous perinatal outcomes and failures. If a viable product is the only thing rewarded in commodity-driven cultures, then productlessness provides nothing to take home, and therefore nothing to talk about. Yet some women (and occasionally men) experiencing pregnancy or perinatal loss *do* speak, and they hope for the gift of being heard.

Pregnancy loss support groups are a mechanism for constructing a stage on which the gift of a lost child and its reciprocal acknowledgment can be performed. As I read Linda Layne's ongoing scholarship on pregnancy loss,[3] I would add that these pregnancy loss support groups also deserve analysis as a specific, historically located form of social solidarity. As American as apple pie, the voluntary support groups (especially in health-focused organizations) teach lessons in self-help that often oppose market-based evaluations of failed production and their producers. Whether it be the support for pregnancy loss, Alcoholics Anonymous, or genetic disorders support groups,[4] we are becoming a nation of twentieth-century survivors. Such groups both undercut and sustain notions of individual achievement, articulating a doubled discourse that both accepts difference and misfortune and normalizes it. Surviving abnormality, misfortune, unhappy endings makes one a valuable individual. This lesson of dialectical worth is the gift support groups bring to their members.

Such groups may speak the truth of solidarity to the individualizing power of marketplace evaluation. But they also depend on that same marketplace for sustenance: how would they have developed without the army of twentieth-century social workers, social psychology's stage theories of problem resolution, newsletters, conventions, and, increasingly, cyberspace? Socially speaking, opposition to the judgment of marketplace culture is complicated business, often dependent on the very discourses and practices it arises to subvert.

This is surely true of the surrogate mothers among whom Heléna Ragoné is working. Surrogacy is a relatively recent product of market-place culture (despite journalists' conventional opening paragraphs about biblical surrogacy and the gift of a child), and the cultural and legal debates surrounding surrogacy index substantial anxiety. As the bits and pieces of life forms, including, of course, human life forms, become commoditized, what are "we" to make of our moral trajectory? Of course, we also need to interrogate the "we": the discourse on infertility or organ donation or fetal imaging looks substantially different when viewed from non-U.S. locations and sometimes different class, religious, or racial/ethnic positions within the United States, as anthropologists have increasingly reported. Brought together through market contract, surrogate mothers and their donor/adopting families spontaneously utter the language of gift to describe the redemption of their promissory notes. Surrogate mothers "give the gift of life," which is, of course, priceless. At least, the payment they receive for hypermaternity is too nugatory to mention. And it is interesting that when California legislators considered banning surrogacy, they approved, in principle, free or voluntary maternal contracts while preserving "customary fees" for doctors, lawyers, and other professional agents involved in these transfers of assisted reproduction. Only maternal labor, it seems, is priceless. In speaking this language of "gifts," surrogate contractors accomplish at least two things: they elevate the status of givers (who are usually drawn from socioeconomic circumstances far less wealthy than the couples for whom they are having babies); and they insist that it is the diffuse solidarity of kinship, rather than the cold cash of the marketplace, that binds surrogate and contracting couple together. The surrogate's gift is at once a resistance to the utilitarianism of the market and a masking of it. The imbrication of market and nonmarket exchanges is continuous.

The same can be said of the gifting in the open adoption practices to which Judith Modell's essay is addressed. As guides to the new map of the political economy of U.S. adoption, open adopters—on both sides of the contract—benefit from the language of the gift. United in diffuse solidarity against the "stranger" model of agency-managed anonymous adoption, both parties now agree: open adoption is not only a gift of a child, but also a gift to the child, whose best interests it is alleged to serve. Instead of giving up a child (in both senses of the term: relinquishing, and accepting defeat and hence, moral inferiority), the birth mother in open adoption now gives. Her status is elevated, indeed, if she was once "dysfunctional" or a "bad mother" because she gave up a baby, now she is reclassified as morally superior, for she gives the baby with love. The originality of Judith Modell's argument lies in her insistence that this change is actually not so much about the gift of the baby, but rather about the gift of newly forged, potentially enduring solidarity among the concerned adults, who speak openly of and sometimes to one another; they may intend to stay in contact throughout their lives. Behind their own backs, they have enacted a contract that is more than they have bargained for: they have broken the genealogical grid of fictive kinship, replacing it with open questions: can a child have two mothers? Children raised by lesbian couples frequently say "yes." Are we here on the terrain of what some have called "post-Schneiderian" kinship studies?[5] Or might we be located on the terrain so clearly mapped by that eminent pre-post anthropologist Esther Goody, who long ago suggested the multiple and flexible strands that adoption may entail, when viewed cross-culturally and transhistorically (Goody 1970)? Can the wholly symbolic nature of the genealogical grid be deconstructed through emergent popular practices that unmask both sides of David Schneider's equation, that is, substance and contract; diffuse solidarity and the rule of law? But let us not forget that this particular popular process uses the language of the gift to streamline more efficient market practices facilitating supply and demand. Open adopters are kinship entrepreneurs, intent on breaking through archaic, unprofitable monopolies, committed to a newly public, morally superior gift economy that challenges the stranglehold of adoption agencies through flexible investment. Such strategies can be tracked in the expenses incurred in running "personal" column advertisements, the cascade of mailings and emailings, the newly installed phone lines, answering machines, lawyers' fees, coverage of maternity expenses and travel to pick up the gifted baby that accompany this opening of a new market.

But who holds the monopoly on foster children, as opposed to the open market now emerging for adoptees? The state both represents and substitutes for the market, placing children temporarily and paying for their upkeep. By definition in the United States, fostered children are children in crisis, their bonds of sociality already shattered. Yet foster mothers see themselves as healers, repairing society's social fabric rent asunder, as Danielle Wozniak tells us in her moving essay on gifts and burdens in the context of foster mothering. Often, especially in African American communities, foster mothers consider themselves as gifted, that is, they have the gift of knowing how to foster. And they often come from fostering lineages: women in their families have fostered through the generations, and today's foster mothers have served as apprentices to these gifted fosterers. Above all, fosterers give the gift of healing, trying to repair the socially induced damage wreaked upon very vulnerable children. Yet the intense solidarity created by these mothers and other parental figures with and for these children is often held in bureaucratic contempt. As one mother says of a social worker's labeling in Wozniak's essay, "I'm not a substitute anything. I'm the real thing." Another, shopping for glasses for a foster child who is offered the "state rate" reimbursable frames, says, "We don't have 'state' children. We have children." Full stop. Might the biggest gift of all be teaching resistance to the diminished personhood that welfare dependency is construed to designate in contemporary U.S. culture?

Where else might the multidirectional flows of diffuse, intergenerational solidarity be mapped in gift language? Who else might be using gifting discourse to elevate the value of their child-centered exchanges, and in that process, resist utilitarianism through state and market value claims? Many sites for attentive investigation come to mind: transnational adoption, which yields exoticized, often racially marked gifts from America's debtor nations to those U.S. families whose childlessness they can repay; teen mothers "having a baby for" their boyfriends, whose preposition inverts their status from inferiority to superiority; lesbian and gay same-sex couples parenting against the legal and social odds all come to mind as instances where the gift economy is imbricated with state and market, simultaneously resistant to and reproductive of its productivist biases. Analyses at these and other sites would surely yield valuable intellectual gifts. The essays collected here are provocative in the best sense of the word: they provoke us as readers, writers, and practitioners to imagine solidarity with the anomalous parents and children on whose gifting they report, and to uncover other social relations in which such gifts are also being imagined, procured, and reciprocated. And that, surely, is a gift worth receiving and for which we are all indebted.

Notes

1. Marshall Sahlins should be credited with this formulation, which turned a classic Maori example into an American pun. I first heard it in his classroom lectures at the University of Michigan in the early 1970s.

2. Once again, I learned this example in Marshall Sahlins's graduate lectures on Mauss.

3. See, e.g., Layne 1990, 1992, 1997, and forthcoming.

4. See, e.g., Rapp, Heath, Taussig 2000; Heath 1998; Taussig, Heath, Rapp 1999.

5. I thank a generation of New School graduate students for this nomenclature, and their insistence on the novelty and potential transformations that the present moment in kinship studies portends. See also Franklin and MacKinnon 2000.

References Cited

Douglas, Mary
1990   Foreword. The Gift by M. Mauss. Pp. vii-xviii. New York: Norton.

Franklin, Sarah, and Susan MacKinnon, eds.
2000   Relative Matters: The Anthropology of the New Kinship. Berkeley: University of California Press.

Goody, Esther
1970   Forms of Pro-Parenthood: The Sharing and Substitution of Parental Roles. *In* Kinship. J. Goody, ed. Pp. 331–45. Harmondsworth, U.K.: Penguin.

Heath, Deborah
1998   Locating Genetic Knowledge: Picturing Marfan Syndrome and Its Traveling Constituencies. Science, Technology, and Human Values 23(1):71–97.

Layne, Linda L.

1990   Motherhood Lost: Cultural Dimensions of Miscarriage and Stillbirth in America. Women and Health 16(3):75–104.

1992   Of Fetuses and Angels: Fragmentation and Integration in Narratives of Pregnancy Loss. Knowledge and Society. Hess and Layne, eds. 9:29–58.

1997   Breaking the Silence: An Agenda for a Feminist Discourse of Pregnancy Loss. Feminist Studies 23(2):289–316.

forthcoming   Motherhood Lost: The Cultural Construction of Pregnancy Loss in the United States. New York: Routledge.

Rapp, Rayna, Deborah Heath, Karen Sue Taussig

2000   Genealogical Dis-ease: Where Hereditary Abnormality, Biomedical Explanation, and Family Responsibility Meet. *In* Relative Matters: The Anthropology of the New Kinship. Sarah Franklin and Susan MacKinnon, eds. Berkeley: University of California Press.

Taussig, Karen Sue, Deborah Heath, Rayna Rapp

1999   Soft Eugenics: Discourses of Perfectibility in Late 20th Century America. Anthropology in the Age of Genetics. Paper presented at Terresopolis, Brazil: Wenner-Gren Foundation.

Transformative Motherhood

The Child as Gift

New Directions in the Study of Euro-American Gift Exchange

Linda L. Layne

Consumer culture sets standards and norms that define an ideal child. The often brutal realities of life create children and childbearing and rearing circumstances outside the ideal. The essays in this volume richly convey the experience of women in the United States whose reproductive lives do not correspond to these cultural standards. In some cases, such as women who choose to become surrogate or foster mothers, this is voluntary; in other cases, such as women who give birth to children with disabilities or those who experience pregnancy loss, the experience is entirely involuntary. In each case we see the various ways women appropriate the rhetoric of the gift to creatively meet the challenges posed by their nonnormative mothering experiences. In the process, they redefine conventional understandings of the institution of motherhood, of the mother/child relationship, and of children as products of biologically or legally determined kinship. At the same time they use "the gift" to articulate, with various degrees of explicitness, a critique of consumer culture.[1]

A staple of anthropological theory, "the gift" is enjoying renewed anthropological interest. (See, for example, the National Humanities Center conference on "the gift and its transformations" held in 1990 and the School of American Research seminar on a related topic in 1996). At the same time, "philosophers, literary critics, and literary theorists [are] with increasing frequency joining anthropologists . . .

in their attempt to theorize gift exchange" (Schrift 1997:1).[2] This volume contributes to these current interdisciplinary discussions of "the gift" and at the same time represents a new direction in anthropological studies of gifts and giving.

Notwithstanding the notable exception of Lévi-Strauss's depiction of women given in marriage as "the most precious possession" and therefore "the supreme gift" (1969:62, 65),[3] historically, anthropological theories of the gift focused on the exchange of goods and services. The armshells and necklaces of the kula (Malinowski [1922]; Mauss [1925]), the coppers of the Kwakiutl potlatch (Mauss [1925]), the Melanesian yams and pigs, banana leaf bundles and fiber skirts, as well as the labor of preparing gardens and tending corpses (Strathern 1972; Weiner 1976), are the stuff on which classical anthropological theories of gift exchange, and their early feminist revisions, were built.

As anthropologists have turned their attention to gift exchange in industrialized societies (Carrier 1991, 1997), the focus has been on consumer goods.[4] To give just a few examples, the collection *Unwrapping Christmas* (Miller 1993) describes the rituals of Christmas giving in the United States, the United Kingdom, Japan, and Trinidad; Foster and Foster (1994) have explored elementary schoolboys "consumption work with Marvel Super Heroes Trading Cards"; and Miller (1998) describes the ways North Londoners select consumer goods for their families as acts of love. This current anthropological interest in consumption is also evident in several recent North American studies of reproduction. After a decade of fruitful research on the influence of production metaphors on the experience of reproduction in the United States (e.g., Katz Rothman 1982, 1989; Martin 1987, Davis-Floyd 1992), a number of feminist scholars have begun to investigate the substantive role consumer goods play in contemporary reproductive practices (Anagnost 1997; Layne in press, 1999; Taylor in press, 1998, 1992; Wozniak 1998).[5]

In comparison with goods, much less attention has been given to other types of gifts. It is precisely these other, non–consumer good gifts (e.g., people, services, and transcendental gifts) that form the focus of this volume. The most important of these is the child as gift. As these essays amply illustrate, in contemporary North American culture, children are commonly understood to be "a gift." There are multiple versions of this notion. Babies are frequently described as gifts from God to their parents or to the world. In addition, mothers (and sometimes fathers) often think of their child as a gift from themselves to the world, or as in the case of adoption or surrogacy, to other parents. In the case of pregnancy loss, fosterage, or children with disabilities, the child is also sometimes thought of as giving "the gift of self" to the parents.

As with blood donation (Titmuss 1972) and organ transplantation (Fox and Swazey 1974, 1992; Joralemon 1995; Sharp 1995), in the case of surrogacy (Ragoné, this volume; Narayan 1995), adoption (Modell, this volume), and fosterage (Wozniak, this volume), the rhetoric of the gift marks a discomfort with the commodification of life. Joralemon likens the rhetoric of the gift to the drugs that suppress the biological rejection of transplanted organs. He argues that "gift ideology" serves to inhibit "cultural rejection of transplantation and its view of the body" (1995:335). In the context of surrogacy, adoption, and state-sponsored fostering, the ideology of the gift may serve a similar role, that is, in suppressing the rejection of reproductive arrangements that violate the Euro-American ideological separation of the reproductive and domestic sphere from that of commodity exchange.[6] But as the essays on pregnancy loss and children with disabilities show, the notion of the "child as gift" is not restricted to cases where payment is made in exchange for the child or childbearing/rearing services. While the notion of the child as gift is one that can be used to describe any child, the value-ladenness of the "gift" clearly helps parents of fostered, disabled, or dead children deal with the fact that their children do not meet the standards set by consumer culture.

The essays also illustrate how the "gift" inflects the meanings of goods and services, as well as transcendental benefits like "spiritual" or "personal growth." Dead and foster children do not enjoy the same social recognition as other children, and the purchase of presents for these children helps foster and bereaved parents assert the "realness of their relatedness" in the face of social contestation. Similarly, families that adopt children who have been in foster care may try to erase this nonnormative moment from their children's lives through the replacement of goods from that era with the gift of new (not previously owned) consumer goods (Wozniak 1998).

The giving of motherly labor is also an issue in many of these essays. Foster children and those born with disabilities require even more "giving" from their parents than other children. Wozniak describes how foster mothers understand themselves to be "gifted" with the mothering skills required to undertake the healing of the damaged children who enter their homes and of the families and communities from which they come.[7] As Landsman tells us, the exceptional giving required of mothers of children with disabilities is socially acknowledged, but in this case, as in the case of fostering, mothers are quick to point out how much the children give in return. But not all motherly labor apparently qualifies for the edifying rubric of "gifting." We see in the essay by Ragoné that when surrogate mothers provide the ova as well as their womb, their role in producing a new child is often described by themselves and the commissioning couple in the language of the gift, but when surrogates "simply" provide the "service" or "labor" of gestating a fetus and birthing a baby to which they are not biologically related, the language of the gift is withheld.

Several of the essays (especially Layne and Landsman) highlight the centrality of transcendental gifts in the rhetoric of mothering.[8] Members of pregnancy loss support groups describe a host of transcendental gifts they understand as coming either from their dead children or from the experience of their death, including greater faith in God, an improved set of priorities, greater appreciation for what they have, and so forth. Landsman discusses how mothers of children with disabilities emplot themselves as the recipients of gifts from their children such as "enlightenment" and "knowledge of unconditional love."

So why is it that gifts other than consumer goods (whether it be children, services like mothering, or intangibles like "love" and "enlightenment") have been undertheorized in studies of Euro-American gift exchange?[9] One source of explanation may be found in the overlapping meanings in English of "gift" and "present." Carrier notes that in English the word "gift" "calls up images of presents, usually nonutilitarian *objects*, given consciously and with some degree of ceremony"; this, he suggests, is why labor, "which can be a gift (just as it can be a commodity)," is not normally considered a "present" (Carrier 1991:122; emphasis added). A related point can be found in Strathern's use of Melanesian ethnography to interrogate the anthropological concept of gift. She notes that the anthropological notion of "gift" has "seemed readily applicable to self-evident and concrete 'gifts' [because] the term trailed a reassuring visualism. One could 'see' gift exchange because one could see the gifts, the things that people exchanged with one another" (1997:293). Although children can be readily seen, domestic labor has been notoriously invisible, and "love," "maturity," and "inner strength" lack the helpful, self-evidentiary concreteness and unmediated visualization of consumer goods.

I would argue that another reason for this neglect is the clear association of these types of gifts with Christianity. Although since Mauss, theories of gift-giving in tribal societies have generally acknowledged that gift items possess a spirit (Mauss 1969), gift-giving and consumption theories relating to capitalist societies have rarely taken into account the "spiritual" or "religious" dimensions of "giving" in Euro-American culture.[10] As the religious studies scholar Leigh Schmidt (1997:69) notes, "For all of the multidisciplinary discussion of gift economies, historians of American religion have rarely . . . concern[ed] themselves with gifts, their complex moral and political economy, their polysemous rituals and symbols."[11] Yet, as we come to the close of what Haraway (1997) refers to as "the Second Christian Millenium," the meaning of "the gift" is still very much colored by Christian understandings of this notion.[12]

"Gift" is an important concept in the New Testament.[13] The *Concordance to the Revised Standard Version of the Bible* lists twenty-one entries for the New Testament, as compared with only five entries for the Old Testament.[14] In comparison with the Old Testament, where "gift" refers primarily to material gifts or services (the topics historically covered in anthropological analyses of giving), the New Testament Scriptures refer to gifts like "eternal life," "God's grace," "the gift of the Holy Spirit" and "Christ Jesus," notions more akin to "the child as gift" and "unconditional love." In addition, these Scriptures refer to a set of special abilities as "spiritual gifts," including the gifts of speaking in tongues, healing, and prophesying.[15] It is this sense of the term by which people like the foster mothers described by Wozniak can be understood to be "gifted" with special talents.

These Scriptures contain a number of themes that bear on the moral economy of gift giving in the contemporary Euro-American context. One such theme is the structural opposition of gifts and commodities; the spiritual and the material. Several of the New Testament Scriptures contrast God's gifts with commodities. For example, the Book of Acts recounts the story of Simon, the magician, who tried to pay the apostles to teach him the trick of the laying on of hands. Peter rebuked him, "Your silver perish with you, because you thought you could obtain the gift of God with money!" (Acts 8:20). Another example is found in an oft-quoted excerpt from Romans, where the secular notion of "wages" is structurally opposed to that of "gift"— "the wages of sin is death, but the free gift of God is Eternal life in Christ Jesus our Lord" (Romans 6:23).[16] This type of comparison is echoed in the narratives of bereaved mothers who contrast the transitory nature and lesser value of the consumer goods they would have been buying for their child had it lived (for Christmas or Chanukah) with "love," which is "eternal," or the "best gift" of being with God in heaven (Layne 1999).

A related theme is the way the Christian "gift" offers an important resource for those whose social status is inferior. As these essays illustrate, this is as true for those whose status is diminished because of the poor "quality" of their children or because they got or had their children in a nonnormative way as it is for "the poor," "the persecuted," "the reviled," or "the meek" who will "inherit the earth."[17]

Another theme concerns the moral obligation to use God-given talents, like the gift of mothering shared by the foster mothers described by Wozniak. Using such gifts for the benefit of others is clearly defined as a Christian act. For example, in Peter's first letter to "the exiles of the Dispersion" he urges Christians to share their gifts with others, "as each has received a gift employ it for one another, as good stewards of God's varied grace" (1 Peter 4:10).[18]

However important the notion of the gift may have been for early Christians, the theme became richly developed during the middle of the nineteenth century, decades during which consumer goods were proliferating and Romantic authors were formulating critiques and apologies for the expanding gift economy. Today, "the gift as a trope is pervasive . . . [in] the theologies, liturgies, pieties, and practices" (Schmidt 1997:70) of American Christians.[19]

To use an example with which I happen to be familiar, one finds the notion of "gift" and the related notions of "giving," "sharing," and "offering" running through every service of the First United Presbyterian Church in Troy, New York. These ideologically charged terms are inscribed weekly in the printed bulletin members use as a guide through the service (e.g., the time for "*Sharing* of Joys and Concerns," "The *Sharing* of Faith with Children and Youth," "The *Offering* of our *Gifts and Ourselves*"; emphasis added). In addition to these regular instantiations, the concepts are worked into particular services in a variety of ways. Perhaps the most dramatic example can be found in the Thanksgiving service which in 1998 began with a call to "*give* thanks to God," and was followed by a prayer based on the words of Chief Seattle, which ended with the plea to "accept our thanks for your *gift of life*." The sermon was entitled "All *Good Gifts* around Us," the title of which was taken from the chorus of the assigned hymn, written by Matthias Claudias (1740–1815), which thanks "our provider, for all things bright and good" and concludes that we, in return, have no "*gifts*" to offer except "our thankful hearts." The "prayer of dedication" given when the "*offering*" was collected read, "Loving God, with these *gifts* we bring together the full circle of life—the material and the spiritual, worship and work. Help us to use all your *gifts* wisely so that they may bring healing and wholeness to our broken world" (First United, November 22, 1998).

The theme of gifts and giving was less developed during their Christmas service, but there one finds multiple, explicit references to the notion of the child as a gift. In 1998 the litany for Christmas Eve began, "Loving God, on this holy night we thank you for the gift of the Christ child and thank you for the gift of children everywhere" and goes on to list all the things about children we have to be grateful for, like their "enthusiasms, energy, trust." The prayer concludes, "You have given us the gift of Christmas . . . may we, your children, give you the gift of ourselves" (First United, December 24, 1998).

Such Christian inflections of the gift are not restricted to church settings but are diffuse in popular culture. Take, for instance, the promotional material provided with the best-selling Backstreet Boys' CD, which includes a lengthy acknowledgements section, "Thanks from the Boys." Each of the five performing artists begins by thanking God for "the gift" of his "talent," and for his "family" and "friends." One also thanks God for "the gift of life," "the gift of song," and "the gift of a dream."[20]

Given its pervasiveness in contemporary culture, how can we account for the scholarly neglect of the Christian dimensions of "giving" in societies like the United States and the United Kingdom that have a dominant Christian heritage? This neglect is clearly part of a broader trend in anthropology. According to Huber, until "the 1970s the anthropological literature on Christianity was quite thin" (Huber 1997:96). Although since that time "a wider range of anthropological work on Christianity has appeared," "the evangelical spread" of Christianity has continued to provide "the dominant focus for anthropological reflection" (Huber 1997:96).[21] With the important exception of Miller's recent book *A Theory of Shopping* (1998), which interprets shopping as a devotional rite, a form of sacrifice, I know of no other anthropological study of Western consumption that takes into account the way religious cosmology influences consumption ideologies and practices; the spheres of economy and religion being assumed to be completely distinct and even antithetical. In her book on religion and popular culture in America, McDannell suggests that the reason "the material dimension of American religious life [has] not [been] taken seriously" is that the dichotomies between "the sacred and the profane, spirit and matter, piety and commerce" have constrained "our ability to understand how religion works in the real world" (1995:4). These same dichotomies have obscured the religious dimensions of contemporary gift exchange.

The same blind spot is found in recent studies of reproduction.[22] In the extensive body of anthropological research on reproduction in Britain and North America published in the last twenty years, the greatest emphasis has been on how biomedical models of reproduction and new reproductive technologies affect the experience of women. Paradoxically, in their focus on the "medicalization of birth," anthropologists have contributed to the dominance of the medical model and have been blinded to other interpretative systems. For example, Strathern (1997) and Ragoné (1994) discuss the "gift of life" and "the ultimate gift" in the rhetoric of surrogacy, and Strathern (1997) discusses "charitable altruism" in the context of egg, sperm, blood, and organ donations, without acknowledging the roots of these concepts in Christianity or exploring the extent to which a Christian cosmology may still inform the meanings of these practices for those who engage in them. Similarly, Franklin's (1997) fascinating discussion of the "miracle babies" resulting from the "medical miracle" of in vitro fertilization does not consider the ways Christianity may also inform the meaning of these "miracles" for parents, medical staff, and newspaper reporters.[23] As I have argued elsewhere (Layne 1992), despite the tendency to assume a rigid separation of science from religion and to study these discursive systems in isolation, ethnographic analysis reveals that laypeople may not experience their lives in this fragmented way, and, through personal narratives, often actively weave together these domains.

The Essays

Although the essays in this volume can be read individually, there is a logic to the order in which they appear. Rayna Rapp's foreword begins, appropriately enough, with a revisit to Marcel Mauss's book *The Gift*. Drawing on Douglas's foreword to the new edition of *The Gift*, she situates *Transformative Motherhood* in terms of Mauss's political polemic against English utilitarianism. Rapp focuses on the political significance of gift giving's potential for diffuse social solidarity as critique and counterweight to liberal individualism. She notes, however, that the cases explored in this volume illustrate how the rhetoric of the gift is strategically used as an alternative to the ideology of market exchanges but is, at the same time, imbricated in it.

The essays by Modell and Ragoné look at surrogacy and adoption. In both cases, it is the child-getting method that is nonnormative; the child is presumed normal.[24] "In a culture in which parenthood is created by birth," adoption creates parenthood "by law" (Modell 1994:2). "A made relationship" instead of a "natural" one, American adoption relies on law to create the "fiction" of kinship; the child is treated "as-if-begotten," the parent "as-if-genealogical" (Modell 1994:2). The extent to which our adoption laws and practices "mirror" biology indicates the ongoing importance of this cultural interpretation of kinship.

In surrogacy, the need for "making" an "as-if-begotten" relationship is both greater and less than in the case of adoption. In traditional surrogacy, the child is biologically related to the father but not to the mother, who typically adopts it once the surrogate mother has relinquished it. This creates a structural imbalance in the family. In her book *Surrogate Motherhood: Conception in the Heart*, Ragoné described how "all the participants" "de-emphasized, even devalued" blood relatedness "in order to make surrogacy [more] consistent with American cultural values about appropriate relations between wives and husbands" (Ragoné 1994:136). With in vitro fertilization, used in gestational surrogacy, there are a number of possible combinations for biological relatedness—the child may be biologically related to both parents, to the mother only, to the father only, or to neither. All that is certain is that it will not be biologically related to the woman who bears it. Ragoné's comparative study of these two types of surrogacy starkly reveals the primacy of the blood tie in North American kinship.

These essays are followed by Wozniak's study of foster mothering. Her essay is a pivot point between the first two essays and the two that follow. Wozniak's work illustrates the problems foster mothers have in getting their motherhood to be seen as legitimate parenting. As with surrogacy, adoption, pregnancy loss, and the parenting of children with disabilities, in fosterage who counts as a "real" mother is at issue. Although Wozniak's focus is on the mothers and not the children, she discusses how the labels of "foster child" or "state child" connote "an inferiority" and how these children can be tainted by their association with families that failed to meet "patriarchal nuclear family" ideals (this volume). At the same time, her gripping account (1998) reveals the "special needs" of many of the children placed in such homes. "Children entering foster care seldom do so without having experienced serious and complicated emotional and/or physical trauma" (this volume).[25]

Whereas in the first three cases women's motherhood is challenged primarily because of the nonstandard route by which they have formed their families, in the last two cases it is the way the child differs from the norm that challenges mothers' status. Despite the expectation that one will end up with a perfect baby if "one follows the latest expert advice" (Landsman, this volume), some babies die, some are born disabled. Women who give birth to children with disabilities and women whose babies die before or shortly after birth find that although society had encouraged them to think of the baby they were carrying as a precious person, a valued subject, when the baby they produce doesn't measure up to expectations, the personhood previously attributed to the "baby" is revoked or at least diminished, and by extension, so too is the status of the woman qua mother.[26]

In all five essays, we see how women whose experience of mothering is at odds with the normative standard are exposed to the judgment of others. Given that these women are themselves members of society, it is not surprising that they may have internalized these norms regarding motherhood and may judge themselves (and sometimes their children) against those standards as well. Because of how closely motherhood and womanhood are still tied in our culture, these judgments concern womanhood as well as motherhood; they present an assault on the self. The virtue of these women is questioned in brutal ways: What kind of woman would rent her womb, would allow herself to be impregnated with a stranger's sperm and then give her baby away after growing it for nine months? What kind of woman would get pregnant out of wedlock, would give her baby to strangers? What kind of woman can't produce a child of her own and must buy a baby or rely on the charity of others to give her a baby to raise? What kind of woman would mother other people's children for pay, would accept into their homes to mingle with their "real" children severely troubled children, the dregs of society? What kind of woman produces a defective or deformed child? What kind of woman kills her own child while in the womb or mis/carries this most precious cargo? What kind of woman produces a baby that is so flawed that people tell her it was a blessing that it died, or nature's way of protecting itself from such aberrations?

The answers to these question are no less unkind. Such a woman must be "in it for the money" or an "unwitting, naively altruistic victim of the patriarchy" (Ragoné 1994:52). In the case of birth mothers, she is presumed to be "irresponsible, vulnerable, young, [and] mistaken," in need of "the chance to redeem her error and start over" (Modell, this volume). Adoptive mothers do not always fair better: although in comparison with birth mothers, adoptive mothers are generally deemed more "fit," infertile women who adopt are often characterized as "desperate" and "obsessed" (Sandelowski 1993).[27] Foster mothers are considered neither "real mothers" nor "professionals" by the state. As "non-" or "fake mothers," they are routinely treated as if they do not have "legitimate rights to knowledge, information, and expression based on a kinship relationship with their foster children" (Wozniak, this volume). Mothers of children with disabilities are often assumed to be "bad mothers," "epitomized by the unwed teenage drug-addicted girl who irresponsibly brings crack babies into the world, or who brings disability into her life through child abuse" (Landsman, this volume).[28] Women whose babies die during pregnancy sometimes describe feeling like "a baby killer," "a human coffin," or "a living tomb" (Layne 1992), and some women whose babies die at or shortly after birth describe feeling like "a freak" (Layne 1997).[29]

In the face of these debilitating judgments, the rhetoric of the gift provides a powerful defense. Just as "the concept of gift restores virtue to adoption" (Modell, this volume), so it does for surrogacy, fostering, pregnancy loss, and children with disabilities. The opposition in North American culture between the ideologies of gifts and commodities provides an effective resource for valorizing nonnormative family-making practices and experience. Foster, birth, adoptive, and surrogate mothers, mothers of infants with disabilities, and those who have suffered a pregnancy loss use idioms of the gift to construct (or reconstruct) themselves as exemplary women and mothers in and against a context of capitalist consumerism.

The rhetoric of the gift facilitates a number of transformations in the way these women understand and explain their experiences. Three aspects of gifts and gift giving are crucial in this regard: (1) their efficacy in forging and maintaining social relationships, (2) the gendered status implications of giving and receiving, and (3) the ideological opposition between commodities and gifts, and the related oppositions between things and persons, the material and the spiritual.

Although in the surrogate arrangements studied by Ragoné, participants do not intend to continue the relationship after the birth, surrogates assume that in giving "the ultimate gift" of a child, "they are creating a state of enduring solidarity between themselves and their couples." As in the case of traditional adoption, the birth mother tends to be in a socially and economically subordinate position to the couple to whom she gives the child, and the rhetoric of the gift serves "as a leveling device" for the class differences between couples and surrogates (1994:91). Since "all gift giving creates a degree of gratitude," and given the fact that "the gift of life" cannot be reciprocated, "by acknowledging that the surrogate child is a gift, the couple accepts a permanent state of indebtedness to their surrogate." Ragoné also interprets the rhetoric of the gift as an expression of "resistance to the conflation of the symbolic value of family with work."

Modell shows how, in contrast to traditional closed adoptions where the transfer took place "between strangers" and once the transfer was complete there was no future interaction (aspects more characteristic of commodity relations than those of gift exchange), the rhetoric of the gift as employed by proponents of open adoption suggests "an enduring solidarity" among the members of the adoption triad (birth mother, adoptive parents, child). Seeing adoption as a "gift-based transaction" shifts the focus from "kinship" (based on something "mystical, fated, or inherent" in any of the participants) to ties forged through the chosen, purposeful "flow of social relations" (this volume). In addition, the rhetoric of the gift in open adoption emphasizes "respect, reciprocation, gratitude, and appreciation," and in so doing alters the hierarchical dimension in American adoption practice in which the adoptive parents have been viewed as socially superior to the birth mother (Modell, this volume). Finally, "gift" addresses the "fear of commodifying human life" by "humanizing the transfer" and offers a counterweight to the bureaucratic intervention of the state (this volume).

Wozniak has shown how foster mothers use their "gifts" of love and caring to establish three types of relationships. Through "the gift of motherhood" they cement "bonds of connectedness" with their new children. Once given, the gift of mothering cannot be revoked. Even after a child has died, or been returned to her/his family of origin, or been moved to another home, the "kinship" established through their giving endures. In addition to the primary relationship established in this way between foster mother and child, Wozniak describes how some foster mothers engage in "social repair" by extending their emotional gift giving to the children's mother or grandmothers. Foster mothers also understood their gift of mothering to create social bonds across multiple generations of caregivers: they inherited their gifts from their own mothers and grandmothers, and pass on their gifts to their children, who may one day do the same.

Unlike the case of adoption or surrogacy, where the gift exchange is understood to take place between people situated differently in the social hierarchy, and despite the clear power differences between parents and children, according to Wozniak, foster mothers conceived the gift-giving relationship with their children as "always bidirectional exchanges between two equally valuable and valued parties." Not only are the participants in the relationship cast as equals, but that which is exchanged is thought of as equivalent. "Both got something and gave something of equal value . . . through their presence, children were gifts to women; in return women gave mothering gifts to children" (Wozniak, this volume). Whereas the exchange between mother and child is understood as egalitarian, the rhetoric of the gift helped foster mothers assert their virtue in the face of "degrading social relations with the state" (Wozniak, this volume). As with surrogacy, fostering challenges the gender ideologies that bifurcate mothering and wage labor. Whereas surrogates try to resist the conflation of the two by downplaying the importance of payment, foster mothers embrace the conflation, arguing that mothering can be both socially valuable and an economic activity (Wozniak, this volume).

In the final two essays, where it is the qualities of the child that are nonnormative rather than the way the child entered the family, the emphasis on the social relationship-building qualities of the gift are not as salient. Here, it is the ideologically gendered social and moral status of givers and receivers that is of particular importance.[30] Landsman shows how the rhetoric of the gift helps restore virtue to children with disabilities and to their mothers. When seen through the lens of commodity production and consumption, neither the child nor the mother fares well; recast in the language of the gift, both emerge as exemplary moral actors. Landsman found that the notion that God gives "special" children to "special parents," though sometimes accepted by parents early on, is usually later replaced by the notion that the child is not the gift, but rather the giver. Persons with disabilities, like children, are emplotted as "dependent" in a culture that values autonomy and independence (and in which those valued qualities are associated with masculinity; cf. Cixous 1997). By redefining her child "as a giver of gifts," the mother "raises the value of her child" not only back to the level of the "normal" child she expected, but beyond (Landsman, this volume). "To recategorize as a 'giver' an infant previously interpreted as either the just consequence of a mother's morally inferior life or a tragedy she was chosen by God as strong enough to bear, is to reestablish the full personhood of the child" (this volume).[31]

In the final essay we see how bereaved mothers use the power of the gift to deal with the moral problem pregnancy loss poses for women in a culture that often understands pregnancy in terms of capitalist production and consumption, and deems moral stature and worldly success to be the result of purposeful, individual effort. In casting themselves as "givers" of the child to God, the world, or themselves and their families, or as givers of support and expert knowledge to those who suffer a loss after theirs, they reassert their moral status as active agents, a status challenged by the out-of-controlness of pregnancy loss. In so doing, they reinforce the status quo by confirming the privileged position of the giver/doer as a moral agent. Similarly, in casting their dead child as a "giver" of moral enlightenment and the gift of self, they enhance the personhood of the child by drawing on the moral association of giving and agency. But at the same time, in casting themselves as "receivers" of God's gift of the child, and of their child's morally uplifting lessons, they undermine this dominant, masculinist ideology by asserting the Christian alternative that the ideal Christian is one who is dependent on and receptive to the grace and blessings of God.[32]

Transformative Motherhood illuminates the ways women who, whether or not by choice, experience these particularly challenging forms of mothering employ the rhetoric of the gift to valorize their experience. While the gift enables them to make their experience match more closely society's (and their own) expectations about normative mother/child relationships, at the same time many mothers use the gift to challenge the reasonableness and justice of those norms. The sacred qualities of the gift make it a powerful resource for women who would change the status quo. Modell describes "gift" as "a powerful weapon in the arsenal of those who wish to change American adoption practice, custom, and law" (Modell, this volume). Wozniak describes a number of foster mothers who use their gift of mothering as part of an explicit political/social activist agenda. Members of pregnancy loss support groups are outspoken about their desire to change the social response (or lack thereof) to pregnancy loss, and the rhetoric of the gift provides a forceful language for narrativizing this tabooed topic. Mothers of children with disabilities discuss the broader transformative potential of experiencing, firsthand, the full personhood of individuals who are subject to discrimination.

To end, then, let us return to the beginning of the beginning—Mauss's first chapter of *The Gift*. Anthropological treatments of the gift continue to be indebted to Mauss's seminal work, the most influential aspect of which has been his discussion of the "hau." What is systematically overlooked is the fact that Mauss chose to begin his book with a discussion of other beginnings—childbirth and the rituals that accompany it (1969:6–7). Mauss precedes his discussion of the "hau" with an account of the child as gift in Somoa (cf. Miller 1995:157). Samoan children are considered "tonga" ("feminine property"), and are given to the father's sister and her husband to be raised. A birth stimulates an elaborate exchange of goods too, and thenceforth, the child facilitates a lifetime of giving between her maternal and paternal families.[33] Furthermore, although Mauss himself glosses "hau" as "the spirit of the *thing* given," he ends his discussion of the "hau" with the reminder that the "magical and religious hold over the recipient" entailed by the notion of "hau" applies to "whatever it is [that is given, be it] food, possessions, women, [or] children" (1969:10, emphasis added).

In other words, as this volume so abundantly displays, if we are to fully appreciate the meaning and import of giving, whether it be in "archaic" or "contemporary" societies, the realm of childbirth remains a good place to start. A greater comprehension of giving (and gifting) in this context will enrich our understanding of the burdens and pleasures of mothering and the tension-fraught and generative dynamics of consumer culture alike.

Notes

I am grateful to Daniel Miller, whose probing comments on a draft of my essay "True Gifts" prompted me to interrogate the imperfect fit between anthropological theories of the gift and the types of gifts that feature in this volume, and for his apropos "gift" for this essay. I thank Mary Huber for generously sharing with me her expert knowledge on the anthropology of Christianity and Melanesian exchange, and Gail Landsman and Pamela Klassen for their wise advice on an earlier draft.

1. This paragraph was adapted from the session abstract coauthored with Danielle Wozniak for the 1997 American Anthropological Association panel.

2. Schrift considers the gift "one of the primary focal points at which contemporary disciplinary and interdisciplinary discourses intersect" (1997:3).

3. See Strathern (1988:312–13) for a discussion of the feminist critiques of Lévi-Strauss on this issue.

4. See Miller (1995) and Carrier (1997) for useful reviews of this literature. Anthropological analyses of gift exchange in the North rarely mention the exchange of services. However, although not generally described in these terms, the selecting, buying, wrapping, and later preserving or disposing of consumer products, what are colloquially sometimes referred to as "gifts of love" (cf. Miller 1998), could be thought of in terms of the exchange of services.

5. The 1998 American Anthropological Association's double panel "Kinship as Consumption: A Productive Reproductive Paradox," organized by Janelle Taylor, Danielle Wozniak, and Linda Layne, includes additional examples.

6. See Kopytoff (1986) for a discussion of how peculiar (both geographically and historically) this distinction is.

7. Fox and Swazey discuss the labor required to run a home dialysis unit by one member of a family for another as involving "a gift-exchange relationship . . . that is analogous to donating and receiving a live kidney . . . in that home dialysis requires a family member to make an extraordinary gift of herself (or himself) so that a close relative may survive" (1974:227). Like mothering, and in contrast with transplantation, this is not "a single act of giving, . . . but rather . . . a continuous donation of time, energy, skill, and concern" (1974:228).

8. I came across another example of use of the notion of the gift relating to motherhood and death in the letter a woman I know passed out at her mother's funeral. Wendy had cared for her mother during a long, agonizing terminal illness and she ended her letter by describing how much she learned

from the experience. "Being with her these last months has enriched my life . . . as I never would have thought it could. My views on people, my views on life and death are changed forever and it is my mother once again I have to thank for the gift."

Another example of a "transcendental" gift in popular culture can be found in the 1999 American Cancer Society fund-raising sale of daffodils which used the slogan "The Gift of Hope."

9. Some important exceptions include Miller's (1998) treatment of shopping as a "devotional rite" and Hyde's (1979) work on the gifts of artists.

The connections are most clearly elaborated in the literature on organ donation. Although it is not the focus of their work, Fox and Swazey explicitly acknowledge the religious connections of the "most literally sacrificial act" of donating an organ to another and the "religious kind of experience" that this is for many donors (1974:25). Although many clinicians were suspicious of donors' motivations, Fox and Swazey point out that "to be of use in a way that helps others is an expression of our at once pragmatic and humanitarian Judeao-Christian Tradition and that families of cadaver donors have frequently stated that they felt impelled to assent to donation for essentially religious motives" (1974:29). "Organ donation is an ultimate expression of a sublime value in our society: the Judeao-Christian injunction to give of one's self to others, sacrificially if need be, that they may live and flourish." Joralemon notes how reference to the "gift of life" links the medical procedures of organ transplantation to "the foundational values" of "generosity, altruism, and selflessness" but does not explore the relationship of these values with the predominant U.S. religious traditions. He also observes that proponents of organ donation have sought and received the approval of religious authorities. "Most religious leaders worldwide consider organ and tissue donation the ultimate charitable act" (National Kidney Foundation quoted in Joralemon 1995:343). Ohnuki-Tierney (1994) ends her insightful comparative discussion of brain death and organ transplantation with a scathing critique of "the gift wrap[ing]" of the new biomedical practices such as these in the "morality of Western civilization" when they are transported to other cultures. She objects to the rhetoric of the gift in these contexts, not only because it "misrepresents the practice" of organ donation, but also because in presenting it as "an altruistic practice, an expression of Christian love," it seeks to impose "the superior morality of the West" and in so doing, "further restricts the freedom of choice of the people to whom the technology is introduced" (1994:241–42).

10. This holds true for the meanings of the anthropological concept of the gift as well. Huber has remarked on the influence of Christianity on anthropo-

logical concepts such as "progress," "person," "religion," "ritual," "sacrifice," "symbol," and "belief" (Huber 1997:96–97), noting that "the ways
these concepts have been inflected by their specific Christian histories . . .
have not yet been fully explored." The same clearly holds true for "gift."

11. Instead, according to Schmidt (1997:71), the "ascendant paradigm" in
religious studies has been "the free market model . . . in which growth, competition, entrepreneurialism, and market share have been foregrounded," and
he points out that this "supply-side model" has been of "limited use when it
comes to the study of popular or lived religion."

12. Of course, this in no way is meant to diminish the rich religious diversity found in the U.S. or to suggest a unitary Christian stance on the issue.

13. Of course, I am not attempting to infer how early Christians understood these passages but simply to point out the resources the Bible provides
contemporary Christians in this regard.

14. One of the Old Testament scriptures refers to sacrificial gifts offered at
the altar (Leviticus 17:4). Two others convey a Middle Eastern concern with
the honor involved in giving and receiving—the speaker asserts his honor by
the fact that he has not asked anything of another party (2 Samuel 19:42; Job
6:22).

15. According to Schmidt, such gifts were at the core of the late-nine-
teenth-century Holiness and Pentecostal movements. "The pieties of the Holiness and Pentecostal movements were . . . an extended reflection on a divine
gift economy" (1997: 71).

16. This Christian opposition between God's gifts and commodities created a rhetorical challenge for the apostles, for they needed believers to do
some of this more mundane giving if the fledgling church was to survive. In
his second letter to the Corinthians Paul urges them to be generous. (It is
here one finds the famous line, "God loves a cheerful giver.") And in his letter
thanking the Philippians for their generosity, he belittles the importance of
those very gifts.

17. The democratic, egalitarian ethos of Christianity most closely associated with the Beatitudes is also found in other New Testament Scriptures regarding the gift. For example, when the "brethren . . . in Judea heard that the
Gentiles also had received the word of God they complained to Peter and he
confirmed that 'God gave the same gift to [the uncircumcised and by implication, undeserving] as he gave to us when we believed in the Lord Jesus
Christ'" (Acts 11:17). One finds another instance of this in Paul's first letter
to the Corinthians, where he develops a body metaphor to explain the value
of diversity (in this case, the diversity of the spiritual gifts God has given his
followers): "If the whole body were an eye, where would be the hearing? . . .

The eye cannot say to the hand, 'I have no need of you' nor again the head to the feet 'I have no need of you.'" While this makes the point that all types of people and talents are valuable, he goes on to reverse the normal hierarchy of social distinction: "the parts of the body which seem to be weaker are indispensable, . . . God has adjusted the body, given the greater honor to the inferior part" (1 Corinthians 12:17–31).

Huber has remarked on how the recent return of Christian fundamentalism to the public arena in the United States underlines "the continuing capacity of people acting in the name of Christianity to challenge powerfully a status quo" (1997:98).

18. Another example is found in Paul's first letter to Timothy, where Paul instructs him, "do not neglect the gift you have," a gift he had received when the elders laid their hands on him (1 Timothy 4:14).

19. "It is there in rituals of thanksgiving. . . . It informs the rhetoric and practice of benevolence, charity, almsgiving, and stewardship. It is present in the language and ritual of the Eucharist as recipients partake of the gifts of Christ's body and blood. . . . It underpins Protestant soteriology, the 'free gift' of salvation, righteousness, and eternal life, the atoning sacrifice of Christ that can never be balanced, [and it] haunts the ceremonies of church weddings in the form of the bride as gift. . . . As scriptural precept and simple proverb, the gift works its way into the day-to-day wisdom of Protestant folks" (Schmidt 1997:70–71).

20. One of the "boys," Brian Littrell, starts with a reference to Philippians (4:13): "I can do all things through Christ who gives (me) strength. Without my Lord and Savior, Jesus Christ, I would not have the gift of song, (or life) to share with you. Thank you Lord for my many gifts: The gift of family. . . . [and] the gift of a dream."

21. See, for example, the special issue of *American Ethnologist* edited by Schneider and Lindenbaum (1987).

22. Religion is rarely considered except when the subject is abortion (e.g., Ginsburg 1989; Duden 1993). Pamela Klassen's (1998) work on the spiritualizing of home birth is an important exception.

23. This summer while visiting the field site of one of my students I witnessed an in utero fetal surgery. One of the most pressing questions the husband/father-to-be had for the attending nurse before his wife's surgery was the *exact* time that the surgery would take place, since members of his church and the thirty-nine other churches of this denomination planned to engage in "targeted prayer" for their daughter, i.e., they met in homes and prayed collectively during the procedure for the health of this child. The daughter sur-

vived and was given "Miracle" for her middle name. The parents attribute the miracle of her birth to the skill of the physicians, the efficacy of modern medical technologies, the work of God, and the power of prayer (cf. Blizzard in prep.).

24. Of course some of the pregnancies of would-be surrogate or birth mothers end in pregnancy loss or the birth of a child with disabilities. This raises a number of interesting questions: Are the miscarriages or stillbirths of surrogates or birth mothers mourned in the same ways as those of other women? What becomes of the infants with disabilities born in adoption or surrogacy arrangements? What difference does it make if one's disabled child was born to another?

In addition, the normalcy of the adoptee's personhood may be affected by her/his nonnormative origin story and family. The adoptees that Modell interviewed tell of the "moment they realized they were different from everybody else" (1994:117).

25. Some have suffered sexual, physical, or emotional abuse; others have congenital malformations and/or developmental delays. According to Wozniak (this volume), most foster mothers "conceded that their children were not like other children (i.e., like "normal" children) in terms of their abilities, histories, or needs."

26. Members of pregnancy loss support groups tell of how people acted as if nothing had happened, as if there had never been a pregnancy at all. When this happens, the status of both the mother and child is threatened. As one woman put it, "a mother without a child. What am I? I had a baby, but she's gone. Am I a mother? What am I?" (Chaidez quoted in Schwiebert and Kirk 1985).

Similarly, Landsman (in press:10) describes how one first-time mom whose premature child suffered a serious bleed in the brain missed out on "all those rituals" of motherhood. Nobody congratulated her, "nobody like oohed and aahed" over her baby as they did for the babies of her friends, and they didn't send out birth announcements "because what's there to announce? That you have a one-pound-five-ounce baby" (Landsman in press:9).

27. According to Modell (1994:87), both birth mothers and adopted children (even those who grew up happy) often think of adoptive parents as "greedy, possessive, and selfish."

28. Society also provides alternative narratives to counter the damning causal stories for mothers of children with disabilities and bereaved mothers: God chose a special parent for this special child (Landsman, this volume) or God needed this baby in heaven (Layne, this volume). In addition to these

religious explanations, in both cases there is usually post facto medical reassurance that there was nothing the woman could have done to cause this unfortunate event. But these reassurances contradict all the messages women received before and during their pregnancies about the supreme importance of maternal behavior for the welfare of the child.

29. Their infants may be regarded as freaks by others.

30. Euro-American women have historically held contradictory positions vis à vis gift exchange. On the one hand, financially and legally "dependent" on their husbands or fathers, they have been emplotted as receivers. On the other hand, in their roles as wife and mother, they are the archetypical givers. Modell notes the contemporary association of gift giving with the "familial, domestic, feminine, private, and archaic" (Modell, this volume). See Giddens on the development of "maternal affection" and the "essentially feminized love" of "romantic love" (1992:43).

31. Similarly, Wozniak reports that foster mothers often felt that the state saw the children "as objects that needed to be 'placed,' 'moved,' or 'returned home' but not as full-fledged human beings imbued with subjectivity and needs" (this volume). Casting their foster children as givers helps restore to these children their full personhood.

32. The New Testament Scriptures make clear that Christians are fundamentally receivers. Matthew likens believers to children and compares the "good [material] gifts" that flow from parent to child with the superior spiritual gift that come from the heavenly father (Matthew 7:11). Romans (12:36) makes clear that in return we have nothing to offer—"who has given a gift to him that he might be repaid? For from him and through him and to him are all things."

33. "Heaps of property are collected on the occasion of the birth of [a] child," yet "the husband and wife are left no richer than they were," except with regard to honor (Mauss 1969:6).

References Cited

Anagnost, Ann S.
1997   Dream Child. Paper presented at the annual meeting of the American Anthropological Association, Washington, D.C.

Blizzard, Deborah
in prep.   The Socio-Cultural Construction of a Fetsocopy Network. Doctoral dissertation, Department of Science and Technology Studies, Rensselaer Polytechnic Institute.

Carrier, James G.
1991   Gifts, Commodities, and Social Relations: A Maussian View of Exchange. Sociological Forum 6(1):119–36.
1997   Exchange. *In* Encyclopedia of Social and Cultural Anthropology. Alan Barnard and Jonathan Spencer, eds. Pp. 218–21. London: Routledge.

Cixous, Hélène
1997   Sorties: Out and Out: Attacks/Ways Out/Forays. *In* The Logic of the Gift: Toward an Ethic of Generosity. Alan D. Schrift, ed. Pp. 148–73. London: Routledge.

Davis-Floyd, Robbie E.
1992   Birth as an American Rite of Passage. Berkeley: University of California Press.

Duden, Barbara
1993   Disembodying Women: Perspectives on Pregnancy and the Unborn. Cambridge: Harvard University Press.

First United Presbyterian Church of Troy
1998   Church Bulletin. November 22 and December 24.

Foster, Nancy, and Robert Foster
1994   Learning Fetishism? Boys' Consumption Work with Marvel Super Heroes Trading Cards. Paper presented at the annual meeting of the American Anthropological Association, Atlanta.

Fox, Renee C., and Judith P. Swazey
1974   The Courage to Fail: A Social View of Organ Transplants and Dialysis. Chicago: University of Chicago Press.
1992   Spare Parts: Organ Replacement in American Society. New York: Oxford University Press.

Franklin, Sarah
1997   Embodied Progress: A Cultural Account of Assisted Conception. London: Routledge.

Giddens, Anthony
1992   The Transformation of Intimacy: Sexuality, Love and Eroticism in Modern Societies. Stanford: Stanford University Press.

Ginsburg, Faye D.
1989   Contested Lives: The Abortion Debate in an American Community. Berkeley: University of California Press.

Haraway, Donna
1997 Modest_Witness@Second_Millennium.FemaleMan_Meets_OncoMouse. New York: Routledge.

Huber, Mary Taylor
1997 Christianity. *In* Encyclopedia of Social and Cultural Anthropology. Alan Barnard and Jonathan Spencer, eds. Pp. 96–98. London: Routledge.

Hyde, Lewis
1979 The Gift: Imagination and the Erotic Life of Property. New York: Random House.

Joralemon, Donald
1995 Organ Wars: The Battle for Body Parts. Medical Anthropology Quarterly 9(3):335–56.

Katz Rothman, Barbara
1982 In Labor: Women and Power in the Birthplace. New York: Norton.
1989 Recreating Motherhood: Ideology and Technology in a Patriarchal Society. New York: Norton.

Klassen, Pamela E.
1998 Dilemmas of Consumption in the Spiritualizing of Home Birth. Paper presented on the panel "Kinship as Consumption: A Productive Reproductive Paradox" organized by Taylor, Wozniak, and Layne at the annual meeting of the American Anthropological Association, Philadelphia.

Kopytoff, Igor
1986 The Cultural Biography of Things: Commoditization as Process. *In* The Social Life of Things: Commodities in Cultural Perspective. Arjun Appadurai, ed. Pp. 64–91. New York: Cambridge University Press.

Landsman, Gail
in press "Real" Motherhood, Class, and Children with Disabilities. *In* Ideologies and Technologies of Motherhood. Heléna Ragoné and France Winddance Twine, eds. New York: Routledge.

Layne, Linda L.
1992 Of Fetuses and Angels: Fragmentation and Integration in Narratives of Pregnancy Loss. Knowledge and Society. Hess and Layne eds. 9:29–58.
1997 Mother Nature/Freaks of Nature. Paper presented at the electronic conference "Cultures and Environments: On Cultural Environmental Studies," Washington State University American Studies Web site.

1999   "I Remember the Day I Shopped for Your Layette": Goods, Fetuses and Feminism in the Context of Pregnancy Loss. *In* The Fetal Imperative/Feminist Practices. Lynn Morgan and Meridith Michaels, eds. Pp. 251–78. Philadelphia: University of Pennsylvania Press.

in press   "He Was a Real Baby with Baby Things': A Material Culture Analysis of Personhood, Parenthood and Pregnancy Loss. *In* Ideologies and Technologies of Motherhood. Heléna Ragoné and Winddance Twine, eds. New York: Routledge.

Lévi-Strauss, Claude
1969   The Elementary Structures of Kinship. Boston: Beacon Press.

Malinowski, Bronislaw
[1922] (1961)   Argonauts of the Western Pacific. New York: Dutton.

Martin, Emily
1987   The Woman in the Body: A Cultural Analysis of Reproduction. Boston: Beacon Press.

Mauss, Marcel
[1925] 1969   The Gift: Forms and Functions of Exchange in Archaic Societies. New York: Routledge and Kegan Paul.

McDannell, Colleen
1995   Material Christianity: Religion and Popular Culture in America. New Haven: Yale University Press.

Miller, Daniel
1993   Unwrapping Christmas. Oxford: Clarendon.
1995   Consumption and Commodities. Annual Reviews in Anthropology 24:141–61.
1998   A Theory of Shopping. Ithaca: Cornell University Press.

Modell, Judith S.
1994   Kinship with Strangers: Adoption and Interpretations of Kinship in American Culture. Berkeley: University of California Press.

Narayan, Uma
1995   The "Gift" of a Child: Commercial Surrogacy, Gift Surrogacy, and Motherhood. *In* Expecting Trouble: Surrogacy, Fetal Abuse and New Reproductive Technologies. Patricia Boling, ed. Pp. 177–201. Boulder: Westview.

Ohnuki-Tierney, Emiko
1994   Brain Death and Organ Transplantation: Cultural Bases of Medical Technology. Current Anthropology 35(3):233–42.

Ragoné, Heléna
1994   Surrogate Motherhood: Conception in the Heart. Boulder: Westview.

Sandelowski, Margarete
1993   With Child in Mind: Studies of the Personal Encounter with Infertility. Philadelphia: University of Pennsylvania Press.

Schmidt, Leigh Eric
1997   Practices of Exchange: From Market Culture to Gift Economy in the Interpretation of American Religion. *In* Lived Religion in America: Toward a History of Practice. David D. Hall, ed. Pp. 69–91. Princeton: Princeton University Press.

Schneider, Jane, and Shirley Lindenbaum, eds.
1987   Frontiers of Christian Evangelism. A special issue of American Ethnologist 14(1).

Schrift, Alan D.
1997   Introduction: Why Gift? *In* The Logic of the Gift: Toward an Ethic of Generosity. Alan D. Schrift, ed. Pp. 1–24. London: Routledge.

Schwiebert, Pat, and Paul Kirk
1985   When Hello Means Goodbye: A Guide for Parents Whose Child Dies before Birth, at Birth or Shortly after Birth. Portland, OR: Perinatal Loss.

Sharp, Lesley A.
1995   Organ Transplantation as a Transformative Experience: Anthropological Insights into the Restructuring of the Self. Medical Anthropology Quarterly 9(3):357–89.

Strathern, Marilyn
1972   Women in Between: Female Roles in a Male World. London: Seminar Press.
1988   The Gender of the Gift: Problems with Women and Problems with Society in Melanesia. Berkeley: University of California Press.
1997   Partners and Consumers: Making Relations Visible. *In* The Logic of the Gift: Toward an Ethic of Generosity. Alan D. Schrift, ed. Pp. 292–312. London: Routledge.

Taylor, Janelle S.

1992   The Public Fetus and the Family Car: From Abortion Politics to a Volvo Advertisement. Public Culture 4(2):67–80.

1998   Of Human Bonding: Obstetrical Ultrasound, Commodity Fetishism, and Love American-Style. Paper presented on the panel "Kinship as Consumption: A Productive Reproductive Paradox" organized by Taylor, Wozniak, and Layne at the annual meeting of the American Anthropological Association, Philadelphia.

in press   An All-Consuming Experience: Obstetrical Ultrasound and the Commodification of Pregnancy. Feminist Studies.

Titmuss, Richard M.

1972   The Gift Relationship: From Human Blood to Social Policy. New York: Vintage Books.

Weiner, Annette B.

1976   Women of Value, Men of Renown: New Perspectives in Trobriand Exchange. Austin: University of Texas Press.

Wozniak, Danielle F.

1998   What Will I Do with All the Toys Now? Consumption Practices and the Signification of Kinship and Loss in U.S. Fostering Relations. Paper presented on the panel "Kinship as Consumption: A Productive Reproductive Paradox" organized by Taylor, Wozniak, and Layne at the annual meeting of the American Anthropological Association, Philadelphia.

| O N E |

Freely Given

Open Adoption and the Rhetoric of the Gift

Judith S. Modell

Introduction

"If human life itself must become an item of commerce, transferred
from person to person or house to house, then it must be gift property
and the 'rights of action' must be those that appertain to gifts, not to
commodities" (Hyde 1983:95). By law and by custom, in American
adoption a child is transferred from person to person and from house
to house. The rules of the transfer have always been ambiguous and at
the moment are under fire. My chapter argues that a rhetoric of gift is
central to the controversies surrounding American adoption policy
and that the use of the concept is crucial to proposed changes in adoption practice. I describe the people and issues involved in the controversy and discuss its far-reaching implications for the changing language of child placement policy. Rhetoric is never simple, and in this
case the meanings of the terms extend through the lives of many individuals.

As the literary critic Lewis Hyde suggests in the opening quotation,
human life must not be treated as a "commodity." Fear of commodifying human life haunts American adoption even as—or maybe because—the transaction is presumed to be based on love, need, care,
and generosity. In American cultural discourse, adoption should not
be a market phenomenon, but in many ways it is. In American culture,
although a child should not be priced, the differential value of particular children influences adoption practice. Overall, while adoption is

not supposed to be based on selfish interests, individual wants often motivate the transaction of a child.[1] These ambiguities determine the debate over "opening" adoption that has been going on in the United States since the 1970s.

The argument for opening adoption is an opposition to closed adoption, to the confidential, anonymous, sealed-record adoption characteristic of American society since the early twentieth century. Pertaining only to stranger, or nonrelative, adoption, the custom of forbidding contact between adopted child and relinquishing parent provides the stereotypical picture of adoption in the United States.[2] Against both the custom and the cliché of secrecy, supporters of change argue for opening records, providing information to participants in an adoption, and encouraging contact between child and relinquishing parent. They make the argument by applying the rhetoric of gift to the transfer of a child from person to person.

These are big changes in American adoption, and "gift" is core to their significance. My essay examines the use of gift by those who argue for change: the intentional meaning accorded the concept as well as its unintended consequences. "Intentional" refers to meanings that are articulated and elaborated in the rhetoric; "unintended" refers to the implications for child placement policy, American kinship, and dominant cultural ideologies. Like other authors in the volume, I show that moving toward a gift model has profound implications for understandings of child placement, parenthood, and kinship.

If we consider gift the representation of social relationships, a gift model in adoption will "socialize" the exchange in a way that removes it from an ideology of blood-based kinship. Adoption, I argue, will be a social and not a kinship transaction. In addition, if gift should become the model for child exchange in a modern, diverse American society—faced with an increasing number of children needing homes (Wozniak, this volume)—the concept of gift itself will be transformed: no longer "just" a matter of private, emotional, domesticated, and feminized exchanges, gift would be restored to its classic meaning of "social exchange." I claim that the application of a gift model to adoption changes child placement practices, and ultimately changes the bases on which Americans transact "human life" altogether.

Organization and Methods

I start by suggesting why "gift" impinges so dramatically on American adoption practice, referring in part to the literature on gift exchange in anthropology and, to a lesser extent, in sociology. I then discuss the development of a rhetoric of gift by proponents of change within the adoption triad; in this section, birth mothers take the lead. My data come from the research I have been doing on American adoption for the past decade (Modell 1994). My fieldwork includes participation in birth parent groups and adoptee groups, meetings with birth parents and adoptive parents through agencies, as well as extended interviews with all members of the adoption triad. Many adoption groups put out newsletters, and those constitute a fair proportion of my data as well.

I attended a branch of Concerned United Birthparents (CUB) for almost ten years, taking notes on meetings and interviewing a number of members. I also joined an adoptee support group, and there too members were generous with both their stories and their time. In addition, I continue to interview the social workers, lawyers, and judges whose decisions about placement are crucial to the way participants in adoptive relationships understand their own situations. My interviews are entirely loose—I encourage my interviewees to create their own narratives, testify to their own experiences, only asking questions when absolutely necessary. In the case of members of the triad, interviews often lasted the good part of the day.

I am grateful, too, for the hours of observation judges permitted me in courtrooms, social workers at meetings, and families in their households. All material is confidential, and all details presented with a respect for anonymity.

Based on the research, I interpret the meanings of "gift" to individuals whose experience of adoptive kinship forms the groundwork for a profound critique of American customs for transferring a child. Next I analyze the implications of a rhetoric of gift for the debate over "openness." Some of the implications are articulated and some are not by those who use the rhetoric. In the end, I argue that these implications extend well beyond proposed revisions in American adoption custom and law.

Background: Why Open Adoption?

The trend toward opening adoption came out of three phenomena—the last two closely intertwined and perhaps ultimately inseparable. The first phenomenon is the search movement of the 1970s and 1980s. The second and third are the turn from agency adoption to independent adoption and the baby "scarcity" that gave birth parents a leverage over the transaction they had not had before. The second and third phenomena are connected: one of the most frequently cited reasons for the rise of independent adoptions is the greater availability of babies along that route—a matter of supply, demand, and competition. I will discuss these three phenomena briefly and then show that the origin of openness in a market shift has a lot to do with the inclination of participants to use "gift" as a central element in their rhetoric. The significance of market, I also show, is not a full explanation for the attractiveness of a concept of gift.

The term "search movement" refers to the increasing efforts by adoptees to find the parents who relinquished them years ago. Adoptees were followed quickly by birth parents, who similarly pursued a search for the babies they had once given up. (Incidentally, all adoption language is loaded, including what is borrowed from other domains—for instance, the use in the search movement of phrases like a "need to know" and a "right to information.") Over the past three decades searches have been increasingly successful, in that more adoptees have found a member of the birth family and more birth parents have learned about and even met the children they relinquished. The whole arena of search begs for further investigation; for example, I should put the word "successful" in quotation marks to indicate existing uncertainty about the impact of searching on individuals, on families, and on interpretations of child placement policy in the United States. Little is yet known of the ongoing consequences of these contacts. At the same time, searching has had a tremendous impact on adoptive arrangements and attitudes toward adoption. Demands for information, publicity about long-lost relatives, and spectacular dramas showing tearful reunions shook the American adoption world.

One response by agencies was to one-up the search movement by making information available at the onset of an adoption. The birth parent would receive more information about the people adopting her child and the adopting couple would receive more information about the birth parents (here, again, I really need quotation marks for both "more" and "information"—neither word is unambiguous in this context). The child, of course, depended on the good graces of parents for what she or he learned, but at least information was available, secrets were diminished, and "lying" a less appropriate descriptor for the adoptive transaction.

A number of commentators argue that agency sympathy for disclosing information (at the onset or later in an adoption) would not have occurred without the competition independent adoptions prompted. Simultaneously with the search movement, in the 1970s and 1980s adoptive parents began to turn away from public and private agencies for adopting. They turned instead to lawyers, doctors, social workers, and other professionals who could arrange the transfer of a child from birth to adoptive parent. (To be legal, independent adoptions have to go before a judge and be granted approval in terms of the child's best interests.) During this period, adoptive parents expressed displeasure with agencies for the red tape, exclusive criteria, and general fussiness of their policies. Adoptive parents claimed they had "no choice" in agency adoptions, though one might say the real truth was they were not easily getting the babies they wanted. In an independent adoption, parents got the babies and they also got a lot more information about a birth parent than social workers were permitted to provide.

Birth parents, too, turned away from agencies. They expressed similar dissatisfactions with agencies: too much intrusive control, too little choice about the most significant decision of their lives, too little information about the families that adopted their children. Like adoptive parents, birth parents argued for choice, facts, and respect. Finding these lacking at agencies, they turned to independent mediators in order to place a child.

Birth parents, however, had a further edge. They had the babies others wanted. And here the second factor blurs into the third factor: the so-called baby shortage. An issue too complicated to detail here, the baby shortage has to do with legalized abortion, increased benefits for unwed mothers, decreased stigmatization of the parent raising a child on her own, and general shifts in attitudes toward relinquishment. At the receiving end, a shortage has to do with what is perceived as the desirable and valued item. The term "baby shortage" reveals that the desired adoptee is an infant and, as we know, often a certain kind of infant.

But the criteria for a desirable child are not the subject of my essay—not directly, at any rate. Rather, I am pointing to the demands adoptive and birth parents made on the transaction itself—on the terms and the process of the exchange. In the 1970s and 1980s these demands involved requests for choice and control over the transaction: more input, parents said, in deciding who the other parents of a child would be. Parents asked for leverage and agencies responded, in part, by opening adoption—letting chinks appear in the wall social workers had previously maintained between the relinquishing and the adopting parents.

One view, then, is that open adoption came about less for ideological reasons than because agencies were threatened by changes in the adoption market. Birth parents were turning elsewhere to place babies (the few that selected this option) and adoptive parents were turning elsewhere for the children they "really" wanted. Grown-up adoptees, too, publicized the disadvantages of existing arrangements; if they did not withdraw patronage, they did expose the limits of the institution.

In essence, competition drove adoption agencies to alter their practices so as not to go out of business altogether. In the next section I consider the importance of this market factor to the use of "gift" in open adoption rhetoric. That section is followed by one in which I show the implications of "gift" beyond its deliberate use by advocates of openness.

The Significance of "Market"

Open adoption arose out of market concerns: an imbalance between supply and demand, a scarcity of the desired product, and dissatisfaction on the part of primary consumers (birth parent, adoptive parent, and adoptee). From this perspective, the decision on the part of agencies to open the transaction arose largely from venial motives—fear of losing customers—and only politely from notions of the well-being of a child. The motivation produced compromises and the not-quite full embrace of openness characteristic of agency adoptions. For advocates, open adoption means meetings and ongoing contact between birth and adoptive parents. Advocates apply the rhetoric of gift to open adoption in order to distinguish "true openness" from agency practice and policy.

Existing studies of open adoption scrupulously outline the different arrangements covered by the phrase. Forms of open adoption currently include an exchange of identifying information at the onset of the adoption without any meeting; initial face-to-face meetings between birth and adoptive parents, without any (necessary) further contact; ongoing contact between birth and adoptive parents during the child's lifetime (or childhood).[3] So far, none of these arrangements are contracted or legal; they all depend on the will and willingness of the participants. Agency publicity does not admit to the impact of market factors or competition on changes in practice, though social workers I interviewed talked about losing business, meeting client demands, and dealing with a severe shortage in the available, adoptable population. In their comments, adoptive parents clearly evoked a market metaphor by characterizing themselves as "deprived" by the shortage of babies, subject to the whims of middlemen, and vulnerable to the demands of—though they did not use this word—producers. Behind these comments by adoptive parents lies a fear that birth parents have all the power in contemporary adoptions.

The fear is counteracted by a rhetorical emphasis on gift, giving, and generosity. The rhetoric appears in statements made by adoptive parents, and for good reason. The concept of gift distances adoptive parents from a situation they describe and dislike: engagement in a market for babies. A concept of gift also, I argue, softens the uncertainty of the new arrangement many find themselves in, an arrangement that feels like bowing to the demands of birth parents (e.g., McRoy, Grotevant, and White 1988).

In interviews, some adoptive parents claim they would not have been able to adopt a baby unless they agreed to meet the birth parent or to tell her their names. Others claim they felt coerced by a vague emphasis on the benefits to the child of having information. Overall, however, most adoptive parents end up saying they appreciate openness and recognize its value for the child. The gist of approval comes down to the well-being of the child—with references to love, sharing, and generosity that (in American culture) translate into "giving" even when the word "gift" is not used.

Birth parents have been outspoken in support of open adoption. Those who voice their views put the advantages of openness in terms of an ability to "get over" the trauma of relinquishing a baby. Birth parents claim "it helps" to have chosen the parents who will raise the child and that knowing the child's fate during the years of her or his growing up eases the pain of loss. This does not mean a birth parent has contact with the child: inasmuch as the definition and implementation of open adoption remain informal and consensual, birth parents still depend on adoptive parent permission to see the child. But the constraint does not appear to limit the closeness birth parents say comes from knowing who the adoptive parents are.

Like adoptive parents, birth parents use language that emphasizes the well-being of the child, the benefits of honesty over secrecy, and the importance of choice in such a life-shaking decision. Yet the outstanding feature is closeness, the birth parent's sense of connection with the parents who "share" the child. It is closeness that makes the idea of gift profoundly significant, whether expressed directly or in metaphor.

Advocates of open adoption do use the word "gift." The word is especially important in arguments made by those who claim that the only true form of open adoption is full disclosure and ongoing contact between the parents.[4] Advocates of this position include birth parents, adoptees, adoptive parents, and professionals who support changes in American adoption practice. Throughout, the ideas of humanizing adoption and making the transaction honest are intertwined with and deepen the meaning of gift.

Behind the public testimonies favoring open adoption—whether volunteered or elicited in a study—lies an innovative interpretation of American adoption. The concept of gift captures this interpretation even when the word itself is not used. Why is gift so powerful a descriptor for open adoption in all its forms? The answer is that a concept of gift makes open adoption better than closed adoption. This is not because of what gift says about the child—that's not my argument at the moment—but because of what gift says about the adoptive and birth parents. The answer needs elaboration; I now move to that part of my discussion.

The Rhetoric of Gift

"Gift" transforms American adoption. This blanket statement needs to be unpacked. In an American context, a gift model seems so logical as to be natural for the transfer of a child from one parent to another. After all, a child is a person and should not be commodified. If for whatever reason a child has to be transferred, the rules should be those that appertain to gifts. Yet in many respects, as critics of adoption claim, a version of commodity has ruled the turf: the child has a value, the transactors are strangers to one another, the interaction ends once the transfer has been completed: "In commodity relations the parties are not linked to each other in any enduring or personal ways" (Carrier 1995:11). Given up, or relinquished, by one parent and taken in, or received, by another, the child-as-item does not constitute a bond between the parties. Rather, in traditional closed adoption, bonds between the parties are sharply severed.

"Gift" is a powerful weapon in the arsenal of those who wish to change American adoption practice, custom, and law.[5] To put it simply (though it is not simple at all): appearing in arguments, the concept of gift restores virtue to adoption. Besides "humanizing the transfer," as proponents say, gift eliminates the weight of bureaucracy, the intervention of the state, and the selfish interests of individuals from adoption. In order to delineate these negative aspects of American adoption, supporters of open adoption emphasize particular qualities of gift giving: love, generosity, reciprocity, and permanent connections (enduring solidarity) between the parties. Above all, "gift" inserts the child-as-person into the transaction; the rhetoric implies that the child disappears from conventional, closed adoption. For staunch opponents of closed adoption, the child had become a product, ignored as a person, and treated as an item whose worth is calculable and visible. A rhetoric of gift both explains and justifies the proposed opening of adoption.

"Gift" also rearranges the hierarchical dimension evident in twentieth-century American adoption practice. The dimension to which I refer appears clearly in the imagery surrounding American adoption. Birth mother and adoptive parents are viewed as occupying totally different socioeconomic positions, having different characters, and making different kinds of life choices. In each category, the adoptive parent is "better" than the birth mother. The images are only tenuously connected to empirical and demographic reality, but they are crucial to adoption: the superiority of the adopting parents provides an indicator of the otherwise virtually indefinable "fitness" of the parents that justifies the transfer of a child.

The presumed and assigned superiority of adoptive parents to birth mothers is reiterated in the language of American adoption literature. Birth mothers are described as irresponsible, vulnerable, young, mistaken, while adoptive parents are described as responsible, stable, and, in a word, adult—stereotypes to an extent shared by participants.[6] As a letter to the *New York Times Magazine* in the spring of 1998 noted, birth mothers are presumed to be incompetent, wild, less than proper citizens of the world: a couch dancer and not a concert pianist.[7] Gift dismantles those stereotypes by altering the bases for the transfer of a child, from a comparative measure of fitness to an individualized gesture of solidarity.

In a classic gift relationship, donor and recipient are personally linked and enduringly solid with one another. An appreciation of this ideal lies behind the use of a gift rhetoric, and in adoption includes the assumption that persons thus bound will not engage in negative name calling. Used by members of the adoption community, a rhetoric of gift implies the disappearance of derogatory classifications and stereotypes. As a model for adoption, "gift" is thought to eliminate the stigmatizing signs of difference that are historically a consequence of legally enforced separation between birth and adoptive parents. In addition, in the context of adoption "gift" emphasizes particular personal qualities that are presumed to be absent from commodity exchange: respect, reciprocation, gratitude, and appreciation. These are implications of the rhetoric of gift. The transfer into people's lives through adoption practices is another question.

Open Adoption

Why is a gift rhetoric applied to open adoption in particular? "Gift" reveals the core goal of openness: to establish a relationship between birth mother and adoptive parents, or, as it is sometimes put, birth families and adoptive families. The primary rhetorical use of gift is to constitute a relationship between the parents, whatever the form or timing of openness. That is, in practice an adoption may be "opened" at its onset, so birth parent and adoptive parent make the arrangements in person, face to face. Adoption may also be opened later, with, at minimum, letters and photos exchanged between birth and adoptive parent and, at maximum, visits between the parents, and the parents and the child, maintained over the child's lifetime. To date, openness has not been standardized in American adoption policy and practice.

Like all other child placement practices in the United States, open adoption is evaluated in terms of its benefits for the child. Advocates of open adoption claim that the arrangement serves the best interests of the child: contact between all parents is deemed good for the child, helping her or him to achieve mature adulthood since there are no mysteries or questions in his experience of adoption.[8] Some commentators claim that knowledge and contact between birth and adoptive parents ease the burdens of adoption for those adults, and that a child thrives in an environment of security. Opponents of open adoption also refer to the principle of best interests: for them, closed adoption serves the child best by giving her or him a family as much like the as-if-begotten family as possible. The child in a closed adoption does not worry about who her or his "real" parent is. Both positions rest without much supporting data; open adoption (in whatever form) is too new for much hard evidence of its impact on participants to exist.

Used by advocates, the concept of gift makes up for lack of data by orienting the debate in a clear direction. For supporters of opening adoption, the rhetoric of gift proves the rightness of the arrangement by emphasizing that the child is person not product. In addition, the rhetoric of gift indicates that the child belongs to the birth mother, and is hers to give. For opponents, the rhetoric of gift proves the dangers in the arrangement: gift giving represents random and retrogressive mechanisms for transferring goods. Supporters of open adoption staunchly use the word, recognizing its capacity to convey the flaws in a closed arrangement that mandates a systematic (and absolute) severing of ties between parties to the transfer of a child. Among supporters of open adoption, birth mothers are the most ardent.

There is another aspect to the debate. The rhetoric of gift not only argues for a change in the relationship between birth and adoptive parents but also redefines the nature of the "object," in this case a child. "In gift transactions, the object is linked to the giver, the recipient and the relationship that binds and defines them" (Carrier 1995:11). The child remains attached to giver and receiver, attaching them to one another. A gift, in other words, cannot be alienated from either party: "objects are never completely separated from the men [*sic*] who exchange them" (Mauss 1969:31). Phrased in psychological terms, the adopted child in an open arrangement is alienated neither from his "blood" parent nor from his "legal" parent; the child has the opportunity of knowing and experiencing all aspects of his or her identity. In an American cultural context, this is deemed "healthy." These last points are precisely what make gift rhetoric attractive to birth mothers and especially pertinent to their advocacy of open adoption.

Changing American Adoption

"If I had it to do over, I would choose the family. The agency made all these promises and they didn't come through. They said it was all because I delivered early. They promised me pictures, lots of pictures, and all they sent was five. They [the adoptive couple] can't even write me a thank-you letter. I write a thank-you for a birthday card. I give them my baby and there's not even a thank-you" (Lindsay 1987:101). The statement was made by a birth mother, thinking back to the original adoption arrangement. Although the word does not appear, a concept of gift emerges from the particular complaints she has. The text reveals the several reasons birth mothers draw on a gift model in advocating open adoption.

Three elements can be extracted from the quotation. First, "gift" condemns the bureaucratic procedures many birth mothers experienced; gift represents autonomy and individuality in contrast with agency-imposed impersonal rules. Second, "gift" implies the existence of trust and honesty in a relationship, in contrast with the antagonism and self-interest likely in a contracted arrangement. Third, the concept of gift accords priority to feelings and to a perceived familiarity between the parties to a transaction rather than to the material circumstances (or willingness to pay) agencies depend on in placing a child. These components are central to the birth mother critique of agency adoption, and behind them lie ideologies of choice and of bonding that provide energy to the critique. The quotation above also reveals how difficult it is for birth mothers to extract themselves from a rhetoric that has dominated adoption in the United States for nearly a century.

"The agency made all these promises and they didn't come through." Representing the state and its rules, agencies come in for a lot of complaint on the part of birth mothers who are rethinking the terms of their decisions. "Naturally they're covering the tracks and they don't tell you anything," a birth mother said to me (Modell 1994:82). From this point of view, agencies represent the coldest, least personal, most venial aspects of American adoption. "We were all such vulnerable prey for the baby market!" (Modell 1994:77). Agencies, birth mothers told me in interviews, want babies at all costs. "This woman in authority didn't care about me or my child, what I was feeling or what my child would feel later. . . . Her main concern was not my hurt at that point, only my name on the contract" (Modell 1994:80).

In the 1950s and 1960s, American adoption did seem to favor the adoptive parent—the consumer, as it were—and social workers bent over backwards to find the "right" baby for the right family. The policy known as matching—fitting child to adoptive parents—had as a consequence a systematic scrutiny of the visible traits and potential capabilities of a child. Concern with successful placement led to discussion of healthy babies, desirable adoptees, and "good" birth mothers. Such assessments made the child seem more a product than a person. This was the heart of the complaints that fueled the 1970s and 1980s critique of placement practices, culminating in proposals to open adoption.

According to the critique, a "market" in babies favored the consumer and subjected the birth mother to an evaluation appropriate for a producer. A so-called adoption market also exposed the discrimination in American adoption agencies, where financial independence, marriage, and stability were most likely to qualify a parent. "I was given the Hollywood version of adoption" was the way one birth parent summed up those qualifications (Modell 1994:82). Measurable traits in the parents determined decisions about the placement of a child, traits critics argued were not germane either to the item (a child) or to the distinct content of the transfer (from parent to parent). The perceived missing elements lent themselves to the rhetoric of gift: love, compassion, and generosity.

Images of agencies sharpen by contrast the meaning of "gift." Agencies represented a marketplace of babies. "Gifts, and the spirit of reciprocity, sociability, and spontaneity in which they are typically exchanged, usually are starkly opposed to the profit-oriented, self-centered, and calculated spirit that fires the circulation of commodities" (Appadurai 1986:11). In birth mother rhetoric, these "baby-markets" deprived relinquishing mothers not only of "reciprocity, sociability, and spontaneity" but also of any leverage in the transaction. In the worst view, birth mothers are mere cogs in the wheels of consumer-driven child placement practice. At best, they are victims of circumstances, without control over the fate of their children. And though Uma Narayan (1995) suggests that lack of reproductive control is true in some respects for all women in Western societies, adoption makes the fact stark: the child disappears and the transaction is forever closed. A rhetoric of gift provides a countervailing sense of control.

Gift underlines the equation of agency adoptions with a market in babies by offering an alternative way of conceptualizing the movement of a child from person to person. Rather than following the principles of commodity transfer and letting "money" determine the movement of a child, gift acknowledges the importance of the personal qualities of the parties involved. Like parents who experience pregnancy loss (Layne, this volume), birth mothers assert the spiritual dimension of parenthood in place of the materialistic (and consumerist) calculations attributed to agencies. From their perspective, agencies concern themselves with efficient distribution and not with, in Hyde's term, "human life itself."

The interpretation of agency-as-market constitutes a purposeful criticism of closed adoption. In closed adoption, after legalization the transfer ends permanently, as if the child had been bought and no more contact with the seller was appropriate or required. As in a classic commodity transfer, the parties do not maintain contact, have no further obligations, and make no emotional demands on one another. Drawing on cultural understandings, gift rhetorically communicates the opposite: contact, reciprocity, and ongoing obligations between the parties. Along with this assumption, gift pushes forward notions of trust, honesty, and integrity.

"They promised me pictures, lots of pictures, and all they sent was five." The birth mother's remark condemns the agency for its strenuous efforts to keep her from seeing the baby, the new parents, the adoptive family: the agency would not even send snapshots. Keeping back any tangible signs of who they are, the agency renders the "other" parents virtually nonexistent for a birth mother. Not seen, they remain strangers, unfamiliar, and therefore hard to trust. In an article on garage sales in the United States (1997), Gretchen Herrmann suggests the importance to sellers of seeing the recipient of an especially valued item. Seeing, with its accompanying (presumed) insight, reassures the seller, seals the bargain, and provides a groundwork for trust that the item will be valued. Closed adoption, according to its critics, deprives parties of exactly the sight (and knowledge) of one another that similarly sets the foundation for trust, honesty, and openness.

Herrmann also notes that when an item is especially valued, the seller will often simply give it away. It is more important to know who is receiving the item than to make a profit from it. "They actually want to see those to whom they give" (Herrmann 1997:922). Face-to-face contact provides the confidence that a gift will be well cared for. As an interpretation of giving and its connection with knowing the recipient, this is applicable to adoption rhetoric. In her ethnography of garage sales, Herrmann offers a version of cultural theories of giving that birth mothers also realize. The very difference between a garage sale item and a child underlines the compelling logic of applying gift to adoption, where the precious item is, after all, a person.

In American culture, gifts imply or create familiarity between giver and recipient: you "know" to whom you give a gift.[9] "If I had it to do over," the birth mother quoted above said, "I would choose the family." Unlike closed adoption, open adoption practices usually include an opportunity for birth mothers to select the adoptive parents. Birth mothers who have had the experience report that they instinctively recognize the right parents for their children. Advocates of open adoption assume, in turn, that the instinctive basis of selection creates an enduring and unconditional bond between donor and recipient, as if they were already close. A rhetoric of gift makes the birth mother and adoptive parent familiar—if not, as I discuss later, family. "It was as if we had known each other before," one birth mother said about the adoptive parents (Belbas 1986:194).

Frequently the basis for choice is a perceived similarity. Studies show that many birth mothers choose adoptive parents who seem to be "like" themselves (e.g., McRoy, Grotevant, and White 1988; Gross 1993). What does that really mean? It seems that birth mothers who can choose guard against the danger of selecting the wrong parents by identifying in advance with the recipient of the child. That is, in open adoptions even before the "gift" is made, a birth parent establishes her identification with the recipient. "The more completely it is a gift the more completely it declares an identification of the giver with the recipient" (John Noonan quoted in Carrier 1990:20). When birth mothers use a rhetoric of gift, they underline these aspects of open adoption, which not only personalizes the transfer but also intensifies its emotional content: the transfer of a child occurs between persons who are intimate with one another. The rhetoric predicts enduring solidarity.

In birth mother rhetoric, then, "gift" releases adoption from the red tape, regulations, and presumed consumer-oriented goals of an agency. Incorporating notions of individuality, spontaneity, and choice, "gift" represents a whole new relationship between birth mothers and adoptive parents—one built on trust and honesty, familiarity and intimacy. But even the "freely given" is not without obligation. Return gifts and gratitude are central to the application of a gift rhetoric to open adoption.

"They [the adoptive couple] can't even write me a thank-you letter. I write a thank-you for a birthday card. I give them my baby and there's not even a thank-you." From this birth mother's point of view, reciprocity has been zero. She blames the agency for closing off contact so that the adoptive parents could not thank her if they wanted to, and she also suggests that in general adoptive parents show no gratitude for the babies they receive. From this perspective, adoptive parents are following the rules of commodity exchange and violating the norms of gift giving: few people write thank-you notes for a recently purchased automobile.[10] But a baby? Open adoption encourages the expression of gratitude: "We love you for the life you've given us," wrote an adoptive couple (Silber and Speedlin 1982:140).

Gratitude enhances the bond between birth and adoptive parents, and it diminishes the distance agencies and social workers (as well as cultural stereotypes) put between them. Gratitude also represents the obligation birth mothers embrace in using the concept of "gift." Birth mothers do not reject but rather appreciate the compulsion to return that gift implies; they expect and demand a "thank you" for the precious gift they have given, like surrogate mothers asking for recognition of value (Ragoné, this volume). Being thanked gives a donor her "due," in the birth mother instance removing the stigma attached to her act.

Giving always has rules, and in American culture thank-you notes are one rule. So is the duty not to take back what you have "freely given." Birth mothers who utilize the rhetoric of gift acknowledge the strong cultural taboo against taking back what has been "freely given." They are not the "kidnappers" of American adoption lore; a rhetoric of gift asserts their honor and faithfulness in the transaction. Social workers who support open adoption make the same point: "Somehow, if she gives the baby to them [adoptive parents] in the hospital, they aren't likely to think this mother is someone who will take the baby away from them" (Lindsay 1987:216). In the ideal world that the rhetoric of gift envisions, adoptive parents are assured of permanent possession of the gift they have received.

The Child as Gift

The concept of gift changes not only the terms of a transaction but also the "nature" of the gift itself. "In gift transactions objects are not alienated from the transactors. Instead, the object given continues to be identified with the giver and indeed continues to be identified with the transaction itself" (Carrier 1995:20–21). The implications of this affect adoption practice and, too, link the critique of adoption to cultural understandings of "human life itself."

A rhetoric of gift argues for a continued connection between birth mother and child. In gift transactions, the object is not alienated from the donor; applied to adoption, this insists that the child in an adoptive family maintain an identity with her birth mother. Identification between adopted child and birth mother contravenes the major principle of American adoption practice, the severing of ties that came with laws of confidentiality in the early twentieth century. A violation of this principle exists regardless of whether the identification is enacted or considered an aspect of the child's nature. For birth mothers who use the rhetoric, the dual identification in "gift" is crucial.

Gift theory offers a further interpretation of the way the transaction itself affects the bonds an object forms between donor and recipient. In his history of gift giving in capitalist societies, James Carrier points to the importance of circulation: "to address circulation [as gift does] entails addressing the nature of the relationship that links those who transact the object and the nature of the relationship between person and object" (Carrier 1995:viii). Carrying this idea into adoption, gift rhetoric suggests that the bonds between parties increase as the child grows up. In a kind of circulation-effect, the traits a child develops over time attach her or him more thoroughly both to birth parent and to adoptive parents; inalienable from each, the child's evolving personality locks them more closely together. "I do know one thing, that love grows and grows each day. More and more [love grows] as I look at Dan's [the adopted child] pictures and more and more as I read your [adoptive parents] letters. I hope and pray that we will be able to continue writing and exchanging pictures" (Lindsay 1987:123). Through this connection to the child, the birth mother is bonded with the adoptive parents: "I feel that as his real parents, you are a part of me" (Silber and Speedlin 1982:47).

Carrier also notes that the focus of gift giving on circulation de-emphasizes the attention to object-as-product. Movement from person to person is more important than the use or exchange value of the product. His argument is an elaboration of the Maussian point that gifts are less made than makers of social relationships. Gift operates in birth mother rhetoric in this way as well: an announcement on the one hand that a baby is not a product and, on the other, that adoption is not a distribution of valuable items. In using gift this way, birth mothers protest the language of conventional adoption, in which their babies were assessed in terms of placement potential. "Because I also thought," a birth mother remembered, "'what if she had never been adopted?' But I didn't think that would be the case because she was a beautiful baby. Anybody would have wanted her" (Modell 1994:74). As this statement also suggests, the rhetoric of product is powerful for birth mothers: anyone would want a beautiful baby—just as few want a defective one (Landsman, this volume). "And because your baby is so beautiful it makes you feel better about yourself because you can see something so beautiful that you have produced" (Modell 1994:73).

Gift provides an alternative interpretation, a weapon in the battle against the controlling stereotypes of adoption discourse. Gift transforms the baby from a product into a sign of sentiment, from something made or manufactured into something that comes from the "heart." As Ralph Waldo Emerson presciently wrote, "The only gift is a portion of thyself. Thou must bleed for me. Therefore the poet brings his poem; the shepherd, his lamb; the farmer, corn"; and a birth mother would add to his list, "the woman, her baby" (quoted in Carrier 1995:147). Such an extension of the meaning of gift widens out into a protest not only against American adoption customs but also against a cultural equation between having a baby and making a "good," between the parent's child and the worker's commodity. The equation, as Emily Martin and others suggest, diminishes the affective qualities of motherhood (Martin 1987).

For birth mothers, then, the rhetoric of gift combines the general experience of being a mother in a culture in which a baby is compared to a product with the specific experience of relinquishing a child. By emphasizing a gift, a portion of thyself, birth mothers plead their particular case: the inherent attachment of mother and child that justifies opening adoption. Referring to "human life itself," the rhetoric of gift also refers to the popular dictum in American child placement practice, "the best interests of the child." Birth mothers use the rhetoric of gift not only to personalize the relinquishment and add attachment to its terms, but also to (as it were) protect the object, the child. Open adoption is said to be in the child's interests, inasmuch as it permits the child full access to all aspects of her or his identity.

The inalienability of a gift serves a psychological purpose in arguments for open adoption. The assumption drawn from the rhetoric is that the child who is alienated from a birth mother loses a substantial part of her or his identity and the potential for mature adjustment (Lindsay 1987; Silber and Dorner 1990). The argument gains force from its exploitation of notions of roots, ancestry, heritage, and genetic background that have a substantial place in contemporaneous cultural discourse. The rhetoric has selfish ends as well.

"Gift" Transforms the Birth Mother

"They said it was all because I delivered early." In repeating the agency's excuse for breaking its promises to her, this birth mother reveals the difficulty of extracting herself from existing, official rhetoric. She had failed to produce a good product. "First of all, my baby had a temperature problem so she was under the heat lamp for quite a while." Her product was not good enough in the eyes of social workers. Her own assessment hints at an alternative interpretation: love enhances the "nature" of the object. "You know, I love that baby. If I didn't love her, I wouldn't have placed her for adoption" (Lindsay 1987:101).

The rhetoric of gift alters interpretations of relinquishment, the "object," and the birth mother herself. Behind a focus on the terms of adoption and the nature of the child, birth mothers use "gift" to present a new image of themselves and their roles in adoption. Gift accords the birth mother status and rights in the transaction of a child. Moreover, in its dependence on the concept of gift, the birth mother critique of placement practices expands into a revision of American notions of parenthood, autonomy, and kinship. Much of this revision is directed at adoptive parents and symbolically rearranges the hierarchical structures of American adoption.

Birth mothers took on the rhetoric of gift at a time of changes in child placement policy as well as in American culture more broadly. Specifically, the appeal of a gift rhetoric accompanied the so-called baby shortage of the 1970s and 1980s that gave birth mothers an increased say in adoption decisions.[11] Their products scarce and in demand, mothers who relinquished babies became bolder in their demands for a revision of the standard policies of adoption agencies and experts. At the same time, and as part of the plea for input, birth mothers took on a concept that removed them from the (perceived) marketplace in children. With "gift," birth mothers simultaneously emphasized their positive role in the transaction and removed the transaction from the very situation (a shortage) that provided them with an opportunity to shift the terms of adoption.

Gift "humanizes" or decommercializes the transaction. Gift also transforms the figure of birth mother from passive victim into willing participant, the donor of a precious item. The importance of this reversal is unmistakable in the context of a phrase that is nearly cognate with "gift," giving up.

In American adoption discourse, the mother gives up a child and the child is given up for adoption. The birth mother's gesture is rarely called generous and her baby almost never deemed a "gift." In recalling their experiences, birth mothers equate giving up with surrendering, losing, being a victim of circumstances and not a real player in the game. "I thought I gave in really easy and I felt so guilty about giving in. If I had really given them a fight I may not have felt so bad" (Modell 1994:70). Giving up has nothing positive in it, regardless of the benefits that accrue to birth parent, child, and adoptive parent from an adoption. Scenes of surrender dominated the birth mother stories I collected, and emphasized the failure of those in charge to recognize the elements of self-sacrifice and generosity involved in giving a baby.[12] Gift is a different world entirely.

Most of the birth mothers I met experienced another aspect of official adoption rhetoric that diminished any positive interpretation of their action. They were far more likely to hear themselves described as receivers than givers. Typically, a birth mother is told she is "getting the chance" to redeem her error and start over. She is reminded that she is being "offered the opportunity" to ensure her child's future. She is made into the recipient of redemption, help, and sometimes generosity. As one birth mother put it, "I realize that when I signed that paper I pretty much relinquished all my rights. Paul and Sharon [adoptive parents] have given me a lot more than they really have to give me" (McRoy, Grotevant, and White 1988:109).

A concept of gift communicates the true—experienced—significance of relinquishment for the birth mother. Gift conveys the spirit of her decision to place a baby and the generosity behind her role in the transaction. With a demand for reciprocity and return, gift also imposes norms of behavior on adoptive parents. A gift renders recipients beholden; under its script, adoptive parents return in kind and in gratitude—not through a calculation of less or more to give. Reciprocity, however, was not the experience of most birth mothers I interviewed, few of whom had contact with the adoptive family; even those who did felt partitioned off and not welcomed in to an ongoing relationship.

Their experiences, instead, were of stinginess, selfishness, and lack of gratitude on the part of adoptive parents—either imagined hatred or perceived fear of their presence. "Here this person is able to have it [baby] and give it away and, you know, rather than feeling gratitude they [adoptive parents] feel envy and envy, what grows from that but hatred?" (Modell 1994:88). Accepting the conventions of gift, birth mothers condemned those who could or would not express gratitude. "So the biological mother is important, you know, she's making this step [relinquishing]," another birth mother said to me. "And I feel she wasn't selfish in giving her daughter or son away. I don't think they should be selfish about having the child." She continued, "But you know, they're being so selfish with her. It's like I was told, I wasn't selfish when I gave her up and they don't want to have no parts of her, you know, natural background" (Modell 1994:87).

The condemnation is encompassing. Adoptive parents are not grateful for the child; nor, in these interpretations, are they the least bit generous themselves. Most damningly, according to the thrust of the rhetoric, in rejecting the donor adoptive parents are not accepting the whole child. "I was good enough [for them] to take my baby but not good enough to acknowledge." Another birth mother put it bluntly, "If they think we're such trash, why do they take our babies?" (Modell 1994:89). While the main effort is to redeem themselves and their actions, birth mothers use "gift" to protest against closed adoption in particular. It is the outstanding characteristic of closed adoption that no party to the transaction knows the other and that consequently expressed gratitude is impossible.

A rhetoric of gift does more than support the argument for complete knowledge and contact between birth and adoptive parents—the characteristics of open adoption. "Gift" transforms the birth mother, altering the moral and social traits that have commonly described birth mothers in American adoption discourse, absolutely and vis à vis adoptive parents. By emphasizing reciprocity and generosity, "gift" eliminates the unfit/fit discrimination that justifies the transfer of a child in the United States.

The only way to achieve in practice what the rhetoric of gift abstractly advocates is to open adoption. "Like 'to give up'—you don't give up your child, you don't have to build a wall. That's the choice of open adoption, there's no pretense about it." Then this birth mother added, "But people get scared" (Lindsay 1987:176). Her own response to the projected fear is interesting: she does not talk about family or kinship but about work (cf. Wozniak, this volume). "But when you have a chance to build a relationship of love and trust from the very beginning, from the very first possible moment, problems that come up can be worked out" (Lindsay 1987:176).

The effort to equate opening adoption with working on relationships, networks, and new forms of solidarity is an attempt to compromise between the "immaturity" of gift and the "maturity" of commodity. An emphasis on the work all relationships require, I argue, maintains the positive connotations of commodity-based transfers: efficient and unencumbered. Or, to put it another way, emphasizing the work of relating is a (rhetorical) way of making sure "gift" does not get totally tangled in domesticity and the female domain. I will take that point up in my conclusion.

"Gift" captures American cultural beliefs about the transfer of "human life itself," about children, and about the best interests of children. Why then does a gift model for child placement not prevail? Why does open adoption continue to scare participants in American adoption?

Obstacles to a Gift Model

However appealing in an American context the idea of child-as-gift is, opposition to open adoption remains strong. A two-part *New Yorker* essay by Lincoln Caplan provides one explanation.

Caplan begins with a sympathetic account of Peggy's decision to relinquish her child rather than have an abortion or marry her boyfriend. Peggy refused an agency adoption and turned instead to an independent route: she wanted to choose, meet, and maintain contact with the parents of her baby.[13] The essay takes the reader through the ups and downs of Peggy's plan as it impinged on Peggy, her boyfriend, Tom, and the adopting parents, Lee and Dan. The last scene shows the adoptive family happily busy in the kitchen one weekday morning. Peggy has disappeared and Tom is mainly a voice on the answering machine.

Caplan implies that the open arrangement was too complicated for the four parents. The child, Rebecca, is still an infant when the account ends, and Caplan does not focus on her welfare. His subject is the adults and the confusions and uncertainties embedded in their adoption experience. First there is Peggy, looking for the ideal adoption in which she can love the parents who will love her child. Then there is Lee, the eager adoptive mother, willing to embrace the mother who gave birth to the child. And there are the fathers—Tom, young and tentative about the adoption plan, and Dan, sensitive to the ongoing delicacy of the situation. No one, according to Caplan, knows how to negotiate a relationship that has few precedents, models, or maps.

One has to go back to cultural ideas about gift giving for a model, and these ideas are not easily compatible with expectations for raising a child of "one's own." As long as gift giving is interpreted as properly occurring between intimates, individuals who are "in love" or pledging an ongoing, loving relationship, the mode seems to violate American conventions about placing a child in adoption. As long as "gift" suggests that parents like Lee, Dan, Tom, and Peggy are bound together in enduring solidarity and ongoing reciprocity, the rhetoric prompts discomfort. None of the adults Caplan describes wants a continuous reciprocal relationship, despite the choice each originally made of the other.

Is the concern evident in Caplan's account a reflection of the best interests principle? Opponents of open adoption claim that severing the ties between birth mother and adoptive parents best serves the child. Despite rhetoric, a child is not a gift but a developing person in a society in which parents expect to have exclusive possession of their "own" children. To belong to one family, as if begotten, may well be the ideal route to adulthood for a child, as Caplan suggests in the last scene: Rebecca with her mother Lee and her father Dan, cooking breakfast just like a "normal" American family.

In considering the application of "gift," opponents and supporters of open adoption equally lay claim to the principle of the best interests of the child. Behind that claim, use of the rhetoric by opponents and supporters reveals, lie alarms about the nature and the terms of a relationship between birth mother and adoptive parent. As a reigning concept in the debate, "gift" captures the intensity of viewpoints on those who participate in adoption, on interpretations of parenthood, and on the meaning of transferring a child from person to person, house to house. Gift, in other words, crystallizes profound disagreements over the laws and customs by which a child is "transacted." And these disagreements, my essay shows, bear more directly on cultural understandings of birth mother, motherhood, adoptive parents, and fictive kinship than on the interests of children. Furthermore, the choice of "gift" connects these concerns with issues of obligation, reciprocity, fair distribution, and social solidarity. Thus the issue of child placement enters the wider domain of transferring "human life substances."

Described in terms of gift and gift giving, open adoption poses a severe challenge to the accepted assumptions controlling American adoption practice in the twentieth century. These assumptions have to do with the character, social position, and presumed moral status of those who relinquish and those who accept children. That such assumptions are embedded in competing cultural ideologies is apparent in the heat generated by a proposed opening of adoption.

For opponents, "gift" displays all the problems opening adoption would bring. From this vantage point, gift giving represents random, personalized, and impulsive exchange, not suitable to an item as precious as a child. The argument leans on a dominant theme in American culture: gift giving belongs at home, between intimates, not in public and not for matters of personal (and social) survival. Valuable items, in such a calculation, are better distributed according to the "rights of action" pertaining to commodities: objective, efficient, systematic, and predictable. In a capitalist society, gifts are thought to intensify personal connections, not to serve as mechanisms of broad social solidarity. Simultaneously, and somewhat paradoxically, opponents of open adoption predict that a gift model for the transfer of a child will demolish the family American adoption is designed to create. The prediction is phrased in terms of the child's perceptions: open adoption introduces "too many" parents into the child's life, confusing and baffling her. At bottom, gift giving undermines established, presumably neutral criteria for judging parental fitness. Gift lets "wish" into the calculation of where a child should live.

For those who support open adoption, the rhetoric of gift makes exactly the opposite argument, exposing the flaws in traditional, closed adoption. From this vantage point, gift shows the extent to which established adoption practices in the United States operated according to terms appropriate for commodities: children were scrutinized and assessed, to be marketed to appropriate consumers. In the arguments made by advocates of new forms of adoption, the old forms alienated the child from her birth mother, turning the child into a product whose qualities were more or less valuable. As in commodity transfers, in closed adoptions there were no obligations or interactions between the parties once the arrangement was finalized (legalized). For supporters of open adoption, these commodity-like practices not only violate the "person" of the child but also distort cultural notions of parenthood, love, and bonding.

At an abstract level, each position makes sense and each exploits the commodity/gift dichotomy in American culture. At another level, however, opponents of open adoption reveal an anxiety that has more to do with conservative attitudes about parenthood (motherhood) and family than with a child or the best interests of children. Similarly, supporters of open adoption may be more concerned to "right" the birth mother than to ensure the best placement of a child.

Although birth mothers are not alone, they are among the most articulate proponents of a gift model for adoption, and for good reasons. "Gift" replaces the pejorative connotations of "giving up" with an emphasis on generosity, love, and inalienable connections with a child. "Gift" replaces the passivity of surrender with the action of giving and the strangeness of relinquishment with the familiarity of gift giving. Against these positive connotations, opponents of open adoption deem "gift" an immature, wishful, and whimsical (if also loving) mode of acting. From this perspective, gift can be said to reiterate the irresponsibility, impulsiveness, and less-than-adult status of the woman who gives away a child. A rhetoric of gift associates adoption with the "archaic" quality attributed to giving and sharing items. Even garage sales are fringe to the "real" way Americans transact valuable goods. Presents are more so.

James Carrier writes, "Autonomy and reliance on the impersonal market, then, are taken to define the genius of the modern West in opposition to societies in other times and places, at the same time that they define the genius of successful Westerners in opposition to the unsuccessful" (Carrier 1995:203). In conservative adoption circles, birth mothers are the "unsuccessful," nonautonomous and not (yet) self-reliant. They are willing to give a child as if the child were just a present, a product disguised by wrapping paper and bow. The discourse ignores the gift that is a "portion of thyself." For birth mothers who support open adoption, the twist on "gift" is different: a child is not just a wrapped present obscuring a product. Rather, gift de-commodifies the item, restoring a child's status as person. The child is not a "made" object but an inherent part of the donating parent.

That interpretation of gift is ignored because of the dangers it introduces. The danger is not that a child will be confused by too many parents but that birth and adoptive parents will be too closely identified with one another.

In a book on organ transplants called *The Body as Property*, Russell Scott argues for the advantages of a commodity model when a vital substance is being transferred. Under such a model, he writes, exchange is systematic and predictable. The sources of bargaining power are evident, objective, and neutral. Moreover, exchange that follows commodity rules does not bind together individuals who have no other basis for a relationship. He talks of the "rancorous dependency" and "psychological stress" that may develop when donor and recipient of "human life substances" are known to one another (Scott 1981:238). His dire predictions about the consequences of giving rather than marketing precious goods echo the alarms voiced by opponents of open adoption. In addition, he puts a finger on the real difficulty perceived in gift giving in a capitalist society: the close contact between parties based on nothing other than the transaction.

The sociologist Richard Titmuss reaches a different conclusion in an elegant discussion of blood donation. In *The Gift Relationship*, Titmuss argues that the exchange of vital substances is unlike any other in terms of the meaning for participants and the ethical principles the transfer necessitates. Blood transfers, he argues, are appropriately guided by a gift not a commodity model; blood should not be "on the market," its distribution dependent on capacity or willingness to pay, or on an ability to extort. Money is not an "objective" but an unfair criterion for selecting recipients. An analogous claim forms a banner for critics of twentieth-century American adoption practices.

Titmuss adds another element to his discussion. He recognizes the importance of the state for ensuring that a gift model guides the transfer of vital substances. The state oversees the generosity of individuals. In addition, the state "depersonalizes" the nature of the interaction, so that donors give to unknown recipients and do not expect a direct return. "Yet, as we have argued in this study, social gifts and actions carrying no explicit or implicit individual right to a return gift or action are forms of 'creative altruism' (in Sorokin's words)" (Titmuss 1971:212). On this point his argument diverges from the rhetoric of supporters of open adoption. In the instance of adoption, the rhetoric of gift does not lead to altruism and the attention to a "universal stranger."

In adoption circles, the rhetoric of gift implies intimate, one-on-one, highly personalized transfers. The logic of the rhetoric removes the transaction from state supervision, and especially the state's representatives: agencies, social workers, and other experts. "Gift" brings the transaction back home, as it were. Ideally, gift individualizes an adoption—for good or for bad, depending on who uses the rhetoric and why—and "familiarizes" the parties with one another. Yet, I show below, in the rhetoric of supporters and opponents, gift also "de-familizes" the transaction. The logical end and (perhaps) unintended consequence of a rhetoric of gift is to remove kinship from adoption and to replace it with social solidarity. Yet, with kinship so essential an aspect of law and custom, the shift to a notion of social solidarity in child placement practices (as in blood donation and organ transplants) will require the intervention, not the withdrawal, of the state.

The ideal model for the transfer of "human life itself" is neither a free market nor a freely given gift. Neither of those models would satisfy the strictures of American policies toward children-at-risk, the thrust of contemporary interpretations of the family, or new understandings of the flexibility and "interests" of individuals. Out of the debates over opening adoption emerges another model, which interprets "gift" as a statement of reciprocity, gratitude, responsibility, and compulsory solidarity.

Conclusions: Toward a Culture of Open Adoption

"The adoptive mother and I share something. She has the raising of him but I went through the conception, pregnancy, and birth," a birth mother said to me (Modell 1994:195). This kind of sharing has been excluded by adoption policy. It does not accord with the replication of a nuclear family that has been at the heart of American adoption law since the mid-nineteenth century. It is also the scenario that fuels both support of and opposition to open adoption. But the implications of that scenario are not exactly what they seem: this is not shared motherhood but the extension of bonds that are focused on the child.

In the United States, by custom the adopted child is "just like" a biological child and by law the adopted child is as-if-begotten. Adoptive parents take full possession of the child and the birth parent vanishes from the picture. A replication of the nuclear family depends on maintaining secrecy, sealing records, and keeping birth and adoptive parents strangers to one another. If adoption is opened and those components disappear, the just-like, as-if-begotten model also disappears. What does the rhetoric of gift tell about the pragmatic consequences of such a change?

Let me imagine for a moment the impact a gift model would have if implemented in American adoption practice. First, a gift model transforms the birth mother and adoptive parents from strangers into familiars; they owe each other respect, reciprocity, and mutual gratitude. Second, the object is not alienated from either donor or recipient: the child remains attached to his birth parent even while becoming attached to (bonding with) his adoptive parents. Third, over time, attached to the child, birth and adoptive parents intensify their closeness with one another. "There's a very strong bond between me and Steve and Kate [the adoptive parents], almost as strong a bond with them as between me and Shawn [the child]" (Lindsay 1987:242). The result is an enduring solidarity among the adults, and between the adults and the child.

In non-Western societies, a gift model for the transfer of a child often operates either within an already existing kin group (however "kin" is defined) or within small, face-to-face communities. Applied to the United States, the model operates in a large, heterogeneous, diverse society. Rather than complexity rendering the model futile, I am arguing that gift can thrive in such an environment as long as the social—the interactional—connotations of the concept are recognized as constituting its primary meaning.

With a gift model, a common interest in the gift holds giver and recipient together; concern with the well-being of the child determines the nature of a birth and adoptive parent relationship. Birth and adoptive parents do not constitute one family, and the relationship is not one of kinship. The parents do not share a child but a concern with the child's well-being. Ideally, "gift" establishes a relationship between birth mother and adoptive parents in which each identifies with the child and the priority of one parental link over another (biology over law) disappears; the birth mother is not asking to be part of the adoptive family but to maintain her connection with a "portion" of herself; the adoptive parents recognize the "parts" of the child that connect with another parent. This may be an ideal for practice but it is a true rendering of the rhetoric of gift. Wherever they occur, gift-based transactions indicate the ties that bind that are not based in

Freely Given

blood, family, or kinship but rather in the "flow of social relations" (Appadurai 1986:11). The ties in an open adoption stem from the transaction itself, not from something mystical, fated, or inherent to any of the participants. These are precisely the chosen, and obligatory, ties that construct a social relationship.

Two questions must be asked, one about risks to the child and the other about the ramifications of erasing kinship from adoption. The answer to the first question is somewhat easier than the answer to the second. Constructing adoption practice in terms of a generous, reciprocal transaction between adults can be deemed a risk to the child only if begotten or as-if-begotten is considered the best way of ensuring a child's well-being. But American adoption practice already reflects a breakdown in the link between a child's well-being and a replication of the nuclear (biological) family. As adoption takes its place on a continuum with foster care and other modes of securing a child's best interests, kinship takes a back seat to safety, stability, and permanence in assessments of a child's "best place."

"Gift" pushes the significance of opening adoption further even than its advocates imagine. Taken to a logical end, "gift" in child placement practice not only banishes commodity-based rules of transfer but also revises cultural interpretations of gift giving that hold it to be domestic, feminine, private, and archaic—and therefore unreliable and whimsical. Applied to adoption practice, the rhetoric of gift changes the parties who transact a child from fit or unfit parents into moral persons who are responsible to one another through the gift of a child. Too, "gift" represents the obligatory reciprocity birth mothers phrase in terms of an expected thank-you and sign of gratitude, and which affirms the significance of the transaction. "Gift" reminds participants in adoption that a child is not a product and is not absolutely alienable from a mother the way a commodity is from a worker. "Gift" reminds the public at large that individual judgments of well-being and standards of ethical conduct inhere in any movement of a child, and, in turn, that every act of gift giving inscribes "ethics" for the whole society.

Using "gift" to define the connections made and maintained between those who transact a child widens the circle of those who act in a child's interests beyond a genealogically defined and legally repli-

| 59 |

cated related family. Guided by a gift model, adoption would represent the interests of children through the choices made by adults—though in a capitalist, consumerized culture, where gift is suspect, such a change needs revisions in law in order to evolve in custom. The history of American adoption for the past century indicates that legal structures and statutes are a necessary scaffolding for an event that carries so much emotion, subjective interpretation, and (returning to Hyde) the stuff of "human life itself."

Pulling American adoption toward a gift model ultimately breaks down the filaments attaching the transaction to kinship, family, and the symbolism of blood. In utilizing "gift," advocates of open adoption push further an already existing tendency in policy to focus on placement rather than on constructed kinship, to find a home rather than a parent for a child, and to respect rather than dismiss the importance of individual desires in the transaction of a human life. The location of settings into which a child can safely move is less and less a matter of replicating family.

Inserting "gift" into the rhetoric of adoption beautifully represents a growing tendency to place a child rather than replicate a ("natural") family. Bringing "gift" into discussions of American adoption suggests the potential not only for humanizing but also for socializing the transaction; if "gift" were to model practices, then child placement in the United States might be interpreted as a communal act: one evincing a respect for the whole beyond the individuals immediately involved. Simultaneously, American adoption might embrace the motive of altruism, in which an adult takes in a child not to "have" one or to "make" a family, but to care for a person in need or at risk. True parenthood will shift from individuals with designated qualities to individuals with generous motivations.

Have I overestimated the significance of adoption, after all a comparatively "small" phenomenon in the United States? Such a conclusion would be wrong on several counts. For one, it has long been clear that forms of reproduction are as significant as forms of production (to which they are linked) in any society, including our own. Adoption is a form of reproduction, perhaps especially crucial because of its "self-conscious" or deliberative aspect: under American policy, a particular adoption may be secret but the general rules are always open to scrutiny. Last but not least, President Clinton has recently urged adoption as the "best option" for all children who cannot remain with a biological parent. If his urgency truly affects child placement practices, then the way Americans understand "adoption" will become the way they understand a parent-child relationship—not the other way around.

Notes

First of all I thank all the birth parents, adoptive parents, adoptees, social workers, and others who gave me their time, their confidence, and their assessments of adoption. I also thank Linda Layne for asking me to participate on the AAA panel at which I delivered the paper, the commentator and other panelists for their input, and members of the audience who challenged my viewpoints. Long ago, when I drafted an early version of the paper, my colleague Steve Klepper taught me a bit of economic theory and encouraged my thinking about "altruism"; he may not remember, but I do. Recently, James Carrier went over the piece with extreme thoroughness and contributed immeasurably to its final form; I hope he will accept my gratitude without feeling "bound" by it. I am fully responsible for all interpretations.

1. The term "transaction" is borrowed from a volume on adoption in Oceania; Goodenough 1970.

2. In 1992, the last year for which total adoption statistics are available, nearly 130,000 children were adopted; of these, 42 percent were stepparent or relative adoptions and 58 percent stranger or non-relative adoptions. Because the definition of "open adoption" has been so variable, it is impossible at the moment to estimate how many adoptions might fall into that category.

3. The Child Welfare League of America (CWLA), an umbrella organization for child placement agencies throughout the country, officially approved of open adoption in 1986. The paragraphs in CWLA manuals for child placement practice offer a variation on the list I have summarized here.

4. Impressionistically, I would say "full disclosure" is the term professionals use, concentrating on the information. "Ongoing contact" is used by, and is more appealing to, the parents involved in such arrangements.

5. Like American domestic law in general, adoption law is state-based and famously diverse; see Modell 1994; Mason 1994.

6. One might add that in adoption literature "birth mother" appears in the

singular, while those who adopt generally appear in the plural, a couple. Single versus married is another indicator of less fit/more fit.

7. Letter to the editor, *New York Times Magazine*, May 3, 1998. The letter points out that actually birth mothers come from all social niches; in fact, white, middle-class, educated women are most likely to relinquish an unplanned child.

8. Problems of pronoun occur in all writings on adoption. Generally, the birth parent is a mother and therefore "she." Adoptive parents, as noted above, are two and therefore "they." I try to use both "her" and "him" for the child, while avoiding clumsiness.

9. This quality distinguishes gift from charity, a giving in which the donor usually does not know the recipient in any except (maybe) the most abstract way.

10. Interestingly, car salesmen write thank-you notes to recent customers, perhaps to personalize one of the least appealing "exchanges" in American society.

11. The shortage is usually attributed to the legalization of abortion and the greater social, cultural, and financial support for single mothers.

12. See Modell 1992 on how birth mothers utilize the term "surrender" for various ends.

13. Independent, or nonagency, adoptions are legal in most but not all states.

References Cited

Appadurai, Arjun ed.
1986   The Social Life of Things: Commodities in Cultural Perspective. New York: Cambridge University Press.

Appadurai, Arjun
1986   Introduction: Commodities and the Politics of Value. *In* The Social Life of Things: Commodities in Cultural Perspective. Arjun Appadurai, ed. Pp. 3–63. New York: Cambridge University Press.

Belbas, Nancy
1986   Staying in Touch. Smith College Studies in Social Work 57:184–198.

Caplan, Lincoln
1990   An Open Adoption. Parts 1 and 2. *New Yorker*, May 21 and 28.

Carrier, James
1990   Gifts in a World of Commodities: The Ideology of the Perfect Gift in American Society. Social Analysis 29:19–37.

1995   Gifts and Commodities: Exchange and Western Capitalism since 1700. New York: Routledge.

Goodenough, Ward
1970   Transactions in Parenthood. *In* Adoption in Oceania. V. Carroll, ed. Pp. 1–23. Honolulu: University of Hawaii Press.

Gross, Harriet E.
1993   Open Adoption: A Research-Based Literature Review and New Data. Child Welfare 72(3):269–84.

Herrmann, Gretchen
1997   Gift or Commodity: What Changes Hands in the U.S. Garage Sale? American Ethnologist 24(4):910–30.

Hyde, Lewis
1983   The Gift: Imagination and the Erotic Life of Property. New York: Vintage Books.

Landes, E., and R. Posner
1978   The Economics of the Baby Shortage. Journal of Legal Studies 7:339–78.

Lindsay, Jeanne W.
1987   Open Adoption: A Caring Option. Buena Park, CA: Morning Glory Press.

Martin, Emily
1987   The Woman in the Body. Boston: Beacon Press.

Mason, Mary Ann
1994   From Father's Property to Children's Rights. New York: Columbia University Press.

Mauss, Marcel
1969   [1935] The Gift. London: Routledge.

McRoy, R., H. Grotevant, and K. L. White
1988   Openness in Adoption. New York: Praeger.

Modell, Judith S.
1992   How Do You Introduce Yourself as a Childless Mother? Birthparent Interpretations of Parenthood. *In* Storied Lives. G. C. Rosenwald and R. L. Ochberg, eds. Pp. 76–94. New Haven: Yale University Press.
1994   Kinship with Strangers. Berkeley: University of California Press.

Narayan, Uma
1995 The "Gift" of a Child: Commercial Surrogacy, Gift Surrogacy, and Motherhood. *In* Expecting Trouble: Surrogacy, Fetal Abuse and New Reproductive Technologies. Patricia Boling, ed. Pp. 177–201. Boulder: Westview.

Scott, Russell
1981 The Body as Property. New York: Viking.

Silber, K., and P. M. Dorner
1990 Children of Open Adoption. San Antonio, TX: Corona Publishing.

Silber, K., and P. Speedlin [G. E. Myers, ed.]
1982 Dear Birthmother. San Antonio, TX: Adoption Awareness Press.

Titmuss, Richard
1971 The Gift Relationship: From Human Blood to Social Policy. New York: Pantheon.

The Gift of Life

Surrogate Motherhood, Gamete Donation, and Constructions of Altruism

Heléna Ragoné

*Blessed are those who can give without remembering,
and take without forgetting.*
—Princess Elizabeth Asquith Bibesco

In the anthropological literature, one of the first systematic and comparative studies on the cultural significance of gift giving was Mauss's work *The Gift*. As Mauss so eloquently said, "Things have values which are emotional as well as material; indeed in some cases the values are entirely emotional" (Mauss 1967:63). Mauss's assessment of gifts is not dissimilar to that of Lévi-Strauss: "Goods are not only economic commodities but vehicles and instruments for realities of another order: influence, power, sympathy, status, emotion" (Lévi-Strauss 1965:262).

In American culture, a culture in which commercialization penetrates nearly all domains, one cannot help but be struck by the widely varied uses to which the "gift of life" theme has been applied. The cultural significance of the gift theme resides in its ability to provide both a literal and a symbolic counterpoint to the increasing commodification of modern life. While many anthropologists have studied the significance of the gift, it is interesting that the gift for the most part remains understudied in industrial capitalist society (Carrier 1990). Traditionally, in American culture, the gift's application has been confined (almost entirely) to the arenas of blood donation and organ donation, where it has been "lavishly applied" (Fox and Swazey

1992:44). The inclusion of organ donation and blood donation under the rubric of "gift" may be an attempt by participants and by society to retard, at least symbolically, the trend toward the commodification of life.[1]

My own interest in the cultural resonance of the gift of life theme came about somewhat circuitously as I was conducting research on surrogate motherhood. During the course of that research, I discovered that surrogate mothers often conceptualize the child/children they are producing for commissioning couples as a "gift of life" and/or as "gifts." This they do in spite of the fact that they are compensated for their reproductive act.

In "traditional surrogacy," or "artificial insemination surrogacy," the surrogate contributes an ovum and is artificially inseminated with the sperm of the commissioning father. In such cases both surrogates and commissioning couples routinely refer to the children born of these arrangements as gifts. This practice can be understood as related to Euro-American kinship ideology, in particular its emphasis on the importance of biogenetic relatedness. Perhaps not surprisingly, I have also discovered that with gestational surrogacy, where the surrogate gestates the couple's embryos, noticeably less "gifting language" is utilized to describe these children, an issue that I will address in greater depth in a later section of this chapter.

The gift of life theme, when applied to traditional surrogate motherhood, reveals the ways issues such as work, indebtedness, pricelessness, family, and kinship are being reconfigured. In this chapter I explore the multivariant meanings attaching to the gift theme in the context of traditional surrogacy, gestational surrogacy, and gamete (sperm and ova) donation. I also explore how the gift of life theme serves as powerful reinforcement for Euro-American kinship ideology and speaks (at least in the context of traditional surrogacy) to the inviolability of the blood tie.

Background and Methods

When I began my research on surrogate motherhood in 1988, gestational surrogacy was a relatively uncommon procedure (the first such case occurred in 1987). Surrogate motherhood arrangements required that the surrogate contribute an ovum to the creation of the child and be inseminated with the intending father's semen. However, during the six-year period that followed, the practice of gestational surrogacy increased in the United States at a rather remarkable rate, from less than 5 percent of all surrogate arrangements to approximately 50 percent as of 1994 (Ragoné 1994, 1998). In gestational surrogacy, the surrogate does not contribute an ovum, but instead "gestates" a couple's embryo(s); for this reason, gestational surrogates in general tend to begin the process with different concerns and expectations than traditional surrogates. But not all gestational surrogate arrangements involve the couple's embryos; numerous cases involve the use of donor ova and the intending father's semen. The question is why couples who use donor ova pursue gestational surrogacy when traditional surrogacy can provide them with the same degree of biogenetic linkage/relatedness to the child and has a higher likelihood of success. It also costs significantly less. Typically, two reasons are cited by the largest surrogate mother program, which is now also the largest ovum donation program in the United States, with over three hundred screened donors on file. The primary reason is consumer choice, specifically that couples who choose the donor ova/gestational surrogacy route rather then traditional surrogacy have a significantly greater number of ovum donors to choose from than they have traditional surrogates. But of equal importance is that when commissioning couples choose donor ova/gestational surrogacy they are severing the surrogates' genetic link to and/or claim to the child, whereas with traditional surrogacy the adoptive mother must emphasize the importance of nurturance and social parenthood, while the surrogate de-emphasizes her biogenetic tie to the child.

This chapter draws on my research on "traditional" surrogacy conducted from 1988 to 1994, which involved interviews with twenty-eight surrogates and seventeen individual members of contracting couples as well as interviews with program directors and program staff. I also engaged in participant observation of numerous program activities such as staff meetings and intake interviews at three "open" surrogate programs, that is, programs in which surrogates and couples meet in person and select each other, then interact closely throughout the pregnancy.

Likewise, my more recent research on gestational surrogacy has involved observation of numerous consultations between program staff, intending couples, and prospective surrogate mothers in addition to formal interviews with twenty-six gestational surrogates, five ovum donors, and twelve individuals who had enlisted the services of gestational surrogates. Some of these individuals are/were clients at the largest surrogate mother and ovum donation program in the world. I also intentionally included couples who had advertised for and screened their own gestational surrogates rather than contracting with a program in order to compare their experiences against those of couples enrolled in programs.

In my research on both "traditional" and "gestational" surrogacy I have attempted, whenever possible, to select individuals from the various phases of the gestational surrogacy and ovum donation process, for example, individuals who have not yet been matched, who are newly matched and who are attempting "to get pregnant," who have confirmed pregnancies, who have recently given birth, as well as individuals for whom several years have elapsed since the birth of their child in order to assess what, if any, shifts individuals might experience as they go through the process.

Remunerating the Gift

Thus far, the image of surrogate mothers has been shaped principally by media, legal, and scholarly portrayals of surrogates either as motivated principally by monetary gain or as unwitting, altruistic victims of the patriarchy. This tendency to cast surrogates' motivations into either/or, often antagonistic categories may reveal a great deal more about Euro-American culture than it does about surrogacy itself.

Surrogates readily acknowledge that remuneration was one of their initial considerations, although they consistently deny that it was their primary motivation (and nearly all surrogates state—repeatedly—that the importance of remuneration decreased over time).[2] When questioned about remuneration, surrogates consistently protest that no one would become a surrogate for the money alone because, they reason, it simply "isn't enough." Many surrogate program directors report that surrogates telephone their programs unaware that payment is involved, a phenomenon that would seem to reinforce surrogates' claims that remuneration is not their primary motivation. As Jan Sutton, founder and spokeswoman for a group of surrogates in favor of surrogacy, stated in her testimony before an information-gathering committee to the California state legislature, "My organization and its members would all still be surrogates if no payment were involved," a sentiment not unrepresentative of those expressed by the many surrogates I have interviewed over the years.[3] Interestingly enough, after Sutton had informed the committee of that fact, several members of the panel who had previously voiced their opposition to surrogacy in its commercial form began to express praise for Sutton, indicating that her testimony had altered their opinion of surrogacy. In direct response to her testimony, the committee began instead to discuss a proposal to ban commercial surrogacy but to allow for the practice of noncommercial surrogacy (in which a surrogate is barred from receiving financial compensation, although the physicians and lawyers involved are allowed their usual compensation for services rendered, as in organ donation). This perceptual shift on the part of committee members can be understood to result from an overriding cultural imperative that motherhood, reproduction, and family be squarely situated in a noncommercial sphere, a position that also explains why these same committee members saw no inconsistency in permitting "professionals," that is, physicians and attorneys, to receive compensation for services rendered.

The following are typical surrogate responses to questions about how payment influenced their decision to become a surrogate: "It sounded so interesting and fun. The money wasn't enough to be pregnant for nine months," and "I'm not doing it for the money. Take the money. That wouldn't stop me. It wouldn't stop the majority," and again, " What's ten thousand bucks? You can't even buy a car. . . . Money wasn't important. I possibly would have done it just for expenses, especially for the people I did it for. My father would have given me the money not to do it." Surrogates' devaluation of payment as insufficient to compensate for "nine months of pregnancy" can be understood to fulfill two functions. It is, of course, representative of the cultural belief that children are "priceless" (Zelizer 1985), and in this sense, surrogates are merely reiterating a widely held belief when they devalue the remuneration they receive. But their devaluation also serves as evidence that the perfect gift is one that is priceless, one that transcends "material expression and economic worth" and that renders the material immaterial (Carrier 1990:23).[4]

Interestingly enough, when the largest surrogate mother program changed its newspaper advertisements from "Help an Infertile Couple" to "Give the Gift of Life," the new formula attracted the type of woman the program wished to attract and the program received a considerably larger volume of responses from suitable prospective surrogates.[5] The ad struck a chord with surrogates because it acknowledged that their act is one that cannot be compensated for monetarily; instead, it cast surrogacy in a poignant and life-affirming light, more clearly locating it in the gift economy. The above example reveals the highly gendered nature of the gift; it is unequivocally located within the female domain of surrogates and ovum donors, but does not apply to sperm donors.

Surrogates' dismissal of the importance of remuneration also serves an underlying function, as reflected in the following quotes. Here, a surrogate who had earlier dismissed the importance of money offers a more revealing account of her decision to become a surrogate mother: "I wanted to do the ultimate thing for somebody, to give them the ultimate gift. Nobody can beat that, nobody can do anything nicer for them." Another surrogate, who also used the word "ultimate," discussed her feelings about surrogacy in a similar way: "It's a gift of love. I have always been a really giving person, and it's the ultimate way to give. I've always had babies so easily. It's the ultimate gift of love." Another surrogate echoed the gift theme: "They [the couple] consider it [the baby] a gift and I consider it a gift." And here, a surrogate who initially opposed artificial insemination surrogacy explained her decision in this way: "I wasn't using those eggs every month and I realized they didn't mean as much to me as I thought they did. It was like giving an extra gift to the couple, one extra part of me."

We can surmise that when this surrogate used the word "extra" to describe the gift, she did so as a means to underscore the extraordinary nature of the gift. Another surrogate critiqued the very notion of associating the child with a dollar value when she said, "You can't put a price on a baby's life."

The gift formulation holds particular appeal for surrogates because it reinforces the idea that having a child for someone is an act that cannot be compensated; the gift of life narrative is further enhanced by some surrogates to embrace the near-sacrifice of their own lives in childbirth.[6] Thus, when surrogates define the children they are reproducing for couples as "gifts," they are tacitly suggesting that no amount of money would ever provide sufficient compensation. Distributive justice (Swartz 1967) cannot be attained in the traditional surrogacy arrangement. The child as a gift clearly approaches the highest ideals of gift giving since it fulfills the criteria for the perfect gift.

For Euro-Americans it is "gift relations" rather than economic exchanges that characterize the family (Carrier 1990:24). Thus, when surrogates minimize or dismiss the importance of money, they are on the one hand reiterating cultural beliefs about the pricelessness of children, and they are on the other hand suggesting that the exchange of a child for money is not a relationship of reciprocity but of kinship.

With traditional surrogacy, as with adoption (Modell, this volume), the relationship is one of indebtedness. Even though surrogates are discouraged from thinking of their relationship to the couple as a permanent one, surrogates recognize that they are creating a state of enduring solidarity between themselves and their couples. This belief complicates the severing of that relationship once the child has been born, even though the surrogate knows in advance that the surrogate-couple relationship is structured to be impermanent.

Surrogates' framing of the equation as one in which a gift is given thus serves as a reminder to their couples that one of the symbolic functions of money, namely, the "removal of the personal element from human relationships through its indifferent and objective nature" (Simmel 1978:297), may be insufficient to erase certain relationships, and that the relational element may continue to surface despite the monetary exchange.

Of all the surrogates' motivations, remuneration is the most problematic. On a symbolic level, of course, remuneration detracts from the idealized cultural image of women/mothers as selfless, nurturant, and altruistic, an image that surrogates do not wish to lose; in addition, if surrogates were to acknowledge the money as a fair and equal exchange or sufficient compensation for their reproductive work, they would lose the sense that theirs is a gift that cannot be compensated for monetarily.

In Britain, where commercial surrogacy was outlawed in 1985 with the passage of the Surrogacy Arrangements Bill (Wolfram 1987:189), the situation has been framed in moral terms: "The symbol of the 'pure' surrogate who creates a child for love was pitted against the symbol of the 'wicked' surrogate who prostitutes her maternity" (Cannell 1990:683). The idea of "pure" versus "wicked" surrogacy and, correspondingly, good versus bad surrogates is predicated on the belief that altruism precludes remuneration. The overwhelming acceptance of the idea of unpaid or noncommercial surrogacy (both in the United States and abroad) can be attributed to the fact that it "duplicates maternity in culturally the most self-less manner" (Strathern 1991:31). But perhaps even more important, the rejection of paid or commercial surrogacy may also result from a cultural resistance to conflating the symbolic value of the family with the world of work to which it has long been held in opposition. Drawing together those two spheres is the agency of the surrogate who bridges them through her reproductive work. In the Baby M case, for example, the most "decisive issue" was one of "payment to the surrogate" (Hull 1990:155). As David Schneider so succinctly described the equation, "what is done is done for love, not for money. And it is love, of course, that money can't buy" (Schneider 1968:45).

This truth is reflected in one father's remarks about his surrogate: "I realize now that what Jane [the surrogate] gave was a part of herself; that's fairly profound." Thus, the child serves as a point of connection between the surrogate and the father in the same way that it does between the wife and husband. When Swartz pointed out in 1967 that "the gift imposes an identity upon the giver as well as the receiver" (Swartz 1967:2), he could not have envisioned the literalization of this idea through surrogacy. By acknowledging that the surrogate child is a gift, the couple accepts a permanent state of indebtedness to their surrogate. The quote cited above, in which the father refers to the surrogate giving part of herself, also reflects the enduring quality of the blood tie, a relationship that can never be severed in American kinship ideology. This is because, as Schneider noted, blood is "culturally defined as being an objective fact of nature" (Schneider

1968:24). It is therefore impossible for a person to have an ex–blood relative, for example, an ex-mother, ex-father, or ex-sibling (Schneider 1968:24). In addition to the fact that blood is understood to be "a shared bodily substance," there is also the "connection between ideas of blood . . . and ideas of genes" (Strathern and Franklin 1993:20). Fathers cannot help but acknowledge this connection and comment on it, and neither can surrogates and adoptive mothers.[7]

Because all gift giving creates a degree of gratitude, when couples bestow additional gifts on their surrogates (as they do from the moment the pregnancy is confirmed to the moment the child is born and even after), they, like their surrogate, enter into a gift economy. Gifts are given with such regularity and predictability by couples to their surrogate (and to her children as well) that such acts have become encouraged by surrogate programs. However, the actual birth of the child and the surrogate's relinquishment of the child to the couple are viewed by all participants as the embodiment of the ultimate act of giving/gifting. It is therefore of interest that couples routinely bestow upon their surrogates gifts of jewelry that feature the child's birthstone. Much as in the case of pregnancy loss explored by Layne (in press), the gift of such jewelry simultaneously symbolizes the "preciousness" of the child and the enduring relationship between mother and child even in the face of a lifelong physical separation (see also Wozniak, this volume). Worn on the surrogate's body, the jewelry symbolizes and validates the special intimate bodily connection between surrogate and child and represents an acknowledgment that gifts such as vacations are mere tokens of appreciation that cannot repay the extraordinary generosity of the surrogate. In this way, gifts of precious and semiprecious stones stress the permanent connection that prevails between surrogate and child and bespeak the inviolability of the blood tie in Euro-American kinship ideology.

Of critical importance for surrogates is their ability to describe the child as a gift, a description that serves as validation for their reproductive work. But perhaps of even greater importance, the gift formulation acknowledges their unique contribution toward the creation of a family, an act that cannot (and in the view of many participants, should not) be reduced to mere commodification. This perspective also prevails in the world of adoption, where the language utilized by

participants emphasizes the "gift, giving, and generosity" and ultimately softens the idea that adoption creates a "market for babies"
(Modell, this volume).

But surrogates and couples also recognize, at least tacitly, that true
distributive justice cannot be achieved since such justice is possible
only in pure economic exchanges. It does not occur in social exchanges that involve relationships (Swartz 1967:8), and certainly not
in those that involve the gift of life. As Fox and Swazey pointed out in
their research on organ donation, it is not unusual for organ recipients
to feel a "sense of obligation" due to the extraordinary nature of the
gift proffered. Like an organ, a child is a gift exchange that is "inherently unreciprocal" since it does not have a "physical or symbolic
equivalent" (Fox and Swazey 1992:40).

Commodifying Gestational Surrogacy

The children produced through traditional surrogacy arrangements
tend to be viewed by all parties through the gift lens, a formulation
that explicitly rests on the shared acknowledgment that what the surrogate gives is literally a part of herself. However, a shift has occurred
as gestational surrogacy supersedes traditional (which involves either
the implantation of the couple's embryos or donor ova and the husband's/partner's semen into a gestational surrogate), specifically, this
gift rhetoric is much less prevalent. One probable explanation is the
influence of the hegemonic biogenetic model of kinship. The explicit
articulation of relatedness reveals the tendency on the part of commissioning couples to view themselves as "ending up with exactly the
same child that they would have ended up if it were not for the
wife/woman's inability to carry a pregnancy to term," as one resident
psychologist explained to me.

Her assessment demonstrates that with gestational surrogacy there
is a tendency, perhaps a logical one, for couples to place less emphasis
on the role and/or contribution of their surrogate and more emphasis
on the outcome. Because she does not contribute an ovum, or a
"piece of herself," the surrogate's role is increasingly seen by some
participants as that of "vessel" or "vehicle," as reflected in couples'
language.[8] For example, one thirty-six-year-old father offered the fol-

lowing assessment concerning the role of his gestational surrogate and her relationship to him, his wife, and the child: "I don't think about it much. She was *an oven* . . . she doesn't see herself as the mother. We don't see her as the mother and that's the way it is" (emphasis added).[9]

With gestational surrogacy, commissioning couples place less emphasis on the children as gifts and greater emphasis on the processual component of reproduction than do artificial insemination (AI) couples. When I discussed my theory about the absence of gift rhetoric with the director of the largest surrogate mother program, she confirmed my observations. She had observed, for example, that IVF (gestational) surrogacy couples are in her experience "more difficult" and "less kind at the birth and soon after the birth" to their surrogates. Typically, for example, a surrogate wants her own children to see and/or hold the child/children shortly after they are born. This practice is intended to provide the surrogate's children (and the surrogate herself) with closure, and it is encouraged by the program and its psychologists. And here again, this director observed that the only time "I have had couples run out of a hospital [with the baby] is IVF couples. AI couples will stay around for ten days [after the birth of the child and her/his discharge from the hospital]." AI couples, on the other hand, the director noted, "want the [surrogate's] children to hold the babies." By way of explanation, many IVF couples say that they do not want anyone holding their children because they fear contagion or "germs." But the director's observation was that these couples appear to feel that a surrogate's children do not "have the right" to hold their infants and they "almost behave like a stranger situation."

Even when the pregnancy produces a multiple birth, a fairly common phenomenon in the case of gestational surrogacy, a situation that might be expected to produce a heightened sense of gratitude in couples, the director had observed that they are actually less "kind" to their surrogate than when a "singleton" (one child) is born. The center's contract states that for every additional child couples must pay an additional $3,000 and, according to the director's assessment, a new pattern is emerging in which couples who have twins or triplets tend to give their surrogates smaller gifts. Couples frequently propose to give expensive gifts to their surrogate, but very few IVF couples who receive multiple children keep this promise, and it appears (at least initially) that surrogates who give birth to singletons receive more gifts. How do we account for this behavior? The program director's theory is that because a multiple birth means that a couple's family is complete and will no longer require the surrogate's services (or the program's services), such couples therefore "don't care what we think of them either," often flouting program directives concerning appropriate behavior toward their surrogate.

Ovum Donation: Where Have All the Gifts Gone?

My interest in gamete donation was generated by the intersection of ovum donation with gestational surrogacy. The largest surrogate mother program is also the world's largest ovum donation program. Intending couples who are unable to produce their own embryos have the option of choosing from over three hundred screened ovum donors at the surrogate program. It should be noted that what constitutes relatedness in one context and appears to be consistent with Euro-American kinship ideology is, however, inconsistent in other contexts, most notably with gamete donation.

Interestingly, gamete donation programs/clinics/banks intentionally seek to separate gametes from their donors in ways that bear a striking similarity to adoption practices. Like adoption, gamete donation (ovum or sperm donation) arose out of market concerns; an imbalance between supply and demand, a scarcity of the desired product (Modell, this volume), and it was the routinization and naturalization of IVF that resulted in an increased demand for ova. Intense competition among infertility clinics and the prospect of enormous profits coupled with weak regulatory policies (Reame 1998:1) have created a volatile environment. Although a great deal has been written about the practice of inflating their "success rates," at infertility clinics little has been written about the common practice of advertising for ova donors in college newspapers. Acting on the questionable assumption that women in college possess the genetic potential to produce more intelligent children, clinics seek ova from a cohort known to be in need of financial compensation by using financial incentives (just as sperm banks do). It is interesting to note that while gamete donation programs/banks accept donations only from individuals who are currently enrolled in college or are college graduates, no such emphasis exists in the field of blood or organ donation. In an attempt to recruit college-aged women, advertisements for ova donors have changed their rates from a $2,500 payment for one cycle to a single, larger sum of $10,000 (for three to four cycles), a sum of money that is more attractive. These ads do not indicate, however, the number of cycles involved in the larger payment, intending to draw in candidates through the appeal of a lump sum payment. Ovum "donation" then, like sperm "donation," is explicitly predicated on a remunerative model; it may appear to be outside the province of gifting, but it is not.

The idea of altruism in the context of gamete donation, in particular ovum donation, provides a particularly interesting and vital link to an understanding of the complexity of the gift. As we will see, gift rhetoric is not only contextually dependent, it is also highly gendered.

Gendering the Gift

Gender in the world of assisted conception is a crucial, if curiously understudied, variable, particularly with respect to men and gamete donation. For example, studies on sperm donation have revealed that 71 percent of sperm donors are motivated by the following factors: remuneration (Schover et al. 1992), a desire to assess their own fertility (Handelsman et al. 1985; Daniels 1989), altruism (Handelsman et al. 1985; Daniels 1989; Schover et al. 1992), and, interestingly enough, outcomes, that is, donors are interested in knowing whether children were born from their donation (Handelsman et al. 1985; Daniels 1989; Mahlstedt and Probasco 1991; Purdie et al. 1994; Schover et al. 1992). Before a donor is accepted, his semen is accessed for motility, sperm count, and so on, which allows a donor to assess his fertility. These test results are different from those that inform donors about the actual number of births that have occurred as a result of their act of donation. Given a cultural model that equates good mothers with nurturance and altruism, ovum donors are less likely than sperm donors to acknowledge the importance of remuneration. The dictates of this cultural model are mirrored by sperm banks and ovum donation program staff. Clinicians, for example, are "highly influential" in "creating the overall atmosphere . . . in which donors and recipients experience gamete donation" (Haimes 1993b:1518), as revealed in a study conducted by the University of Southern California's oocyte donation program. The clinicians Sauer and Paulson reveal that as part of the screening process for prospective ovum donors the USC program insists that the "primary reason for participation . . . [be] a desire to help an infertile woman have a baby" (Sauer and Paulson 1992a:727). In spite of this policy, which is intended to screen out women who express financial incentive, 76 percent of the women who had completed "at least one aspiration stated that compensation was important for their continued participation" (Sauer and Paulson 1992a:727, 1992b).

Why then are women who express some financial motivation turned away in spite of the fact that approved donors, once accepted, subsequently reveal that remuneration is important to them? And why are sperm donors, who routinely state the importance of financial compensation, accepted? Sauer and Paulson's conclusion was that "oocyte donors represent a rather unique group of individuals. . . . very different from men donating to our sperm bank" (Sauer and Paulson 1992a:726), a conclusion that is questionable in view of the fact that 76 percent of that program's screened and accepted ovum donors appear to value compensation, as do 71 percent of all sperm donors. Such assessments regrettably conflate commonly accepted, essentialist notions about gender, selectively reinforcing ideas of "altruism" and "gifting" only as they pertain to women.

The irony of programs using financial incentive to attract ovum donors and then requiring them to de-emphasize its importance reveals a deep-seated ambivalence in Euro-American culture about commercializing, commodifying, and fragmenting both the body and the family. Ovum donors are the first to reflect this ambivalence. As one twenty-eight-year-old ovum donor's unsolicited explanation illustrates, "Whatever money I acquired I would use in some way to better my children's life." Another ovum donor felt that her donation needed an explanation: "I got brownie points somewhere." As these remarks reveal, it is not uncommon for ovum donors to indirectly apologize for or somehow excuse their having accepted compensation for their reproductive work. Responses such as these hark back to the script-like responses I received from traditional surrogates, who de-emphasized the remunerative component and to foregrounded ideas consistent with feminine/maternal behavior, such as altruism, caring, and sharing (Ragoné 1994, 1996a); such responses can be understood to reflect the tension between market-driven forces that set the price on how much an infertility clinic can compensate a donor for her ova and the altruistic component of donors' acts. One twenty-four-year-old donor provided a fairly explicit synopsis of this cultural tension:

> I was worried what people would think of me. A close friend made a snide comment about me selling off parts of myself. It made me feel like it was a trashy kind of thing to do. What kind of women would do it? Then it became, "I am the kind of woman who would do this!"

Specifically, when programs insist on anonymity, that is, minimal or no contact between ovum donor and intending couple, they tend to reinforce the idea that gamete donation is a quid pro quo exchange, that is, donors receive payment and couples receive gametes. But although psychological studies indicate that the anonymous model is not ideal, most programs respond to the wishes of their paying clients (Baran and Pannor 1989). As the director of the world's largest sperm bank informed me, in spite of his own psychological staff informing him of the importance of abolishing anonymity and moving the bank into a more interactive and open model, there are currently no plans to implement this since he reasoned it is not what his clients want. The beliefs that children's psychological response is healthier when they are informed of their birth origins, that secrecy in the family should be discouraged, and that infertile individuals must come to terms with their infertility are the primary reasons that psychologists recommend more interactive open models for donation.

Anonymous models of donation appear to have produced negative consequences for some donors, as revealed by a twenty-four-year-old ovum donor whose first donation (facilitated by a private physician) was completely anonymous. She described her experience as an emotionally difficult one: "It made me feel like a prostitute. It was disgusting. I left there crying. In the end, I said, 'I will never do this again.' It was a horrible experience." However, she went on to donate two additional times in a program that encouraged open communication between ova donors and recipient couples/individuals. One of the psychologists at the program she chose described the donor's decision to donate again in an open program as one that "help[ed] her to heal." In this case, participating in an open donation program appears to have accorded the donor a greater degree of agency and placed her act of donation into the gift economy.

The decision of many clinics to retain the anonymity model in spite of evidence that it is not necessarily in the best interest of donors or children has produced an untenable situation for many ovum donors since they are required, on the one hand, to view their donation as altruistic, an aspect of the gift model, but on the other hand, because they will never have contact with the couples or women who receive their ova, the relationship resembles an economic arrangement. The previously quoted donor who reported feeling that she had "prostituted" herself, and the other who felt that she was "selling body parts" were expressing feelings remarkably similar to those expressed to me by surrogates participating in anonymous programs, namely, that the process served to produce feelings of fragmentation of self.

Anonymity facilitates the denial of the genetic component of donation for both donors and recipients and permits recipient couples to deny their infertility. The following quote by a thirty-two-year-old, however, reveals the confusion facilitated by an anonymous model that seeks to ignore issues of relatedness: "I thought 'wow, my eggs are going to be a child.' I don't consider it my child. It is in a way my child. It was a weird feeling. Donating eggs is much different than being face to face with what you donated. I don't think of them as related to me." Although this donor later added, "It's a good feeling helping someone have a baby," it is not uncommon for ovum donors to ignore the link between ova and children. This conceptual gap is the byproduct of both anonymity and commodification.[10]

One thirty-three-year-old ovum donor explained her view of the separation between her ova and the potential child in this way, creating a self and other distinction based on that which is inside the body and that which is outside the body: "It [the baby] really isn't mine even though they [the ova] are mine. Once it's not *in* me, I don't consider it mine" (emphasis added).

Her statement echoes the perception embraced by most gestational surrogates, specifically, that the children are not theirs because they do not have any "genetic" connection to the children they produce. The difference, however, between gestational surrogates and ovum donors is that ovum donors are in fact genetically linked to these children, whereas gestational surrogates are not.[11] But what is of fundamental importance is that various versions as to what does or does not constitute relatedness in Euro-American kinship ideology coexist and their coexistence has a great deal to do with the fragmentation and commodification of the body, as illustrated by the following quote by the twenty-four-year-old donor mentioned earlier who analogized her donation experience to that of prostitutes. Placing her gift in context, she added the following: "I compare it [ovum donation] to donating blood, platelets or bone marrow. You aren't *giving* life, but you are *saving* life" (emphasis added). Her statement can be understood as an attempt to reconceptualize her act of donation and to provide a more finely textured, albeit unclear, theory about life: "giving life," we are informed, cannot be understood as the equivalent of "saving life," a distinction that reveals the deep-seated ambivalence some ovum donors experience. One psychologist who routinely screens ovum donors informed me that ovum donors often equate their donation with blood, organ, and bone marrow transplantations, an analogy that is intended to include their act of donation in the gift economy. One particularly astute twenty-four-year-old donor described her experience of trying to separate herself from her ova and the potential child in the following way:

> I was concerned I would have an emotional attachment to the baby. I was concerned down the road if I was the biological mother. If the child wanted to meet you . . . it would be cruel not to. It is something I don't think about a lot. Keeping up that line in my mind I knew that the one thing I had to do was keep an emotional distance in myself . . . I knew I had [to] for my own sanity, I had to do it. I had to draw the line in the sand because I cannot risk an emotional attachment.

The attempt at emotional distancing and the figurative act of "drawing a line in the sand" to separate herself from the child(ren) a donation might produce represent both an explicit acknowledgment

HELÉNA RAGONÉ

of the biogenetic tie and an attempt to deny that connection. In another study that examines the experiences of recipient couples at the Center for Reproductive Medicine and Infertility at Cornell University Medical College, Applegarth et al. inform us that 90 percent of couples in their program use anonymous donation while another 9.7 percent use "known" donation, for example, biological sister donation (Applegarth et al. 1995:576). The authors concluded that only a "small percentage," 10 percent of husbands and 26 percent of wives, "expressed the desire to meet their ovum donor" (Applegarth et al. 1995:577), but the fact that more than one-quarter of the women wanted to meet their donors seems significant, especially in a program where such meetings are in all likelihood discouraged. It is also impossible to ascertain whether the following remarks attributed to several recipient women are typical. According to Applegarth et al., recipients offer thanks for their ovum donation in the following order: to "God," "the wonders of modern medical miracles," and "fantastic technology." Only one of the recipients had expressed thanks to her donor (Applegarth et al. 1995:580).

The attempt by programs and clinicians to argue that anonymity is an acceptable strategy may be understood as an attempt to privilege the desires of paying clients, that is, the recipient couple, a practice that has a long history in the annals of sperm donation. It is disconcerting that, due to the anonymity model, individuals who are able to have children through gamete donation do not feel the same sense of indebtedness to their donors as do those who participate in traditional surrogacy. As we have seen, the practice of anonymity in both ovum donation programs and sperm banks contributes to the further fragmentation of reproduction and the body, a fragmentation that is inextricably connected to the desire to maintain the commodification model.

Conclusion

An exploration of the gift in the context of surrogate motherhood and gamete donation illuminates the many and contradictory tensions that the commodification of life produces, from a resistance to conflating the symbolic value of family with work, on the one hand, to a desire to justify and even embrace the commodification of life on the other. With surrogacy, as with gamete donation, the enduring power of Euro-American kinship ideology continues to surface in spite of concerted attempts to obscure it. As one surrogate program director stated, in the course of discussing the New Jersey Supreme Court's ruling that surrogacy represents a form of baby selling in the Baby M Case, "How can a father buy his own child? He can't!"

Whether it is used in surrogate motherhood or gamete donation, gift exchange is, as Malinowski noted, "one of the main instruments of social organization" (Malinowski 1922:167). It sheds light on the quality and value of human relationships (Titmuss 1971:13), and the multivariant forms that the gift of life takes will undoubtedly continue to puzzle and in some respects confound us, as technology continues to raise previously unimaginable questions.

Notes

1. However, it is important to bear in mind that in spite of the heavy symbolic load associated with the gift of life, 35 percent of all blood donors in the United States were paid for their donation until 1964 (Titmuss 1971:93), and this practice attracts "alcoholics and other unfortunates who return frequently to blood banks" (Titmuss 1971:114). Remuneration is a critically important issue since many blood donors are aware that "they will be deprived of money if they answer yes to questions about jaundice, malaria, and other infectious diseases" (Titmuss 1971:114). It is clear that the practice has affected the safety of our blood supply; and experts have concluded that blood received from noncommercial banks is categorically safer than blood obtained from commercial banks (Titmuss 1971:152). Profit also permeates the field of organ donation and has resulted in the argument that a donor's family is entitled to compensation (for their loss, for their act of generosity, and because all the other parties involved benefit, e.g., the recipient, transplantation teams, hospitals, and so on), a position to which I have expressed strong opposition (Ragoné 1996b).

2. The version frequently put forth by surrogate mother programs is that the importance of money decreases as the pregnancy progresses.

3. Since 1988 I have formally interviewed thirty traditional surrogates and

twenty-five gestational surrogates, and I have also had countless informal conversations with surrogates.

4. This tendency to de-emphasize remuneration has also been found among Norwegian teenage baby-sitters (known as *passepike*, or girls who "look after" children). Marianne Gullestad reports that even though remuneration is important to these girls, they share in a cultural ideology that devalues the importance of payment for such a service. For this reason, when asked, the girls say that "they do not look after children for the sake of money, but because they are fond of children (*er glad I barn*)" (Gullestad 1992:119).

5. The program had changed its advertising copy because the newspaper refused to print an ad that explicitly sought a woman to serve as a surrogate. This policy has since changed.

6. Surrogates frequently discuss their feelings concerning difficult pregnancies and deliveries in terms that suggest "heroic suffering" and "heroism" (Ragoné 1994, 1996).

7. Interestingly enough, in other contexts, all parties intentionally de-emphasize this contribution (Ragoné 1994, 1996a).

8. Tentatively, I would suggest that this appears to be especially true when couples have located their gestational surrogate independently rather than through a program since they do not receive any guidance about appropriate behavior.

9. When this man's wife telephoned me one year later (for information unrelated to our interview), she apologized for the way her husband had spoken of their surrogate. She assured me that he no longer felt that way, although she did not provide specific details; she glossed over his comments and seemed embarrassed by them.

10. Even in anonymous programs, it is not unusual for donors to inquire about the outcomes of their donation. Some programs do inform donors as to whether or not their donation resulted in children. Some also provide information about the gender of the child, while others will not.

11. Fathers who have participated in traditional surrogacy, it should be noted, also tend to downplay the significance of their genetic relationship to the child by forgoing the paternity test (Ragoné 1994, 1996a).

References Cited

Applegarth, L., N. Goldberg, I. Cholst, N. McGoff, D. Fantini, N. Zeller, A. Black, and Z. Rosenwaks
1995   Families Created through Ovum Donation: A Preliminary Investiga-

tion of Obstetrical Outcome and Psychosocial Adjustment. Journal of Assisted Reproduction and Genetics 12(9):574–80.

Baran, Annette, and Reuben Pannor
1989   Lethal Secrets: The Psychology of Donor Insemination. New York: Amistad Press.

Barratt, C. L., M. Chauhan, and I. D. Cooke
1990   Donor Insemination—A Look to the Future. Fertility and Sterility 54:375–87.

Cannell, Fenella
1990   Concepts of Parenthood: The Warnock Report, the Gillick and Modern Debates. American Ethnologist 17:667–86.

Carrier, James
1990   Gifts in a World of Commodities: The Ideology of the Perfect Gift in American Society. Social Analysis 29:19–37.
1991   Gifts, Commodities, and Social Relations: A Maussian View of Exchange. Sociological Forum 6(1):119–36.

Daniels, K. R.
1989   Semen Donors: Their Motivations and Attitudes to Their Offspring. Journal of Reproductive, Infant Psychology 7:121–27.

Fox, Renee, and Judith Swazey
1992   Spare Parts: Organ Replacement in American Society. New York: Oxford University Press.

Gullestad, Marianne
1992   The Art of Social Relations. Oslo, Norway: Scandinavian Press.

Haimes, E.
1993a   Issues of Gender in Gamete Donation. Social Science and Medicine 36(1):85–93.
1993b   Do Clinicians Benefit from Gamete Donor Anonymity? Human Reproduction 8(9):1518–20.

Handelsman, D. J., S. M. Dunn, A. J. Conway, L. M. Boylan, and R. P. S. Jansen
1985   Psychological and Attitudinal Profiles in Donors for Artificial Insemination. Fertility and Sterility 43:95–101.

Hull, Richard
1990   Gestational Surrogacy and Surrogate Motherhood. *In* Ethical Issues

in the New Reproductive Technologies, Richard Hull, ed. Pp. 150–55. Belmont, CA: Wadsworth Publishers.

Layne, Linda L.
in press "He Was a Real Baby with Baby Things": A Material Culture Analysis of Personhood, Parenthood and Pregnancy Loss. *In* Ideologies and Technologies of Motherhood. Heléna Ragoné and France Winddance Twine, eds. New York: Routledge.

Lessor, R., K. Reitz, J. H. Balmaceda, and R. Asch
1990 A Survey of Public Attitudes toward Oocyte Donation between Sisters. Human Reproduction 5:889–92.

Lévi-Strauss, Claude
1965 The Principle of Reciprocity. *In* Sociological Theory: A Book of Readings. Lewis A. Coser and Bernard Rosenberg, eds. Pp. 77–86. New York: Macmillan.

Mahlstedt, P. P., and K. A. Probasco
1991 Sperm Donors: Their Attitudes toward Providing Medical and Psychological Information for Recipient Couples and Donor Offspring. Fertility and Sterility 56:747–53.

Malinowski, Bronislaw
1922 Argonauts of the Western Pacific. London: Routledge.

Mauss, Marcel
1967 The Gift: Forms and Functions of Exchange in Archaic Societies. New York: Norton.

Myers, M. F.
1990 Male Gender-Related Issues in Reproduction and Technology. *In* Psychiatric Aspects of Reproductive Technology. N. L. Stotland, ed. Pp. 25–35. Washington, D.C.: American Psychiatric Press.

Pedersen, P., A. Neilsen, and J. Lauritsen
1994 Psychosocial Aspects of Donor Insemination. Acta Obstertricia et Gynedological Scandinavica 73:701–5.

Purdie, A., J. Peek, V. Adair, F. Graham, and R. Fisher, R.
1994 Attitudes of Parents of Young Children to Sperm Donation—Implications for Donor Recruitment. Human Reproduction 9(7):1355–58.

Ragoné, Heléna
1994 Surrogate Motherhood: Conception in the Heart. Boulder: Westview.

1996a   Chasing the Blood Tie: Surrogates, Adoptive Mothers, and Fathers. American Ethnologist 23(2):352–65.
1996b   Book review of Life and Death under High Technology Medicine. Ian Robinson, ed. Man 2(2):378–79.
1998 Incontestable Motivations. *In* Reproducing Reproduction: Kinship, Power, and Technological Innovation. Sarah Franklin and Heléna Ragoné, eds. Pp. 118–31. Philadelphia: University of Pennsylvania Press.

Reame, Nancy
1998   Unintended Consequences: What America Should Do about Assisted Reproduction. A Health Policy Report to the American Academy of Nursing and Institute of Medicine. Washington, D.C.

Rosenberg, H., and Y. Epstein
1995   Follow-up Study of Anonymous Ovum Donors. Human Reproduction 10(10):2741–47.

Sauer, M., and R. Paulson
1992a   Oocyte Donors: A Demographic Analysis of Women at the University of Southern California. Human Reproduction 7(5):726–28.
1992   Understanding the Current Status of Oocyte Donation in the United States: What's Really Going On Out There? Fertility and Sterility 58(1):16–18.

Schneider, David
1968   American Kinship: A Cultural Account. Englewood Cliffs, NJ: Prentice-Hall.

Schover, L. R., S. A. Rothman, and R. I. Collins
1992   The Personality and Motivation of Semen Donors: A Comparison with Oocyte Donors. Human Reproduction 6:1487–91.

Simmel, Georg
1978   The Philosophy of Money. London: Routledge and Kegan Paul.

Strathern, Marilyn
1991   The Pursuit of Certainty: Investigating Kinship in the Late Twentieth Century. Distinguished Lecture presented at the annual meeting of the American Anthropological Association, Chicago.

Strathern, Marilyn, and Sarah Franklin
1993   Kinship and the New Genetic Technologies: An Assessment of Existing Anthropological Research. Brussels: European Commission (a report

commissioned for the Commission of the European Communities Medical Division [DGXIT] Human Genome Analysis Program).

Swartz, Barry
1967   The Social Psychology of the Gift. American Journal of Sociology 73(1):1–11.

Titmuss, Richard
1971   The Gift Relationship: From Human Blood to Social Policy. New York: Pantheon.

Wolfram, Sybil
1987   In-Laws and Outlaws: Kinship and Marriage in England. Beckenham, England: Croom Helm.

Zelizer, Viviana
1985   Pricing the Priceless Child. New York: Basic Books.

| THREE |

Gifts and Burdens

The Social and Familial Context
of Foster Mothering

Danielle F. Wozniak

Introduction: Gifts and Burdens

This chapter examines constructions of motherhood, mothering work, and kinship articulated by African American and Euro-American women who foster through the state of Connecticut. All the women who participated in this study experienced themselves as mothers in relation to their foster children and developed kinship bonds based on affective claims of belonging. Their caregiving relationships were premised on a conception of motherhood as an empathic and inclusive experience in which their work was to apprehend and meet the needs, wants, and realities of the children in their care. One consequence of caregiving work was to heal children's emotional, psychological, and physical afflictions, and to enhance their chances for survival. Another was to create extended kin and caregiving networks through permanent, though not always physically embodied, relationships that reconstituted fostering from an impermanent and transient caretaking relationship to one of enduring affective and instrumental familial bonds. Fostering also had an important social/moral dimension. Through transformative relationships with children, women healed a portion of their community and contributed to overall social reform. Through mothering work, women saw themselves as family makers, professional caregivers, and community healers (Wozniak 1997a, in press).

Woven through their discourse, as signs of situated womanhood in which one is at once the receiver of special benefits and the bearer of extraordinary hardship, were descriptions of fostering as gendered "gifts" and "burdens." As women spoke about themselves and their experiences, their descriptions of fostering assumed a kind of dualism. Foster mothering, and children themselves, were both a gift and a burden. Fostering was both the best thing they had ever done and the worst; their lives were immeasurably enhanced and forever depleted.

Gifts emanated from embodied, intimate, caregiving relationships. In their narratives, women considered children and the ability to enact caregiving relationships gifts and simultaneously spoke of themselves as gift recipients. Discourses of mothering as a gift intersected discourses of a gendered identity. Foster mothers were able to see, experience, and know the gifts of fostering through the production of a maternal self-in-relation to children that was moral, transformative, and creative in nature. Women spoke of their caregiving knowledge and expertise as gifts of womanhood that made them "special" and "different" from both men and women who were not involved in fostering. Difference was intersected by agency. By choosing to mother through fostering, women chose to facilitate the development of children's unmet potential and in this way they co-created possibilities for individual children and for society as a whole. Thus, mothering was a gift women gave to their communities.

Maternal gifts were always and closely associated with gendered "burdens." To make the sacrifices necessary to care for very difficult children was a burden, as were weathering feelings of being "different," enduring the hardships of failure when a child had to be removed, or mourning the loss when children returned to their families of origin. Women also felt the burden of having their parenting usurped and denigrated by the state and their kinship relations with children ignored or marginalized. Burdens were constructed in metaphors of balance involving payment and costs. As *women*, they found that enduring the painful burdens of fostering was "the price you had to pay" for the gift; it was the cost of being gifted. The cost of the gift was located within the maternal body. Women spoke of broken hearts, of carrying the memories of children who had left or been taken from them in their hearts and heads, of feeling an emptiness in the pit of their stomachs. At other times, the price was paid by conflict and tension in marital relationships or by foster mothers' biological children who experienced the stress of constant comings and goings of household members.

The subtext for burden themes was that being a woman-in-relation was inherently or eventually painful since the world exacted a heavy price from those who valued and enacted caregiving relationships. In particular, foster mothers saw their mothering commodified and denigrated by the state, their caregiving labor equated with "women's" domestic labor and economically ghettoized, and their kinship relations ignored. Women spoke of themselves as thinking, feeling human beings enacting the work of caregiving and kinship but felt that the state saw them as easily interchangeable temporary child care workers and nonmothers who had an exclusively instrumental relationship with foster children. As nonmothers or archetypal "bad mothers," they embodied historically antithetical images of motherhood and wage laborer, or more succinctly, Madonna and whore, women who profited from their nature and being, motherhood. Consequently, foster mothers were not paid for their labor, nor recognized for their expertise as "professionals," nor afforded the rights or authority given to "family" members. The affective relationships between foster parents and foster children were often ignored since state policy and social worker practice consistently defined "family" in exclusively biological or legal terms (Wozniak 1997a, b, in press).

The significance of foster mothering discourses, similar to the significance of mothering discourses on adoption (Gailey 1995; Modell, this volume), surrogacy (Ragoné, this volume), or lesbian maternal relations (Lewin 1993, 1996), is that they transform ideologies of patriarchy in which relatedness is considered to be a matter of the male seed by establishing kinship relations based on claims of belonging within an extended family (Katz Rothman 1994). This, as Christine Ward Gailey reminds us, is done in a "political and cultural climate that reifies kinship as bloodline . . . and integrates biological determinism into the concept of human nature" (Gailey 1995:3). Foster mothers' experiences also redefine gender ideologies that bifurcate mothering and wage labor by consistently positing mothering as a socially valuable and economically important activity.[1]

The significance of gift rhetoric in women's fostering narratives is that it transforms discourses in which foster mothers and foster children are denigrated as "nonmothers" and "failed" children, because they do not mirror patriarchal nuclear family life, into a discourse in which both are inherently valuable. Mothering is acclaimed as important, life-sustaining, transformative work rather than being primarily associated with essentialized, nonproductive, noneconomic domestic labor. In this way foster mothers, like women who have experienced pregnancy loss (Layne, this volume), assert themselves as moral agents and fostering as socially important work in a consumer culture where "traditional morality and its basis in patriarchal familialism both rhetorically and in the field of social policy" (Clarke 1996:76) define foster mothers as immoral producers and foster children as failed products.

Gift rhetoric also transforms women's sense of powerlessness and coercion at the hands of the state into a discourse of agency and control. Women choose to become foster mothers because they have been given a gift to see the value of children and the special skills required to raise them. Unlike mothers of children with disabilities (Landsman, this volume), who did not freely choose an especially challenging form of mothering, and who resist the view that prior to giving birth they must have been special women or they would not have been given "special children," women who foster openly embrace a view of themselves as "special," "gifted" parents. Discourses in which mothering and children are considered gifts enable women, who feel judged and devalued, to see themselves as unique. They have been given the talent and strength to take care of foster children because they themselves are gifted. Inherent in these powerful and transformative gifts is a sense of altruistic responsibility. Those who have the gifts to mother are compelled to exercise them and to effect interpersonal and social change in spite of obstacles or hardship. By asserting mothering as a gift freely given (that is, separate and distinct from the economic remuneration), women create a discourse, antithetical to the reality they experience, in which the state is beholden to foster mothers rather than women being dependent on or subservient to the state. Through gift metaphors, foster mothers transform fostering, themselves, and foster children into singularized agents who cannot be commodified—

whose value is priceless and irreplaceable (Belk and Coon 1993:408; Kopytoff 1986:64–65) in a social context that regards fostering as a commodity exchange.

In their fostering narratives women used images and descriptions of gendered gifts and burdens to talk about their mothering work. Through text analysis four themes consistently emerged: (1) the gifts of mothering and transformative relationships; (2) kinship and social repair; (3) the gift of children and the burden of their care; (4) commodified mothering and missed gifts and loss. I discuss each of these themes in the remainder of the essay.

Methods

My data come from participant-observation and intensive informal and semistructured interviews conducted over the course of three years from 1993 to 1996 in Connecticut. I interviewed fifty-one women in intensive, semistructured interviews, each lasting between two and three hours. I interacted intensively with foster mothers through three conferences, participated in the formulation of a foster parent–run education committee, and was on the board of the professional foster parents' association. Through key informants, I provided baby-sitting services, transported foster children to and from appointments, and participated as much as possible in women's households and daily lives. I also did structured ranking interviews with sixty-nine women to conduct explicit tests on consensus, reliability, and validity, and conducted four focus group sessions.[2] In all, I talked with over two-hundred foster mothers who were licensed by the State Department of Children and Families. My sample came from a random sample drawn from the database of 1,990 foster mothers the state maintains and from a convenience sample recruited through foster mothers.

Study participants (fifty-one from semistructured interviews, and sixty-nine who participated in the structured ranking interviews) were evenly divided between African American (43.5 percent) and Euro-American women (47.8 percent); a very small portion were Hispanic or "other" (1.45 percent). The majority of women were married (about 75 percent), and the rest were divorced or had never been married. Participants were primarily "middle-" or "working-class." Women's ages ranged from twenty-eight to seventy-eight. The number of children women fostered over their careers ranged from those who fostered no children (there were some who had not yet received any) to those who cared for 250. Of the children women currently had in their homes, a small proportion were biological relatives. Study participants also included women who had adopted up to eight children and those who had adopted none. The length of time children stayed with foster mothers varied from as short as an overnight stay to as long as eight years. Foster mothers also cared for children from a wide range of ages, from birth to late adolescence.

All the interviews were transcribed verbatim with the exception of the participants' names.[3] The interviews were coded by Ethnograph and an Ethnograph-like system and a code book was designed. Women's comments included in this essay are excerpts from those transcripts. While I do not wish to portray this group of women as a monolithic or unidimensional group, an analysis of the codes revealed strong patterns in women's conceptualization of foster mothering, parenting norms, mothering, and parent-child relationships. With a few notable exceptions, foster mothers expressed a high degree of consensus on the core features of foster mothering (how kinship is established through fostering, the permanence of fostering relationships, and the criteria for motherhood; see Handwerker and Wozniak 1997).[4]

The Gifts of Mothering: Recognition and Transformation

Many women placed their ability to recognize children in need and their decision to respond through mothering within a historical legacy passed down from their grandmothers and mothers or through close family friends. To mother and to foster was to become part of a continuum of gifted and extraordinary women who transmitted valuable life lessons and knowledge to children and thus who ultimately changed the face of society. Through mothering one could ensure that the upcoming generation received the care, skills, and knowledge they would need in order to face the world with a solid sense of self. It was a *woman's* response to social and community survival since through mothering one altered the life trajectory of another, changed their opportunities, and conditioned who they would become.

Mothering ability was based on embodied knowledge emanating from a woman's heart, blood, and bones. It was knowledge women felt or intuited and, for most, emerged from their earliest life experiences. All the women defined motherhood and foster mothering through the relationships they developed with children, sometimes with children's biological parents. When this occurred, fostering forged kin networks throughout local communities and connected families. As these mothers state,

> It's always been in me. I've always been a person with children. My mother did it, my grandmother did it. My grandmother raised fifty foster kids; she'd just take them in. The kids would be—she don't care. She just take them in. My mother did the same thing. Somebody come, they got no place, she just take them in. It was just something that was in my heart, within me. . . . I'm doing it because I love children, and I felt like they need somebody to take care of them. I've raised children in my home that was not mine. During the run of my lifetime with children, I think there were about fifteen or twenty children that went through my home. I didn't adopt them or nothing like that, but it's just that they didn't want to stay home. Their mother drank, their father drank, they was abusive parents and stuff. They would leave their homes sometimes in the middle of the night and say, "Can we stay? Can we stay?" I mean back then, people didn't report things to the authorities like they do now. So, I would just say, fine. And sometimes I would call the parents and say, "Look, your son is over here. Are you looking for him?" [They would say,] "No, we know where they're at and they're happy over there. Let him stay. . ." And I said, "All right, no problem." And two of the fellows stay in my house until they got grown. . . . One lives in California but he won't miss a birthday. He would phone from California for my birthday. And you know, they all of them call me mom. [S]ome of them will come by here every week to see me. "How you doing, mom?" (Ann Michaels, a divorced African American woman in her late fifties)

> Friends of ours had done it for years. My husband always lived as a child with foster brothers and sisters. So he mentioned that he wanted to do it. And we had decided that when our youngest was school age, we would look into it. And we had neighbors move in, no mom, very busy

dad, and the eight-year-old was just left home constantly alone. So we unofficially fostered him. I mean, he actually lived with us for seven days a week. I took him to school, shopping, I got him ready for school, play, the whole bit. We did everything. And he was just a wonderful little boy, and he fit well into our family and it's just something naturally we did. So after they moved out of the area, my husband said to me one evening, we ought to look into foster care. (Ellen McKnight, a married Euro-American woman in her mid-thirties)

Most women approached fostering relationships through their own familiarity with loss, adversity, or abandonment, and thus empathically *recognized* the painful life experiences of the children in their care. Recognition of a child's pain enabled many women to speak with empathic recognition. Discourses of recognition became entwined with discourses of claiming. Women knew the struggles with which foster children were confronted and claimed both the child and the struggle as their own. As this mother recounts, recognition, claims of belonging, and the gift of kinship are necessarily mutual.

[Bertie] was sexually abused. And she will move her body on this [pole in the basement] and I asked her what are you doing? And she told me, practicing for when she gets married. She is five. She is a grown-up trapped in a kid's body. . . . She is very hard to handle, but she has calmed down a lot since she has been here. . . . She's been shifted around from home to home since she was two years old. She's been in four or five homes. She has to find a place. When she first came to me she used to keep everything in a paper bag. And I still find her resorting back to that once in a while. And the minute she did something that she thought would make me angry she would say, "Well, let me get my bags packed," 'cause she just know that I am going to send her away. I says, "No, I am not going to send you away. . . . This is your home. . . ." Most of the time she calls me auntie. . . . Once she called me mom, and I said, "I'm not your mom and I don't think your mom would like [you calling me mom]." She asks me, she says, "Do a mom put you in bed at night?" She says, "Do a mom dress you in the morning? Do a mom give you the food?" And I said, "Yes." "Then," she said, "Well I guess you're my mom." (Dorthea Hansen, a married African American woman in her late fifties)

| 96 |

Discourses in which women recognized foster children's pain or struggles were closely linked with recognition of the child's giftedness. In many respects, it was the fact that foster children were "different" that made them "special" or "gifted" in foster mothers' eyes. Landsman (this volume) notes similar findings among mothers of disabled children in which children's impairments were integrated into a concept of selfhood that was positively valued. As she points out, through this discourse, women critique delegitimizing aspects of consumer culture by rejecting the ideal that "real" children are perfect products and "real" mothers are those who produce and tend them.

Most women conceded that their children were *not* like "other children" (i.e., like "normal" children) in terms of their abilities, histories, or needs, nor were fostering relationships like other mother/child relationships in terms of the physically enduring or gradual nature of the relationship. But foster children were like other children in that they had immeasurable potential, they could heal, grow, and be loved— they could both transform and be transformed, and this made them gifted. And fostering relationships were like other mother/child relationships in that they were premised on love and intimate knowledge and recognition of the human being. As this mother remembering her foster daughter's accomplishments states,

I loved her *so* much—and they told me that she would probably die. And she died ten months after I had her. But she achieved everything they said she wouldn't. By the time Rachel died, she was going to school every day instead of just three days a month. And she was taking these tests; she had to go and have her blood thinned. And *before* [she came to live with me], it would take the whole day to do it. And by the time she died, we would go at 10:00, by 11:30 we were back home. . . . She only crawled [before she came here], and before she died she was chasing me all over the house. It was not that she couldn't do it. No one had taken the time [with her]. You have to take the time 'cause—I truly believe this—there is nothing that anyone can't achieve. (Dorthea Hansen, a married African American woman in her late fifties)

Recognition of the "hidden gift," buried under imposed labels like "hopeless," "retarded," or "sick," simultaneously designated foster mothers as gifted in their ability to recognize and participate in transformations. This was important since foster mothers often felt judged, and felt that their motives for fostering were suspect and linked to a commercial exchange rather than mothering. One way women contested their designation as nonmothers was to weave the importance of kinship through transformation stories. By defending the legitimacy of kinship through claims of belonging, women transformed "familyless" nonchildren into "real" children while asserting themselves as "real" parents and fostering as a "familial" (versus a commercial) relationship (See Belk et al. 1989).[5] As these women relate,

> Once I was at the hospital with a sick baby. He was going to be in the hospital for three weeks. It was really hard on me to get there every day, I had a four-year-old at home and everything. But that little baby didn't know anyone at the hospital. He didn't know anybody. When I came early in the morning, he would brighten up . . . I got him to eat. I was talking to a nurse, and she said, "If it's so hard for you to get here, you don't have to come. You're *only* the foster mother." I left the room crying and my pediatrician who knew me asked me what's wrong. I told him that she had said I was *only* the foster mother. . . . Only the foster mother? Can you believe that? These kids are part of my *family*. I make arrangements to be there [for them]. (Linda Vanderbrink, a married Euro-American woman in her late forties)

> I have the picture here, right here, what she looked like [referring to pictures of a baby they cared for who had open-heart surgery]. They couldn't get over that we were there every day. They'd say, "Are you sure you're her foster parents?" [We'd say,] Yes. [They'd say,] "Why are you here every day?" [I would say,] "Because it's our child. That's why we're here every day." (Pearl Hobbs, a married Euro-American woman in her late fifties)

Fostering relationships were premised on the ability to not only recognize the gifts one brought to the relationship, and thus to recognize the other as a gift bearer, but also to recognize the other as a gift *sui generis*. "Recognition is a form of return: it gives back a symbolic equivalent and the symbolic equivalent opens and constitutes the order of exchange, and of debt" (Frow 1997:107–8). The debt of recognition in fostering was based on mutual and interdependent need.

Most women, upon hearing about a child, felt they had something—care, knowledge, and experience—to give *that* child that was invaluable and unique. As one woman said when she read about a young homeless girl in the newspaper, "I read about her and I thought, '*That* girl needs me, and what I can give her!'" At the same time women recognized that what they would receive from a particular child was equally distinct. Individual women and children were united in their need for each other. Thus the other side of "that girl needs me" is necessarily "and I need *that* girl."

Unlike gift discourse in adoption (Modell, this volume), which established bonds of loyalty and concern rather than relatedness, gift recognition and exchange in fostering cemented bonds of connectedness through the establishment of kinship. Gifts, such as those found in kinship relationships, were always bidirectional exchanges between two equally valuable and valued parties. Through their presence, children were gifts to women; in return women gave mothering gifts to children. Through participation in the relationship, both mother and children were transformed. As this mother states,

> I think my life is more complete now. A lot changed with them [foster children]. 'Cause it's like when I got Rachel, Rachel needed me so much, and the only way I was going to be able to give it to her is that she let me into her world. And I was not going to get into her world being the person that I was raised up to be. So I had to sort of like, you know, be more affectionate with her, you know, be a *lot* more. (Dorthea Hansen, a married African American woman in her late fifties)

Kinship and Social Repair

As women formed relationships with children based on care-giving and the hope of transformation, they forged bonds of kinship based on claims of belonging. This wove themes of permanence, stability, commitment, and familial legitimacy through a context of physical and temporal impermanence. "Since the purpose of legitimacy is to determine the eligibility of individuals to enjoy certain benefits and advantages" (Bell 1998:243), discourses of kinship legitimated foster children's rights to physical and emotional care, a home, and stability.

Claims of kinship also legitimated fostering relationships as familial, that is, committed, enduring, caring relationships in which one's needs, however articulated, could and would be met. Through fostering, women redefined the nature of kinship from an idiom of relatedness through blood and embodied permanence to one of commitment, affection, and transformation. As this mother states,

> I got her when she was thirteen, and we had just moved into an all-white neighborhood. And you know how it is when you move into an all-white neighborhood. (*She smiles.*) You've got to be cool. Don't make a lot of waves, 'cause people are watching you all the time, seeing how you are, what you like. And I got my last one when she was thirteen, and we had just moved in, and she had seven foster homes before coming to me; they saying she was all out of control and all. And don't you know the first week we was there, she stole $500 from a neighbor. (*Shakes her head, looking down, smiling at the memory.*) And she says to me, "So, I guess now you gonna have me moved, huh?" And I said, "No, baby. You mine now. You one of my children. You gonna stay here. You gonna turn that money back, you gonna go to court. You gonna suffer. But I'm gonna suffer with you. And you *never* gonna do that again." (Delia Johnson, a single African American woman in her early thirties. She is referring to one of her five foster daughters)

Claims of belonging enabled adults and children to form potentially enduring relationships, even if physical presence was impossible. Whether or not a child stayed in a particular foster home, the relationship often endured for foster mothers. Layne (this volume) described similar findings for women who sustained a pregnancy loss. The "gift of motherhood" resulted in a changed status even when the relationship to the fetus/child was fleeting. Foster mothers' constructions of motherhood, like those of women who have miscarried, were not contingent on the physical presence of the child or an ongoing embodied relationship. Instead they were premised on an enduring sense of caring that permanently connected them to a particular child. Thus the gift was an enduring change in selfhood actualized through ongoing *caring* even if *caregiving* was no longer possible. As one mother stated about her foster daughter who left to live with a maternal grandmother, "Just because the child leaves, doesn't mean that our caring stops. . . . Arabelle is still my family. You know, I'm still her mom and I hope she always calls me mom. And if she came up against hard times, I would still be her mom."

Many women also expressed discomfort with the term "foster," believing that it connoted a temporary or fake mother and, reflexively, referred to a nonfamilial relationship with children. This connotation was considered by women to be a misinterpretation of their work and their selfhood. Fostering was mothering; mothering necessitated kinship.

> I don't see myself as a foster mother. Because I don't believe there is anything such as a foster mother. Because I look at the animal world and if they can adopt—if a dog can adopt a cat and he knows that he is not a cat, then I have to say to myself as a foster mother, I am just a mother that had to step into a situation where there was no mother. "Foster" to me means "substitute" and I am not a substitute. I am the real thing. (Beatrice Rollins, a divorced African American woman in her late fifties who accepts only short-term foster care placements)

Women also objected to designations like "foster child" or "state child" and the connotation of an inferiority and impermanence. "State children" lived in the opposite of their "real" families—they lived in foster homes and thus had no claim to kinship, an inferior claim to parental affection, and a subordinate claim to material goods. Foster mothers as "state mothers" were commercial artifacts of industrial capitalism and could be purchased and exchanged at will. Perhaps more important, however, foster mothers were aware that through these designations foster children were signs of failed nuclear family ideals. Children were "state" children because their "real" parents, echoing the words of a nineteenth-century social worker, "didn't love them in the right way" (Zelizer 1994a:72) and failed to meet state-specified parenting standards. As products of failed families, foster children themselves were tainted and seen as damaged, failed, or non-children and could legitimately be excluded from resources.

> When I get them, I tell them that God loves you so He put you where I could take care of you. I just teach them that you know, try to treat them all as if they were mine. Sometimes I forget . . . that they're not

mine until somebody reminds me, that hey, this is a foster child. We had a problem with one girl in glasses, she became a teenager and needed glasses. She wouldn't wear them because the state said only "X" amount of dollars paid for this type of glasses and the children laughed at her, made fun of her. . . . So we went out and put out money and bought her some glasses so she would wear them.[6] . . . I asked them, "what do you have?" to the eye doctor. He said, "these are all we have for 'state' children." I said, "What do you have for normal children? We don't have *'state' children*. We have *children*." (Norma Peel, a married African American woman in her early seventies)

The gifts of kinship and belonging in women's narratives were linked to social repair and obligation. Through mothering individual children, women repaired an element of social brokenness and contributed to community survival.[7] Often this was understood to be limited to healing or raising an individual child, at other times, women effected social repair through the mending of "family" relationships by forging kin networks with children's mothers or grandmothers, enabling children to be a part of both kin groups. In both cases, women saw children, themselves, and their mothering as intimately connected to a larger social fabric. In this way, what they did with and for children mattered; it "made a difference." Through this difference, the "gift" of mothering became a part of the legacy both women and children passed on to future generations. As these women comment, the gift of mothering, kinship, and love is hope for the future.

> Maybe I can love them enough so when they go back that love will keep them and [they can] hold onto it until they'll be big enough to do something for themselves. (Monica Walker, a widowed African American woman in her early sixties)

> I guess the one thing that I *know* I can do for these children is to provide a safe place while they're here. I can't necessarily say that while they're with their mom or dad things are going to be safe because if the law says they have to visit, then they have to visit. But while they're here, in my home, they'll be safe. There will be plenty to eat. Their home will be clean. They will be warm. Their things, their physical needs will be met, as many of their emotional needs as I can. They

won't have to be afraid of any male figures that are going to harm them nor will I harm them. And I just, while you're here, I'm the mommy in the house, and I will do the best job that I know how to do as a mom, and that's all I can say. But I think that's the most important thing I can do.

If they're only here for a little while, they see what's reasonably normal. God knows our house isn't normal. Early in the morning and late in the evening it does not look normal. I mean maybe that's what normal is, everybody running around. But a touch of what seems to be normal, a mom and a dad figure, other brothers and sisters, with people sharing. Maybe it's laughing or maybe sometimes maybe it's crying or even getting angry, but it's emotions and that's what goes on here a lot, emotion. And seeing an interaction with people loving and touching each other in a good, healthy way. And if they only get it for a very short time, they know it exists because they saw it themselves. And I think that's probably, if I can say we ever did anything really good, that would be it. (Graciella Stevens, a married Euro-American woman in her late forties)

The Gift of Children, the Burden of Their Care

In their discourses women described individual foster children as gifts. They were "blessings" and "joys"; and they had become such an irrevocable part of women's lives that many spoke of being unable to envision life without them. Embodied metaphors were often used to locate women's emotional bond to children. One mother described her two-year-old foster daughter as the apple of her father's eye. Another mother referred to her foster daughter as having "won the hearts of so many people." Yet another spoke of embodied loss: "Handing over babies was the hardest part. It was always like handing over a part of your body, like your arm or your leg." The depth of women's relationships was a source of satisfaction and unexpected pleasure. Whether or not women were married, many spoke of their relationships with children as the most fulfilling and rewarding in their lives. Through their foster children, women were intimately connected to another human being. Through that connection, both their and foster children's lives assumed value and meaning. As Lillith Anderson, a single lesbian mother explains,

| 103 |

I have been saying for years [foster parenting] is my primary emotional relationship. I do not have an adult partner and I don't do one night stands either. Now thank God I have a rich friendship network but it's real clear to me that my emotional relationship is with the kid in my house, whenever I take them, one or max two at a time. I have a very real relationship with them. I can't envision what my life would be like without that. I'd be a miserable, lonely person. Having foster kids gives my life meaning. I'm fifty-four years old and I have always had meaning in my life. I couldn't live any other way. (Lillith K. Anderson, a single Euro-American woman in her mid-fifties)

More than anything, women seemed to simply take delight in knowing, watching, and experiencing the personhood of their children. One woman who adopted her foster son with Down syndrome says she is different from the other women in her support group because she does not see her child as "handicapped" or "retarded," nor does she mourn developmental milestones he does not meet. Instead, she sees him and everything he does as a gift.

So no matter what he does, I go [to the group] and say I'm thrilled! He went in the cupboards and pulled out all the stuff in the cupboards. They're angry that their kid did that. But that's a normal thing for a three year old to go and take out all the pots and pans and all the cereal. So we come from a different wavelength, and I waited so long for him anything he does is okay. Where everything that their child does is not "normal" I'm thrilled [at whatever he does], you know? (Linda Thompson, a single Euro-American woman in her late forties)

Most women spoke about the ways their lives and their self-perceptions changed through fostering. In part, this change involved status (for example, from childless to mother of four), but it also involved a change in the way women defined themselves and their life circumstances. Whether fostering increased a woman's financial hardship or consumed her time with difficult caregiving labor, women thought of themselves as fortunate, gifted, lucky. Having children and being able to give the gifts of motherhood were considered worth the sacrifice.

So we don't do a lot of extras financially. I feel we live okay you know, but we don't go on vacation and we don't go to the movies. I don't even go to McDonald's, 'cause McDonald's is expensive. It's cheaper to eat at home. I don't rent videos either, you know. So we manage, you know. But um, I think it's more important for me to be home and I want to be home. I enjoyed these first six years, I can't even tell you. I mean I documented and took pictures of every sneeze, you know. I have a box of pictures I haven't even gotten to [show you yet]. I just enjoy it too much to take the time to work. And I waited too long. Everybody else was twenty when they had their kids. I financially couldn't do that and I don't think I was ready then either. I was more than ready when I got him . . . and I wouldn't give him up for the world and nobody will take him away from me, you know. (Linda Thompson, a single Euro-American woman in her late forties)

At the same time women recognized their foster children as gifts, none of the women spoke about fostering as an easy process or an easy commitment. Most talked about the way in which maintaining the vision of the child as a gift was at times problematic since children's care needs often presented a considerable burden. Children entering foster care seldom do so without having experienced serious and complicated emotional and/or physical trauma. Routine tasks accomplished by other same-aged children often became a matter, for foster children, of painstaking successive approximations and behavior modification programs. Parenting in these cases required vigilant consistency. Parenting was also often a venture shared with therapists, teachers, and social workers. The commitment required of mothers was tremendous, and the personal, familial, and marital costs these relationships exacted were often quite high. Women commonly spoke of feeling emotionally stretched by the care needs foster children presented and in this respect saw the burden within the gift.

I don't think anybody, doesn't matter what they tell you during your classes, can understand what it's really like. I mean . . . when they called me about Arabelle, she was just about six. She had already been in placement with her brother for about four months. They kept the brother but they couldn't handle Arabelle. What am I doing? I've never done this before. But I'm thinking to myself, how is it that somebody could not handle a five-year-old child? What could be so difficult about this? Well, let me tell you. I do know now! At first there was a honeymoon. And then the bottom fell out. And she's a very defiant, very,

very, defiant little girl. She's belligerent. I mean, she just—she's tough. She's tough. And I know that she's giving her grandmother a really rough time right now. . . . I didn't realize how—it's not really a good word, but for lack of something better, damaged, they are. I didn't realize how damaged they are. And each one has—I mean, their needs are so great. . . . And sometimes you feel like peanut butter on a piece of bread, you know, I mean just all over the place. . . . I don't think I really understood the commitment you make when you open the door. (Sarah Perkins, a married Euro-American woman in her mid-forties)

Many women spoke of teaching foster children behaviors they had always taken for granted in family life, like not hiding food, changing their clothes, going to the bathroom, or not lying or stealing money. These tasks, far from being simple expectations that could be laid down to a child, had to be understood in the context of the child's past experiences and as part of a complicated pattern of unlearning, re-learning, or healing. To accomplish their work foster mothers often received additional training offered by community health agencies. They also worked with a host of community mental and physical health professionals. However, foster mothers located the ability to facilitate healing in the foster mother/foster child relationship and saw social workers, therapists, and physicians as tangential to the "real" healing work of mothering.[8] In this way, women maintained the value they placed on the gift of mother/child relationships relative to "professionals" who many times denigrated or reduced foster mothering work to menial acts of physical caregiving, and maintained the value of intuitive and embodied mothering knowledge that was often demeaned relative to "professional expertise." The same mother talks about her knowledge of healing and the transformation that occurred with another foster daughter, Sandra.

I was well aware of the physical and sexual abuse and the abandonment and the beatings. . . . Her room was over a porch that had no heat and only would fit her crib, and her hands were blue and her diapers were three days dirty, and she didn't have three squares and she had a bottle until she was four. . . . And I found that knowing all of that as she screamed around here [made it easier to understand her]—She screamed from the time she came in, she screamed. If you walked by her, she would fold up and scream, like, "Don't touch me, don't touch me." And if you tried to bathe her, somebody would think that there was some horror show going on in this house. And at night she would just stay up. If you tried to put her to bed, she would scream and scream and scream. And that went on for over a month easily.

When asked how she managed a child who screamed and could not comply with daily living tasks, she replied,

Well, she could do what she could do. She didn't go to bed. I would try rocking her, but she was stiff. She wasn't a child that molded to you. She just—didn't want to be held. And then finally it reached a point where . . . [I had] to draw some lines and so I told her, even if she stayed awake, we had to stay up in her bedroom. And we sat there, and I closed the door, and she would play for a while, and then she might scream. But I would just sit there with her. You couldn't hold her. She wouldn't let you. And then gradually [she began to heal]. Now . . . I say, "Sandra it's bedtime." And in she goes and that's the end of it. . . . It seems to me that if a child is frightened about where she is and is frightened about going to bed, and is scared to death of a bath, I mean, she was more than traumatized, and would ball up when I walked by her as though I was going to kick her or beat her [then you give her time to heal. You don't push her.] . . . I don't know. It just seemed right. (Sarah Perkins, a married Euro-American woman in her mid-forties)

As women spoke with concern about the demands on their time and energy, the thankless struggles to raise children with significant emotional or physical challenges, or degrading social relations with the state, no one in the study spoke of leaving fostering because of the impact it had on her or her family.[9] Children were a joy and a burden. Fostering was a gift and it was difficult work. But it was something each woman was committed to and saw as a necessary and vital way to exercise her ability and desire to mother. It was also tied inextricably if essentially, to being a woman. In this way discourses of gendered gifts were linked with burdens and agency. Women keenly valued their ability and responsibility to be empathetic and thus chose to deal with turmoil rather than escape or avoid it. Foster mothers repeatedly articulated that not only did they know *how to* mother, but they knew they *had to*. Burdens were something a woman simply endured.

There are so many times that we know what's [best]—what would work and wouldn't work. DCF does not like foster parents to know more than they do. They don't like [it when you tell them something]. I had a little girl, and then I got her five-year-old brother for about eleven days before I had to have him moved. And that was my first placement—was these two children. So it was devastating for me to call them and say, "I can't handle this." About six months later, they were looking to move the little girl [from Ellen's home to join her brother]. DCF felt these children should be together, 'cause if they were going to get adopted, they were going to get adopted together, so they should be together now.

So I called up DCF and I said, you know, they do not get along [the brother and sister]. They do not even like each other. I really don't see the need to do this to this child [move the child in the middle of the school year, and after she had been with Ellen for over six months]. [The worker said,] "Now I'm going to have you talk to the supervisor, because she is doing the treatment plan, which is due [tomorrow]." And the supervisor said to me, "We know more about these children than you'll ever know. We have books and books on these children. There are things that happened in these children's life that you'll never know. And we know it all."

And I said, "Oh yeah? Who's their third grade teacher? What's the little girl's middle name? Tell me you know it all!" She actually said that to me. "We know more about these children than you'll ever know." But they know nothing about the day-to-day lives of those children. I was very angry. Why do we bother to do this? You know, why do we bother to do this? (Ellen McKnight, a married Euro-American woman in her mid-thirties)

Like many women, this mother asks, "Why do I keep doing this?" and answers by saying, "If I quit, the children would suffer." Thus to some degree the gift of sight is the burden of care, the gift of agency is the burden of constraint. Having recognized children as gifts and understood their needs, women felt obligated to assume the responsibility, often the burden, of foster children's care, and to bear with them their pain. Possessing the gift of recognition *obligated* one to give. As this mother says about her foster daughter,

Bertie has been around so much and she's been exposed to so much. But I am very, very strict with her. What's no today is no tomorrow.

That's the only way you do it. You've got to be very consistent. The other foster moms were afraid of her. . . . because she used to lie, and because of that they were afraid that she was going to fabricate a lie and [cause a Department of Children and Families investigation]. But I let her know I was not afraid of her. She's been shifted back and forth from home to home. I think I remember four or five. I'm not sure.

I can see why the other foster mothers didn't want her, but I feel I will not give up on her. . . . I get enough to keep on going. No, I can't [give up on her]. If I did that, it [her problems] would just keep on going. Someone has to say okay I will go through it, whatever it takes, whatever she needs. And I tell her that all the time. I say, "Bertie, I am determined that you are going to be a nice young lady." I says, "I am determined that you are going to grow up to be proud of yourself, never mind what I think of you, proud of yourself." Oh yeah, she is very mouthy. And she will try me all the time, but I don't give up. I don't let up on her. And see, *I know her.*

And see, she could resent the fact that her mom is not here. I try to put myself in her place. How would I feel at four years old not being with my mom? And how would I, maybe that's what makes me keep her. Somebody has to, 'cause she will go through the system until she is eighteen years old, and then you've really got a problem. And now you don't have a six-year-old anymore, [you have an adult]. (Dorthea Hansen, a married African American woman in her late fifties)

Most women talked about an inability to refuse a child in need even when they were currently fostering so many children that their homes were full or when caring for children presented economic and/or emotional hardship. Through the use of gift discourses women constructed themselves as giving despite hardship and thus established themselves as moral agents in the face of socially defined failure by redefining the nature of success from product to process (see Layne, this volume). In so doing, foster mothers reconstructed themselves from hired mothers-for-the-state into powerful moral agents and reconstructed fostering from a commodity exchange into social action.

My husband has been clean three and a half years now. I have been married to him for two and a half years. Same amount of time I've had the kids. So it's like, as soon as I get him straight, yeah, I take on these kids with some *serious* problems. So I got used to it. I guess I'm a sucker!

Just the way I look at it. I guess I'm just a sucker that can't help myself 'cause I like kids. I tell all these little crumb snatchers around here, "Why do you come to my house?" They won't leave. They keep coming back. This one over here [a mother in the neighborhood] says to me last night, "Could you buy her [daughter] a pair of shoes?" I don't have *enough* kids that I got to buy shoes for? Now you want me to buy your kid a pair of shoes?

Today I'm gonna go to the store and buy the kid a pair of shoes. I can't let the kid go around barefooted. I watched her for two weeks barefooted. I can't do that no more. So it's like, you know, you do what you gotta do. What is the total number of years you been a foster parent? I'm not a foster mother. I'm just a mother because I've got children and I'm their mother. They're mine. (Deleah Smith, a married African American woman in her late thirties)

Disregarded Gifts: Commodified Mothering, Loss, and the State

Foster mothers conceptualized fostering as an exchange in which they both got something and gave something of equal value. Sometimes it was a child's growth and healing in return for love, or companionship and life meaning in exchange for a home and a family. Other times it was money in return for a child's care. In equal exchanges women talked about what they received from the transaction with little embarrassment or shame because there was a symmetry that precluded exploitation. However, mothering as an exchange in which a woman both gave and got something of equal value contests images of the cultural and historical archetypal "mother" depicted in popular media and in the social services foster care literature (see Wozniak 1997a:7–16; b:357–364; and 1996:9–12). In both, "mothering" was a distinctly noneconomic activity. Thus money entered women's fostering narratives as a contradiction.

It was at once part of a fair exchange *and* a sign of their exploitation; it was a symbol of their domestication and control, *and* it was part of their freedom. What distinguished these discourses or conditioned how women constructed them was the relationship between how foster mothers saw the exchange and how they saw themselves being seen relative to it. When the presence of money did not contest women's status as legitimate mothers to their foster children, women talked about the benefits of reimbursements, and the need to be adequately compensated for their expenses, sometimes their expertise. They also talked about mothering, work, and economic need or compensation as inclusive and compatible activities.

When, however, money was a sign of women's nonmotherhood and negated their kinship claims, women complained of the inadequacy of the reimbursements, de-emphasized its importance to their households, and expressed resentment at the way it legitimated their exploitation at the hands of the state. Occasionally these discourses were held separate in parent's narratives. Most of the time they were bound together as a signification of the meaning of foster motherhood and were articulated through complaints about social relations with "the state." The significance of this discourse is that through nonmotherhood women, children, and mothering were commodified and devalued, and recognition and acknowledgment of women, children, or fostering as gifts were rendered impossible.

When discussion of money did not signify commodification, most women saw mothering and money as compatible. Mothering was work, and was an important service; thus receiving money from the state was "natural." In these cases, money was contextualized as an equal exchange for services, a compensation for child care costs, or an exchange of responsibility with the state: women labored to provide emotional and physical care for foster children, and the state had a responsibility to support children financially.[10] In this respect the state entered women's discourse as a partner, and fostering was a partnership between parties who both contributed something valuable to sustain the relationship.

This mother talked about how she got into fostering. In her story she is a woman with a family, and she is a worker who needs to contribute to her family's support. She will provide a service to the state by taking in children, she will increase her family, and she will also make money.

> It's a long story. I moved from Atlanta, Georgia, to here. It was hard for me to find a job at that time. I had a eighth grade education, no skills, nothing but domestic work. That's all I knew how to do. So I decided,

well, I heard it on TV, please open your hearts to children. I decided that I could do this for some money. I would get paid. But little did I know it was $69 a month. That's all they offered me. So I went to it [to apply] but I told them no. But when they sent the references to the people where I had worked and private homes where I had took care of their children, they came back and asked me over and over, the state did, to reconsider. So I still said, no, because it wasn't enough to help us, you know. [Then] they brought these two little twin babies and let me see them. When I *saw* those babies, I just had to have them. . . . From then on, I got into it—and there was another brother and sister, and continued it all the way through [for thirty years and fifty-four children]. (Norma Peel, a married African American woman in her early seventies)

In a discussion about what a foster mother is, this mother uses the language of a mother and a worker who is providing an important service to children. It is ultimately a service that is provided *through* her; in effect she is the service. While she articulates the pricelessness of the gift, mothering through falling in love, she also is clear that this is a service and one for which she accepts money. Unlike the women in Ragoné's sample (this volume) who consistently devalued or dismissed the importance of money, this foster mother pairs paid service and the gift of mothering. She thus articulates a discourse in which receiving money for the embodied gift of falling in love is not prostitution, but a gendered service given to children and the state.

If you look at yourself as a temporary mother, although you know it's a temporary situation, I don't think you can provide the proper kind of service to the kids, because children deal with emotions and they are very susceptible to picking up on things that maybe you don't think about. But if you hold back from them in any way, they can sense that. If you really want . . . to be good to the kids and provide them with all the love and attention they need, you have to put all the other feelings aside and just let yourself completely fall in love with a kid basically. . . . That's what you have to be willing to deal with. You have to be willing to take [the pain that comes from separating after you have fallen in love]. (Lillian Rosebud, a married Native American woman in her mid-forties who has adopted four children and who fosters children of all ages)

Women spoke of state reimbursements as income but often described it as "extra" money or money that "helped" them and their family rather than supported them. Like payments to surrogate mothers in Ragoné's study, state reimbursements often meant that foster mothers could do certain things (care for children, pay the rent or mortgage) or have certain things (a washing machine or a larger car) that they could not otherwise afford. As foster children became a part of women's families, money earmarked for taking care of them was reasonably spent on activities or household expenses that assisted the family. Most women said that their state reimbursement checks were placed in a general checking account used for household management and daily expenses. In this way, payment from the state actually gave women autonomy rather than increasing state control, since the state did not stipulate what the money should purchase or exactly how a child should be taken care of. If a child had become a part of a family and the head of the household deemed it good for the family to remain in a certain house or apartment, then it was good for the foster child, and state reimbursements could be used in good conscience for mortgage or rent payments or home improvements.

At the same time all foster parents were acutely aware through social relations with the state that the exchange of money signified non-motherhood and legitimated their commodification and treatment as unskilled, interchangeable workers. As this couple state,

TOM: They [the Department of Children and Families] [think they're] steering you some money. They think you're not in it for anything except to get the money. I really don't think that they understand that our hearts are right there. I can't say in all cases because I do know some foster parents that do it that way. But in 80 percent of the cases, you know, our hearts are right there.

CANDICE: And I don't think that they understand that when they're shifting a child out of your home it's not only the child suffering. It's us suffering. It's the biological parents [suffering] because their contacts have now been broken.[11] Everybody suffers. It's a no-win situation. But the agency's attitude is "You have to learn to deal with it. It shouldn't bother the child. It shouldn't bother you." [But] you can't just be standoffish. You just can't ignore that child. . . . We were told that they were "foster children." That means emotionally we should be cut off from them because they can come and go. . . . So be standoffish. Don't get attached. Don't fall in love. [But] it just doesn't work that way. (Tom and Candice Gordon, a married Euro-American couple in their mid-forties)

As workers instead of parents, foster parents felt that the state was free to treat them as nameless, faceless drones performing a menial job. These women also voice their sense of powerlessness.

They see you as a caretaker. The whole agency sees you as a temporary caretaker. You're being paid to take care of that kid and feed 'em and clothe 'em and that's as far as it goes. You're not supposed to love 'em; not supposed to get attached to 'em. If you get attached to the child and try advocate on the child's behalf, the department will step in and take that child out of there because they're afraid of going up against you . . . the whole department runs that way from the top to the bottom. (Lillian Rosebud, a married Native American woman in her mid-forties)

I don't think they have no respect for foster parents. And I'm not talking about everybody at DCF. . . . But I think a lot of them either get harden on the system or they drop out because they can't cut it. . . . The whole thing is, their attitude is that you're foster parents and you toe the mark, and do what I tell you to do. And if we tell you to march, you march, and don't go getting any ideas of your own. (Rebecca Echo, a married Euro-American woman in her late fifties)

You have no rights. You're a glorified baby-sitter is what everybody's been saying, and it's true. Their [the state's] first thought is don't get too involved when you take in a child. (Marjorie Johnson, a married Euro-American woman in her late fifties)

[The state treated me as if] I was doing a job and my job was terminated [when a child left]. It was ended and it was over and so that's' the end of it. I don't need to deal with her anymore, as though it was no more than that, you know? (Sandy Wallace, a married Euro-American woman in her late forties)

Most women found their commodification painful because it meant that in the eyes of the state they were neither a "mother," that is, one who had legitimate rights to knowledge, information, and expression based on a kinship relationship, nor a "professional," that is, one who has rights based on skill, experience, and training. As this mother comments, social workers have legitimate rights to make decisions as children's legal guardians even though they approach, in foster mothers' eyes, their "job" with little passion or feeling, and foster mothers, who possess intimate knowledge of children and their needs, and who approach their work with the passion considered "normal" for mothers, have no legal voice. Ironically, foster mothers, like this mother, frequently described social workers in the same way that the social service literature characterized foster mothers—as detached, passionless workers.[12]

> I sit and watch the visits [between natural parents and their children]. You get a sense of who really loves their kids and who doesn't. Workers don't want to hear it. I've got a worker right now who's the pits and her supervisor is even worse. It's like, "it's none of your business. It's our decision to make." That's it. It alienates me and my feelings because there are certain things that we see and we feel and it's like, this worker says, well, "that's our decision and it's got nothing to do with you." And it does have something to do with us. We're the ones who love these kids and deal with them twenty-four hours a day and we're the ones who have the instinct to protect them. That worker doesn't care for that kid. It's a job. She goes home at 4:30 and forgets about it until Monday morning. [She sees the kid] once in two months. You know, she comes out here, spends ten minutes in your home, shows up late for a visit . . . you know, they're supposed to be here at 10:00, they show up at 10:30, and they're supposed to be out of your house by 11:00. They spend a half an hour with the kids and they're the great experts on what the kid needs. They're looking at paper. And heck they stay on the case for six months and then they're gone and another one comes along. (Lillian Rosebud, a married Native American woman in her mid-forties)

Most women spoke vehemently about the marginalization of their personhood and the commodification and degradation of their mothering work. Louise DaSilva, a married Euro-American woman in her early forties, fostered a young child for over a year. During an interview, Mrs. DaSilva described the day her foster daughter left their home. She was asked if the social worker had ever followed up the departure with a progress report about how the girl was doing in her new setting. Mrs. DaSilva angrily and sarcastically comments,

> No. But we didn't expect any. You know, we are a facility. You've got to keep that in mind, because they're going to keep reminding you. You're not a human being, you are a facility. . . . [They say] those exact words. They remind you [by saying] "Hey, look, you know, you're getting too involved, you're a facility." . . . They tell you what your limits are. I mean you just can't go around for a kid acting like its parent. "You're not the parent. You think you're the parent, but you're not the parent. You are a facility." You can't go to the school and tell them to do something, the school doesn't have to listen to you. . . . In the meantime you can have a kid, six months in school who needs reading—who needs reading help, who's not been getting it, or hearing help, or speech help.
>
> [When asked if she sees herself as a facility, Mrs. DaSilva's response is] Of course not! I never stop being a parent. . . . It bothers you sometimes. Like when . . . she broke her finger [referring to a foster child] it took us over a week to get someone who would set it.

These interactions felt especially like violations because children were being hurt. Clearly detailed in every woman's stories were painful accounts of injury inflicted on foster children as a result of social workers' misconceptions of the fostering relationship. Since most women saw protecting children as an important part of fostering and strongly identified with children's pain, injuries they could not prevent were experienced with helplessness and anger and perceived as an assault on their mothering. Most women felt that "the state" failed to see children as gifts, and instead saw them as commodities or objects that needed to be "placed," "moved," or "returned home," but not as full-fledged human beings imbued with subjectivity and needs. Many felt that the state was "squandering" children's lives and futures through social relations in which both foster mothers and children were objects of trade that represented a "social and political agenda of patriarchal family life" (Rapp 1987:129). In each story, the subtext was the same: this could not or would not happen if those in "official" positions could see the relational work of caregiving and foster mothering as gifts and see the gifts foster children represented.

But children were not the only ones hurt through the abrogation of mothering gifts and the construction of fostering in commercial terms. Many women experienced the removal or the threat of removal of children from their care as deaths. This was compounded by the length of time a child lived with a family, the degree of intimacy in the relationship, and the contact women were allowed after a child left. Seldom, when children left, was there any recognition that an affective relationship existed between foster parents and children. Many women complained bitterly about this latter factor, saying that a phone call from the social worker just to let them know the child was all right would both satisfy their concern for a child's safety and affirm the kinship relationship that had existed.

These mothers use embodied metaphors to articulate their grief. The first mother compares the loss of a foster child to the loss of a body part, and thus to the loss of a part of herself. In her statement, she feels not only that her grief was not acknowledged, but that her expertise as a mother was also ignored. The second foster mother articulates her sense of the inevitable nature of the fostering relationships and the inevitable nature of loss.

> Giving up the babies was the hardest part. Every time a baby left, it left quite a hole in our lives, and in our family. . . . It was always like handing over a part of your body, like your arm or your leg. Sometimes I couldn't do it. You would have to go down to the state, and hand over the baby. Sometimes my husband had to do it. I don't know how he ever did it. It was like losing a part of you. You hand the baby over and you don't know what's going to happen to it and you're not allowed to know. *I* had the baby all of its life [when it went to adoption]. *I* was the one who knew why it woke up in the middle of the night. *I* knew what made it cry. *I* knew what to do for it. (Lois Jacobs, a married Euro-American woman in her late fifties)

> Well, I try to say, this child is going to be different. I want to feed this child, clothe this child, give this child a bath, and don't put out too much love because you'll have to cry again. It don't work. It just don't work and it starts all over. When I know that they're getting ready to leave, it just automatically—I feel my heart break—it's just—I can't help it. [I tell them] I say, now, you know that I'll always love you and you'll

always have a space in my heart. (Monica Walker, a widowed African American woman in her early sixties)

A mother who decided it was time to quit fostering after having fostered over 120 children during her career, sums up her experiences of loss and the social relations with the state child welfare agency this way:

> You have the agency on one hand saying, you've got this child coming to your home and you're supposed to love it for however long you have it in your home. Then all of a sudden, a year later, you've got this agency saying, now you've got to stop loving this child because it has to go someplace else, but we've got this other child and now we want you to love it. How do you just say, OK, this one's gone now so I don't have to love her any more. It's like—a part of you just dies. And there were certain kids that left, there were this certain few, that when they left . . . , they say that when your heart breaks, there's no such thing, but you actually feel like there's this part of you that is just dying. And you can't explain this kind of thing. I always said that it's worse than losing someone to death. Because when someone dies, they're gone. And you know that it's permanent and that wherever they are they're OK and you don't have to worry about them any more. But when you lose a foster child, and they go off either back to their biological parents, which is sometimes worse, or off to adoption, you're always wondering—I wonder where they are, I wonder if they're OK, I wonder how they're doing, I wonder if their life is OK and if the parents—if their marriage lasted. . . . You know what I mean? Constantly. You worry about them. But when somebody dies, you don't worry about them any more. (Evelyn Day, a married Euro-American woman in her early sixties)

The expectation that women should "detach" when they were told to by state social workers or judges often violated foster mothers sense of their mothering work. Many relationships ended before foster mothers' felt it was time—or as some women expressed, ended way past the time. In these situations, endings in foster mother/child relationships violated mothers' understanding of time, sequence, cycles, and rhythms, and thus violated their subjectivity (Kristeva 1982:34), but also violated their sense "of how things are supposed to be" or their sense of natural order (Layne 1996:137). Endings also occurred, as many women complained, without their input regarding future plans for the child, which violated their experience of relationships in which they were the experts about the child, and about the child's natural family.

> It's hard. I felt like a person, I guess if you lost a child that died. Nothing you can do about it, you see, but there is nothing you can do about it and you just have a void. I had two children, Kyle and Norman. . . . I took them when they was about a month old and all of a sudden without warning the state was to call me one day and wanted to pick them up the next day. That almost killed me. . . . I wanted them. I felt like they were mine and I felt like, what is this child gonna say when he sees I'm not there? . . . It took me about three years to lose that aching inside. (Norma Peel, a married African American woman in her early seventies)

Women repeatedly stated, "I lost a part of me when that child left," and "something inside of me died," but admitted that they had not shared this with anyone because they did not feel that anyone understood that these feelings could exist. Because the loss was never acknowledged, many women's responses to mourning became defensive as they tried to claim their right to grieve. For example, one woman talked about a baby she had cared for for eighteen months. Because the child was born with numerous health complications, she had to be kept on a ventilator and had to be manually suctioned every twenty minutes. For this reason, the baby slept on the foster mother's chest for over a year. She states,

> [The state] pressured me to adopt her. They figured I had her so long, I would just keep her. And I had her for eighteen months, and then I fought for this little girl. The mother was a paranoid schizophrenic who smelled like beer or booze when she came for visits, and was dirty. They should have [terminated her parental rights] and let that baby go to adoption. I had to consider the whole picture. I have my own children and one adopted child, plus I take care of our parents. I couldn't adopt another. After eighteen months I pushed to have this little girl placed in an adoptive risk home. You know, I wished it could have worked out, I would have loved to keep her. . . . It's real hard when you have a little tiny baby clinging to you. (*She starts to cry.*) And I had my son's feelings

| 119 |

to deal with. He knew he was adopted and he was always asking questions, like, "Why can't we adopt her? Why can't we keep her? We have an extra room. Why are you crying?" and him thinking maybe, you know, we won't want him.

[The child's social worker from the agency] called right after [the child] left. I was crying and I told her, "I can't talk now." The worker asked, "What's wrong? Why are you crying?" I told her, "I know I had to give her up but I have a right to cry too." (Linda Vanderbrink, a Euro-American woman in her late forties)

In the face of invalidation, many women experienced difficulty finding the emotional space they needed to mourn the ending of embodied foster parent/foster child relationships since the time and space to mourn were, for many, premised on some social acknowledgment that an important relationship had existed and been lost. Often a foster mother's time of mourning was eclipsed when she was pressured by social workers to accept more children. Foster mothers who were willing to care for one child after another reinforced for social workers the idea that foster mothers were emotionally distanced workers who didn't need time to mourn because they didn't grieve and reinforced the notion that fostering was more like production line work, where workers interact with a product for a short time, then move on to the next product, rather than parenting.

Foster mothers affirmed for themselves that an important and meaningful relationship had existed by maintaining a personal memory of the child and thus validating the relationship they had experienced. Most mothers talked about the photographs they kept of their foster children. Most homes were cluttered with baby pictures hanging on the walls, children's drawings hung on the refrigerator, children's notes and letters displayed with clay figures, handprints, and scrapbooks. Through their memory of a child, foster mothers could acknowledge, however privately, that the relationship was meaningful, was important—was a gift to them—and consequently was painful when it ended. They could thus make a space to grieve. In this way foster mothers maintained their sense of self as gifted, and the child's presence and absence became a permanent part of women's selfhood.

Like the women in Layne's sample (this volume), foster mothers found that thinking about and describing children and their relationships with children as gifts helped them deal with their sense of loss when a child left, and deal with invalidation of their claims of bereavement. Many women articulated the idea that once a gift (in most cases this referred simultaneously to the memory of the child and the gift of the relationship) had been given, it could not be taken away even when a child left. That is, the gift of the child was permanent through the irrevocable and enduring nature of the affective relationship (see Modell, this volume).

> So [one day sitting in the doctor's office waiting room] Selina said to me, she said, "Miz Monica do you love me?" and I said, "Yes child, I love you." And she said, "All the way up to God Jesus?" Because if you say up to God Jesus it was true. So I said, "I love you all the way up to God Jesus and I will love you with all my heart." She said, "Then why are you making me go?" And I said, "Darling, I'm not making you go. . . ." I said, "But you'll know no matter where you go, that I'll always love you and you're right here (*touches her heart*) and you can put the love from my heart, right here (*motions to child's heart*) and hold on to it forever. And that is my promise . . . always know that I love you." (Monica Walker, a widowed African American woman in her early sixties, relating a conversation she had with her three-year-old foster daughter)

Conclusion

Ironies, Donna Haraway reminds us, "are about contradictions that do not resolve into larger wholes, even dialectically, about the tension of holding incompatible things together because both or all are necessary and true" (1989:173). In popular culture foster mothers are at once an icon of the "good mother," the woman who takes a child in to her home and her heart, *and* the faceless, nameless worker who, feelingless, acts at the state's discretion to nurture and then relinquish children. Foster "mothering" is both naturalized in a Saussurrean sense as it is an affective relationship between a woman and a child, occurring in a home, in a nuclear family, thus in a specific context, and is "denaturalized" as an artifact of industrial capitalism in which the context is no longer part of the natural experience, and can be changed, perhaps purchased at will (Haraway 1989:10). Foster mothers see themselves as women who are engaged in the important work of creating kinship and caring for their families. They also see this as an economic activity and themselves as economic figures. It is the juxtaposition and inhering contradictions of women's self-constructions and knowledge of their social construction that offer important insight into the nature and meaning of women's fostering narratives within a larger sociocultural context.

Most of the women who participated in this study actively contested definitions of fostering imposed on them and their families by "the state." This often took the form of challenging agency rules, marginalizing DCF in their lives, or actively subverting agency policy and social worker practices. Most were also aware that in a consumer culture, nonmaterial and mutual gifts embodied in poor women and children and transmitted through a relationship were devalued when they were seen at all. Most actively contested these constructions of "mother," "child," and "work" by vigilantly and relentlessly maintaining a sense of who they were as valued women who engaged in the important work of caring for one of society's most precious resources. All women saw their mothering and the children they mothered as singular and irreplaceable gifts who could not be commodified or replaced (Kopytoff 1986:73). This was not exclusive of discourses on the economic value of mothering or sometimes the economic value of children.

Most women reported experiencing a sense of fatigue in regard to their fight, and thus, resistance often took the form of an ebb and flow; women chose their battles, backed off, and then chose other battles. What remained constant was women's vision of themselves as important agents of personal and social transformation, and their relationships with foster children as respected, honored, cherished gifts of womanhood. In this way women offered, if not a critique of kinship in a consumer culture, then an alternative to it by redefining children, families, and mothers who are excluded from the "ideal" as precious and thus consistently positing an alternative vision.

Imagery in which women emphasized what they gave to children and what they received from them was very important in helping foster mothers maintain a discourse of fostering as an exchange *while* maintaining their status as mothers. Through gifts women could negotiate tensions between conflicting images of "proper" motherhood as an essentially noneconomic activity and foster mothering as a relationship of exchange. Foster mothers, similar to surrogate mothers (Ragoné, this volume), at times discounted the importance of the reimbursement fee through phrases like "I would do it even if there wasn't money" or "They can't pay you enough for what we do" and simultaneously stressed the importance of kinship relations. By recontextualizing reimbursements within the context of kinship relations, they altered the meaning of money and motherhood, asserted their compliance with cultural norms, and echoed the popular sentiment that children and mothering are priceless and thus supra-economic. As Ragoné states, "when surrogates minimize or dismiss the importance of money, they are on the one hand reiterating cultural beliefs about the pricelessness of children, and they are on the other hand suggesting that the exchange of a child for money is not a relationship of reciprocity but of kinship" (this volume).

In their discourses foster mothers did not mother in order to *get* money (making children objects of production and thus violating images of the emotionally priceless and instrumentally valueless child; see Zelizer 1994a), but received money as a way of "helping" support their burgeoning family. Since as Zelizer (1994b:133) notes, "gift money" has the connotation of something unearned, foster mothers essentially affirmed the noneconomic nature of mothering while still receiving financial support. They also echoed latent cultural beliefs that "real" women's work, that is, motherhood, is noneconomic. That is, women are not *earning* money through fostering—they are receiving a *gift* from the state that *helps* run their household. By recontextualizing money-for-mothering as gift-money-for-family, foster mothers transform themselves from nonmothers into women who can legitimately claim the children in their care as *their* children, and thus claim themselves as mothers.

At the same time, women's narratives are rich with images pairing money and mothering work, wages and the task of constructing kinship. When this occurred, women asserted themselves as economic figures who did not sell mothering, but rather performed an invaluable service and provided a unique gift. Through both their actions and their narratives women created texts of situated selfhood in which the nonproductive labor of interpersonal relationships and caregiving was legitimated and affirmed, and in which socially "traditional" or "state"-supported constructs of kinship, mothering, family, and labor as separate and exclusive activities were actively and ultimately transformed.

As Strathern reminds us, "what constitutes a natural or logical domain of ideas gives an image its cultural stamp. This is equally true of what is thinkable in terms of combinations and syntheses—you can tell a culture by what it can and cannot bring together" (1992:2). Idioms of kinship articulated through conventional nuclear family ideals and the rhetoric of the gift affirm a fairly unconventional kinship relationship—that is, kinship through claims of belonging. Images of the emotionally priceless children coexist with discourses that assert the importance of their instrumental value. The unselfish gifts of motherhood mirror ideals of the "perfect gift" in their immateriality (Carrier 1990:20–21) while firmly embedding the importance of kinship and mothering within an economic/material discourse.

Finally, what is ultimately and consistently conveyed in women's narratives is that they are the possessors of special and gendered gifts that compel them to mother through fostering. Through these gifts they are catapulted into the business and life work of social healing and individual transformations. They thus extend what is socially thinkable and alter, in yet another way, the nature of the society in which they live.

Notes

1. The history of African American fostering in the United States is significantly different from the history Euro-Americans have experienced. As Patricia Hill Collins writes,

> Whether because of the labor exploitation of African-American women under slavery and its ensuing tenant farm system, the political conquest of Native American women during European acquisition of land, or exclusionary immigration policies applied to Asian-Americans and Hispanics, women of color have performed motherwork that challenges social constructions of work and family as separate spheres, of male and fe-

male gender roles as similarly dichotomized, and of the search for autonomy as the guiding human quest. . . . [T]his "reproductive labor" or
"motherwork" goes beyond ensuring the survival of one's own biological children or those of one's family. This type of motherwork recognizes that individual survival, empowerment, and identity require group
survival, empowerment, and identity. (1994:47)
However, it is interesting to note that while the histories have been different,
the Euro-American and African American women in this sample consistently
espoused very similar ideologies relative to the nature, purpose, and meaning
of fostering.

2. The foster mothers who participated in the focus group sessions were
generally drawn from a word of mouth sample and were not interviewed prior
to or after participating in the focus group. In the first focus group, in which
we discussed issues of loss and bereavement, thirty foster mothers and fathers
participated. In the second focus group, twenty foster parents participated in
discussing problems in the social worker/foster parent relationship. The third
and fourth focus groups were attended by ten to twelve foster mothers. The
topics were differences in fostering and biological mothering, differences between African American and Euro-American women's experience with DCF,
and how kinship is created through fostering.

3. Each transcript was between fifty and seventy-five pages in length, sin-
gle-spaced.

4. While there was some variation in women's constructs of parenting relationships and foster parenting, primarily by age, significant differences were
more likely to occur over particular issues, for example, foster mothers' feelings about and relationships to biological mothers, and these were likely to be
related to specific experiences, rather than as a delimitation in the population.

Consensus analysis (e.g., Romney, Weller, and Batchelder 1986; Weller and
Romney 1988) constitutes an explicit test for agreement among informants
by applying minimal residuals factor analysis to sets of cultural data adjusted
for random variation—drawn from text collected by various forms of informal
or semistructured interviews, or from structured interview formats like pile
sorts, triads tests, or ranking scales. When we conduct a factor analysis of sim-
ilarities among what informants have told us, we ask if the responses of each
person constitute just one measurement of an unobserved consensus about
meaning. A large proportion of the variance among individuals explained by a
single factor the eigenvalue of which is three or more times larger than the
next largest—a dramatic scree fall—constitutes initial evidence of a cultural
consensus. Factor loadings tell us how much each informant agrees with the
consensus; their average provides a means of measuring the reliability and

validity of the identified consensus. The consensus analysis procedure identifies the existence of significant agreement differences by the presence of more than a single major factor.

Property-Fitting (PROFIT) analysis confirmed that no life experience marker influenced the ways foster mothers experienced and configured kin relations. Applying the Spearmen-Brown Prophesy Formula to cases rather than to variables reveals that my findings exhibit reliability and validity scores well over .90.

It is possible that I missed some significant variable bearing on women's life experiences and so created selection bias. But I looked hard, and I asked foster mothers what they thought might condition fostering experiences, and we could not think of any other variables. I infer that the findings I report are generalizable to foster mothers in the state of Connecticut who share the life experiences of the women I spoke to, that is, African American and Euro-American women, old and young women, rich and poor women, women who fostered their kin or nonkin, women who fostered for short-term and long-term placements, and women who fostered all ages of children.

5. The idea that foster children are not "real" children, but something less than children or subchildren, was something that not only foster parents were aware of; foster children were keenly aware of it too. I became aware of it when my foster daughter referred to her previous foster family, saying, "they had four real children and five foster children." Later she said she wanted to be adopted, she was tired of being a foster child and wanted to be a "real" child again. While the sample of foster children for this study was quite small, primarily due to the difficulty of accessing foster children without endangering foster mothers' ability to continue fostering, these findings are consistent with the other children I spoke with. To be a foster child, to be in the legal custody of the state rather than a family, was enough to be stigmatized as "different" and inferior. To have some identifiable physical or emotional issue only compounded inferiority.

6. The magnitude of this sacrifice is not aptly represented in the quote. The Peels were one of the poorest families in the sample. The family of seven lived primarily on Mr. Peel's social security income. Since they had adopted most of their foster children, the state "helped" very little through reimbursement payments. Thus to buy their foster daughter glasses required considerable sacrifice and saving.

7. While the historical context and the meaning of community survival are significantly different for African American and European American families (Hill Collins 1994; Stack 1974), both groups espoused these beliefs, often describing their mothering in terms of social responsibility with concern for so-

cial survival. Since no woman's ability to mother a child was conditioned by a child's ethnicity and all women fostered children from different ethnic/racial groups, "community" for both African American and Euro-American women was seen to be both a geographically and racially delimited community and "society" as a whole.

The difference lay primarily in the conception of "community." For Euro-American women "community" was seldom delimited by ethnic boundaries and instead mostly referred to geographic boundaries (i.e., "giving something to my community" most often meant my town or city). For African American women, "community" often referred simultaneously to an African American community delimited both geographically and ethnically and a larger "community," which referred to society as a whole.

8. The knowledge that women are family healers is not an uncommon cross-cultural theme (Spector 1979; Velimirovic 1978; Melville 1980; Clark 1970; Kleinman 1980; Romanucci-Ross et al. 1983; Young 1981; Helman 1984; Martinez and Martin 1979; Finerman 1995; McClain 1995). But healing has not commonly been associated with foster mothering, nor, for that matter, with mothering in the United States.

9. It should be noted that the study sample may skew this finding. These women were "system survivors." The vast majority of them had fostered for more than two years. Most women who leave fostering do so after the first year. Thus, there is something about these women that has made them stay or something about other women that made them leave.

10. When women emphasized the unfairness of the money they received relative to the expenses of raising a child "properly," they referred simultaneously to the impossibility of being adequately compensated for their mothering work and a sense of outrage that the state provides inadequately for children, thereby maintaining them as "less than children" or inferior beings.

11. Mrs. Gordon is referring to the relationship that develops between biological parents and foster parents. In her view of fostering, this relationship is a supportive one and is often lost when a child returns home.

12. Foster mothers' perceptions that social workers were detached, passionless workers were not borne out in my research. While social workers did not form parent/child relationships with children, they often referred to them as "my kid" or "one of mine," and expressed great concern and responsibility for children's welfare. They also expressed an overwhelming sense of powerlessness at being unable to provide or obtain for children what they felt children needed. For more discussion about social workers' relationships to children, see Wozniak 1997a.

References Cited

Belk, Russell W., and Gregory S. Coon
1993   Gift Giving as Agapic Love: An Alternative to the Exchange Paradigm Based on Dating Experiences. Journal of Consumer Research 20:393–417.

Belk, Russell W., Melanie Wallendorf, John F. Sherry, Jr., and Morris B. Holbrook
1989   The Sacred and the Profane in Consumer Behavior: Theodicy on the Odyssey. Journal of Consumer Research 16:1–38.

Bell, Duran
1998   Defining Marriage and Legitimacy. Current Anthropology 38:237–53.

Carrier, James
1990   Gifts in a World of Commodities: The Ideology of the Perfect Gift in American Society. Social Analysis, 29:19–37.

Clark, Margaret
1970   Health in the Mexican-American Culture. Berkeley: University of California Press.

Clarke, Jorn
1996   Public Nightmares and Communitarian Dreams: The Crisis of the Social in Social Welfare. In Consumption Matters: The Production and Experience of Consumption. Stephen Edgell, Kevin Hetherington, and Alan Warde, eds. Pp. 66–91. Oxford: Blackwell.

Finerman, Ruthbeth
1995   The Forgotten Healers: Women as Family Healers in an Andean Indian Community. In Women as Healers: Cross-Cultural Perspectives. Carol Shepherd McClain, ed. Pp. 24–41. New Brunswick: Rutgers University Press.

Frow, John
1997   Time and Commodity Culture: Essays in Cultural Theory and Postmodernity. Oxford: Clarendon.

Gailey, Christine Ward
1995   Making Kinship in the Wake of History: Gendered Violence and Older Child Adoption. Paper presented at American Anthropological Association, Washington, D.C.

Handwerker, W. Penn, and Danielle Wozniak
1997   Sampling Strategies for the Collection of Cultural Data: An Extension of Boas's Answer to Galton's Problem. Current Anthropology 35(5):869–75.

Haraway, Donna
1988 Situated Knowledge: The Science Question in Feminism and the Privilege of Partial Perspective. Feminist Studies 14:576–99.
1989 A Manifesto for Cyborgs: Science, Technology, and Socialist Feminism in the 1980s. *In* Coming to Terms. E. Weed, ed. Pp. 173–204. New York: Routledge.

Helman, Cecil
1984 Culture, Health and Illness: An Introduction for Health Care Practitioners. Bristol, England: John Wright.

Hill Collins, Patricia
1994 Shifting the Center: Race, Class, and Feminist Theorizing about Motherhood. *In* Mothering: Ideology, Experience, and Agency. Evelyn Nakano Glenn, Grace Chang, and Linda Rennie Forcey, eds. Pp. 50–55. New York: Routledge.

Katz Rothman, Barbara
1994 Beyond Mothers and Fathers: Ideology in a Patriarchal Society. *In* Mothering: Ideology, Experience, and Agency. Evelyn Nakano Glenn, Grace Chang, and Linda Rennie Forcey, eds. Pp. 139–57. New York: Routledge.

Klein, Norman, ed.
1979 Culture, Curers, and Contagion. Novato, CA: Chandler and Sharp.

Kleinman, Arthur
1980 Patients and Healers in the Context of Culture. Berkeley: University of California Press.

Kopytoff, Igor
1986 The Cultural Biography of Things: Commoditization as Process. *In* The Social Life of Things: Commodities in Cultural Perspective. Arjun Appadurai, ed. Pp. 64–91. New York: Cambridge University Press.

Kristeva, Julia
1982 Women's Time. *In* Feminist Theory: A Critique of Ideology. Nannerl O. Keohane, Michelle Z. Rosaldo, Barbara C. Gelpi, eds. Pp. 31–53. Chicago: University of Chicago Press.

Layne, Linda
1996 "Never Such Innocence Again": Irony, Nature and Technoscience in Narratives of Pregnancy Loss. *In* The Anthropology of Pregnancy Loss:

Comparative Studies in Miscarriage, Stillbirth and Neonatal Death. Rosanne Cecil, ed. Pp. 131–52. Oxford: Berg.

Lewin, Ellen
1993   Lesbian Mothers: Accounts of Gender in American Culture. Ithaca: Cornell University Press.
1996   Inventing Lesbian Cultures in America. Boston: Beacon Press.

Martinez, Cervando, and Harry W. Martin
1979   Folk Disease among Urban Mexican-Americans: Etiology, Symptoms, and Treatment. *In* Culture, Curers, and Contagion, N. Klein, ed. Pp. 188–94. Novato, CA: Chandler and Sharp.

McClain, Carol Shepherd
1995   Women as Healers: Cross-Cultural Perspectives. New Brunswick: Rutgers University Press.

Melville, Margarita B., ed.
1980   Twice a Minority: Mexican-American Women. St. Louis: C. V. Mosby.

Rapp, Rayna
1987   Toward a Nuclear Freeze? The Gender Politics of Euro-American Kinship Analysis. *In* Gender and Kinship: Essays toward a Unified Analysis. Jane Fishburne Collier and Sylvia Junko Yanagisako, eds. Pp. 119–31. Stanford: Stanford University Press.

Romanucci-Ross, Lola, Daniel E. Moerman, and Laurence R. Tancredi, eds.
1983   The Anthropology of Medicine. New York: Praeger.

Romney, A. Kimball, Susan C. Weller, and W. H. Batchelder
1986   Culture and Consensus. American Anthropologist 88:313–38.

Spector, Rachel
1979   Cultural Diversity in Health and Illness. New York: Appleton-Century Crofts.

Stack, Carol
1974   All Our Kin. New York: Harper and Row.

Strathern, Marilyn
1992   Reproducing the Future: Essays on Anthropology, Kinship and the New Reproductive Technologies. New York: Routledge.

Velimirovic, Boris, ed.
1978   Modern Medicine and Medical Anthropology in the United States-

Mexico Border Population: Proceedings of a Workshop Held in El Paso, Texas. Pan-American Health Organization Scientific Population.

Weller, Susan C., and A. Kimball Romney
1988   Systematic Data Collection. Newbury Park, CA: Sage.

Wozniak, Danielle F.
1996   Strains of a Discourse: An Analysis of Women's Work as It Is Experienced through the Social Relations of Contemporary U.S. Child Fosterage. Unpublished manuscript.
1997a   Twentieth Century Ideals: The Construction of U.S. Foster Motherhood. Doctoral dissertation. Department of Anthropology, University of Connecticut.
1997b   Foster Mothers in Contemporary America: Objectification, Sexualization, Commodification. Women's History Review 6(3):357–66.
in press   They Are All My Children: Foster Mothering in America. New York: New York University Press.

Young, James Clay
1981   Medical Choice in a Mexican Village. New Brunswick: Rutgers University Press.

Zelizer, Viviana
1994a   Pricing the Priceless Child: The Changing Social Value of Children. Princeton: Princeton University Press.
1994b   The Social Meaning of Money. New York: Basic Books.

FOUR

Does God Give Special Kids to Special Parents?

Personhood and the Child with Disabilities as Gift and as Giver

Gail Landsman

A first-time mother whose newborn daughter had recently been identified as being at risk for serious disabilities reflected that she and her husband

> are both very gentle and loving people and maybe we were meant to have a special baby. Someone said to me God never gives babies to parents who don't have extra love to take care of them, sick babies to parents that can't take care of them, and I think, yeah, it does take a special person to have a baby with problems and be there for them and love them and help them out in a way. I'm sure you're one of those good people just by the way you talk about your daughter.

Fourteen months later, with the child still fed by gastric tube and now definitively diagnosed with cerebral palsy and a high likelihood of mental retardation, the very same mother offered this critique of the notion that God gives special kids to special parents: "I'm trying to think what I said when somebody one time, when they said that. Oh, I know. . . . I said well if they're such a blessing how come everybody doesn't pray to have one?"

She continued, explaining that regarding her daughter, "we feel really blessed to have her. . . . We don't feel it's some God-awful curse that's been put upon us or anything like that." "But," she complained,

> it's funny the things people say to you. Either they, you know, assume
> that you know, this is God's wish that you had a special child, or you
> know, that you did drugs and, you know, caused this to your child type
> of thing. So, once again, you know, you just can't take all this stuff too
> seriously because you'd drive yourself nuts.

Contrary to the advice of this mother, in this chapter I do propose to take seriously what cultural meaning is carried by the notion that God gives special children to special parents. I ask what might account for both the widespread dismissal of this notion by mothers who have been raising young children with disabilities for some time, and the fact that these same mothers nevertheless continue to represent themselves as the recipients of blessings and gifts. The exploration will take us through an analysis of the meanings of motherhood in a consumer culture and the relationship between body, disability, and personhood in late-twentieth-century North American culture.

Feminist scholars have addressed Euro-American personhood largely with an eye toward debate over its cultural beginning and end points. Given the current cultural and legal privileging of the fetus over the mother, concern about the implications of the concept of fetal personhood for reproductive choice is justifiable. Fetuses, as Rapp reminds us, have a public presence; images of the fetus "permeate sex education, right-to-life literature, and obstetricians' examining rooms," and "surely contributed to the narrowing of aperture and sharpening of focus on the fetus rather than on pregnant women" (1997:44). Amniocentesis, ultrasound, and the avid consumption of conceptive technologies are now understood by feminist scholars as having at the very least lent themselves to what Morgan refers to as an uncoupling of biological and social birth (1996:59) such that personhood is often constructed prior to birth (see also Layne 1999). No longer must a fetus cross the developmental threshold of being born before it attains the status of person.

However, while analyses of the role of new technologies in conception and pregnancy have done much to develop our understanding of changes and intracultural variation in concepts of personhood, much can be gained from expanding our focus in the domain of reproduction to include mothering. I have proposed that if we shift the starting point of our analysis from *when* in the gestational process Western personhood appears and becomes fixed (at conception, birth, or some point in fetal development such as viability) to the issue of *to whom* personhood is attributed, we find that in the West, far from being an all-or-nothing proposition, personhood can be earned and/or reduced in increments (Landsman forthcoming). The same woman whose body held a "person" in the womb during pregnancy may later find herself the (diminished) mother of a "less than full person" upon giving birth to a baby identified with a defect or upon her child's subsequent diagnosis of disability. When we examine personhood through the lens of the abortion controversy, there seem to be in North American cultures two distinct categories—"nonpersons" (who can be morally aborted) and "persons" (those to whom the protection of the state applies)—with the debate being where to locate the boundary between categories; when we expand our view to include the birth of children with disabilities, what appears instead are *gradations* of personhood. From the perspective of a feminist agenda, the idea that personhood can be attributed to a human entity prior to birth is often seen as a social and political problem;[1] for individuals with disabilities and the mothers who give birth to and/or nurture them, the problem is that personhood can be diminished for a living infant by virtue of disability.

This diminished personhood of the child with disabilities serves as the jumping-off point for my analysis in this chapter. McMahon (1995) makes the argument that whereas in earlier decades of the twentieth century the moral value of motherhood was associated with mothers' roles as protectors of innocence (children), since World War II the moral worth of motherhood has been reduced to its association with valued children. If indeed a mother's moral value rests on her association with *valued* children, the cultural expectation of, and exclusive maternal responsibility for, attaining perfection in fetal outcome links the diminished personhood of the "defective" child with disabilities to an experience of diminished motherhood for the woman who nurtures it. In the United States, mothers of infants with disabilities are not seen as morally equivalent to mothers of normal children. As the quote that begins this chapter illustrates, compared to mothers of normal children, mothers of children with disabilities are seen either as

worse—"bad" mothers who use drugs and cause imperfect children—
or better,—"special" mothers chosen by God to have special children.
My research suggests that while this dichotomy represents the beliefs
with which most American women approach their pregnancies, it is
challenged by the transformative experience of mothering a child with
disabilities. The purpose of this chapter, then, is to reach an understanding of the strategies whereby some women, through the
metaphor of the gift, negotiate and transform the meanings of personhood and perfection, and thereby reinstate their own motherhood.

Methods

This chapter is based on a two-year study during which over 120 evaluations of infants and children with or at risk for disability were observed
and recorded at a hospital-based newborn follow-up program in upstate
New York. The hospital has a twenty-five-county catchment area, including urban, rural, and suburban communities. The program evaluates
those infants who were discharged from the hospital's neonatal intensive
care unit (NICU), as well as those who were referred from sources including pediatricians, child care providers, and parents themselves.

The Newborn Followup Program serves as an evaluation site to determine children's eligibility for early intervention services. In compliance with the section of the Individuals with Disabilities Education
Act (IDEA) that requires states to provide services to children ages
birth to three years, the program provides a free evaluation of a child
for disability or developmental delay; if a child is diagnosed with a disability or significant developmental delay, the child qualifies for (but
parents are not required to accept) early intervention services such as
physical therapy, speech therapy, nursing care, occupational therapy,
teachers of the visually impaired, audiology, nutritionists, and special
education. Because early intervention services are themselves also provided at no expense to parents, a wide cross-section of socioeconomic
class in the area is represented in those bringing their children to the
Newborn Followup Program for evaluation.[2]

During each evaluation session, physicians discuss their diagnosis of
disability with the mother. Sixty mothers whose children were diagnosed as having or being at risk for disability were interviewed in

depth in their own homes within a month of the visit to the physician. Interviews lasted from one to four hours. While data were collected on variables such as the mother's age, marital status, religion of up-bringing, current religious affiliation, education, and work history, the bulk of the interview was devoted to collecting mothers' own stories of their experiences of giving birth and coming to learn about their child's disability.[3] Twenty-one (over one-third) of these mothers were interviewed a second time approximately one year following the initial interview. Mothers to be interviewed were informed that the re-searcher's child has a physical disability. While the absence of this fac-tor would not have precluded the research, its presence had some pos-itive effects on rapport; if women's comments are to be believed, it re-assured participants that they were likely to be understood despite any differences in our religious backgrounds, educational levels, or socioe-conomic class. Phrases revealing assumptions of common identity or experience—as in "I'm sure you're one of those good people" in the opening quote—were peppered throughout the interviews.

Maternal Responsibility and Blame

While maternal drug abuse, alcohol consumption, child abuse, and lack of prenatal care are all associated with childhood disability, and while each of these was implicated in some of the cases observed at the Newborn Followup Program, among the mothers *interviewed,* none had children whose disabilities were attributed by medical professionals to maternal behavior. Nevertheless each mother's narrative reflects her awareness of expert knowledge regarding the effects of maternal behav-ior on the health of the fetus.[4] With few exceptions (including the two adoptive mothers in the study), each mother had searched her past to de-termine what she had done wrong to bring about the disability, and/or complained that others judge her as having done something wrong. The possibilities for having done something wrong usually involve specific events during the pregnancy, such as once having taken a pill or a drink of an alcoholic or caffeinated beverage, or longer-term behaviors such as continuing to work at one's job. Women showed surprising precision in locating what they interpreted as their violations of the prescribed pre-natal diet. One mother remembered drinking half a glass of wine on her anniversary and wondered whether it could have caused her child's autism; upon learning of her daughter's seizure disorder and developmental delays a mother immediately recalled having beer, junk food, and cigarettes at a Super Bowl party before she knew she was pregnant; a mother of a boy with spina bifida tried to remember what she was doing on the twenty-eighth day of her pregnancy, when, she had heard, the spinal cord closes; a mother of a child born without a hand tried to determine whether fetal development of the hand coincided with the night she had three drinks at a party before she knew she was pregnant. This excerpt from a woman whose child has mental retardation is common:

> People kind of assume if there's something wrong with your child that you did it, and you struggle with that enough yourself. Did I eat the right things? I mean, I went over everything. I took one Tylenol when I was pregnant. One, and it haunted me. Just one Tylenol. Some of them do crack through their entire pregnancy and manage to have a perfectly normal baby.

The possibilities for a mother doing something wrong to cause disability are extended beyond her lack of compliance with prenatal diet to include broad moral issues regarding life choices as well.

> Sometimes I think well, since my daughter's thirteen, and people said, I told you you shouldn't have waited so long—those sort of comments or remarks come to mind—like I should have stayed with one, or why didn't you get your tubes tied? And why did you wait so long? (Mother of a boy with spastic diplegia [cerebral palsy])

Maureen's story is an example of how broadly the notion of making the right choices is interpreted and incorporated into stories of mothering. She has two sons diagnosed with pervasive developmental disorder, a disorder on the autistic spectrum. Although as a child Maureen was beaten and lived in a home "with no love,"

> I made the right choices with my life when I was a teenager . . . and I saw people all around me, you know, in the '70s or so, all the teenage girls, you know what I mean, pregnant; it was like why do you want to ruin your life? I've met a lot of people, you know, throughout my life that, you know—I thought of, but I didn't do drugs—but I told them, I said, you can be anything you want to be. You just go find out how to

do it, and do it. And I've always believed that. And so, here I had to come smack up in my life of I made the right choices and yet I still have to deal with stuff. So, that was why I was so mad at God.

Like Maureen, most mothers in the study volunteered that they had, after all, done "everything right." Consistent with the findings of Press et al. (1998), during their pregnancies most women in this study had conceptualized the hypothetical disabled child as "the other," as something that happens only to other people. Their narratives reveal more than just feelings of shock or tragedy at the birth outcome; they also expose a sense of profound injustice and betrayal.

The expectation of having perfect baby if one follows the latest expert advice is the manifestation in the domain of reproduction of the society's general faith in progress and individual responsibility (cf. Layne, this volume); it is in a sense the ultimate expression of a belief in the possibility of control over nature. To fail to exercise that power by implementing the available expert knowledge and technology borders on the criminal. Medical professionals, who themselves are often called upon to explain to distraught and guilt-ridden parents that sometimes such things "just happen," nevertheless also hold women accountable for their failure to exert control, and assume that compliance with expert advice affords protection. One mother told how after being informed that her child was born missing one hand she was reminded by the doctor that she had not, after all, wanted an ultrasound offered to her during pregnancy. In a case I observed at Newborn Followup, a mother brought her daughter in for an evaluation because of her concerns regarding the girl's development and physical appearance; concerns that had been brushed aside for over a year by the girl's pediatrician. The developmental specialist examined the child and quietly gave the mother his catastrophic prognosis: the child's symptoms pointed to a storage disease, a fatal diagnosis. The young girl would soon start to deteriorate both physically and mentally, and in all likelihood death would occur within a few years. In addition, the mother was five months pregnant at the time, and there was a high likelihood that the new baby would also have the disease. The burden of bearing such painful news weighed heavily on the staff, and the case became the topic of much discussion among residents and nurses. But despite sincere sympathy for the mother, the issue of her responsibility for exerting control over nature remained. "The thing I don't understand," said a nurse, "is that if she knew there was something wrong with her kid, why did she go ahead and get pregnant again?"

Sensing that they are being judged, mothers often feel called upon to justify themselves to medical professionals, and to distinguish themselves from those who are "rightfully" held accountable for their child's disability. A mother of an infant girl with cerebral palsy and a swallowing disorder complains,

> Here I am, you know, fruits and vegetables, don't drink, don't smoke, you know, walk and get my exercise and . . . prenatal care the whole time I was pregnant and stuff and people treat you like you're some like little teenager who was out doing drugs and have this kid with all these problems and good for you.

Mothers are particularly aware of the image of the "bad" mother, epitomized by the unwed teenage drug-addicted girl who irresponsibly brings crack babies into the world, or who brings disability into her life through child abuse. As one mother described her experience with doctors at a hospital to which her child had been transferred, "They talked down to me until I told them, wait a minute here. I pay my taxes, and I'm a good mother. I didn't put my child here. I didn't shake my child. I didn't neglect her to put her here." Drawing on the work of Shellee Colen, Faye Ginsburg and Rayna Rapp (1995) employ the concept of "stratified reproduction" to encourage us to see the ways "by which some reproductive futures are valued while others are despised" (1995:3). As this mother's story reveals, especially in her use of paying taxes as justification for better treatment, mothers are well aware of this stratification as it relates not only to the valuation of reproductive futures but to the valuation of children already born. By their association with either "perfect" or "imperfect" children, some mothers are assumed to be valued contributors to society, and others to be the deadbeat takers.

Mother blame itself is neither new nor specific to North American culture.[5] However, as the narratives of mothers reveal, the routine availability of prenatal screening for fetal abnormalities, development of new reproductive technologies, and widespread dissemination of expert knowledge regarding the impact of maternal behavior on pregnancy outcome have affected in new and specific ways women's accountability for the failure to produce "perfect" babies. The discourse of responsibility for control of reproductive outcome does not emerge exclusively from the medical community. A counterdiscourse, one that resists the authority of the medical system, professes to empower women by advocating that a woman take control over her own pregnancy and assuring her that if she "listens to," is "in tune with," and "trusts her body" rather than medical authorities, all will be well (cf. Layne, this volume). What both approaches maintain, however, is the illusion that nature is and should be controllable by pregnant women. The situation of the mother of a child with disabilities who did in fact "do everything right" to control her pregnancy outcome thus in either case cries out for an explanation. It is precisely to this situation that the statement "God gives special kids to special parents" speaks.

Special Children for Special Parents

Davis documents the historical transition whereby perfection, once understood as an ideal visualized in the arts and attainable only by the gods, has now become conflated with the norm (1995:23–49). In the arena of reproduction, new technologies and public recitation of expert knowledge (for example, that "alcohol causes birth defects" and that "folic acid prevents them") provide the means through which women can attain the perfect/normal child if only they choose to do so. A woman's exertion of proper control over the uterine environment through proper diet and screening out of fetuses with genetic defects should, the current American story reads, result in the birth of a perfectly normal child.[6] But if indeed perfection is conceptualized as a goal attainable by all women who have access to prenatal care and who comply with medical advice (Landsman 1999), what can we make of the birth of a child with "defects"? One explanation, we have seen, is that the mother is to blame. The other explanation is that she was chosen.

The belief that God chooses to give special kids to special parents removes reproductive outcome from the domain of biological facts for one unique category of people ("special" parents), while leaving intact faith in its functioning for "normal people." The concept thus supports the belief that the normal state of affairs is indeed that nature is in our control and that progress itself is natural. It enables its speaker to retain faith that we increasingly know so much more now about how to create healthy children, that increased knowledge results in increased control over pregnancy outcomes. Linda Layne (1996) has discussed a similar belief regarding progress in the field of neonatology. Regardless of public perception, however, the fact is that despite genetic screening and the decreasing age of viability in prematurity, childhood disability rates have *not* declined (Malone, personal communication 1997). The mortality of both extremely immature infants (those born at or before twenty-six weeks' gestation) and extremely small infants (those with birthweights of eight hundred grams or less) has decreased significantly over time since 1972; however, because the rates of disability among survivors have not changed, there has been a "steadily increasing prevalence of children with disabilities" (Lorenz et al. 1998:425; also see Holzman and Paneth 1998).

With the statement "God gives special kids to special parents," the rhetoric shifts from what the mother *did* during pregnancy (which should have resulted in perfection) to what she *is* (special); the "fact" of her specialness is validated and made visible by what she received (a special child). The mother shifts from being defined as a careless producer of a defective product to a purposely chosen recipient of a special gift. The statement in this way not only maintains intact the belief in the possibility of quality control, but also supports both the cultural mandate to have perfect babies and the "othering" of disabled children and the mothers who give birth to them.

In the narratives collected, the statement "God gives special kids to special parents" is always reported by mothers as having been told to them by others. Many women had been exposed to the idea by having read in the paper, or having been sent by well-meaning friends or relatives, a reprint of an Erma Bombeck column originally published in 1980; in the column Bombeck envisions God engaged in a conversation with an angel in which He explains to the angel why a particular woman should be sent a handicapped child. The woman is chosen because of her particular inherent qualities and, according to Bombeck, will have God always by her side (Bombeck 1993).

As in the example with which I opened the chapter, those mothers who found the notion comforting generally did so in the early days of learning of their child's disability. Some mothers at that time responded to it as a reassuring statement of faith on the part of friends or family that they were strong enough to cope with the difficult news and with the struggles that loomed ahead of them; the line thus appears as another version of the saying that God never gives you more than you can handle. Regardless of their religious beliefs, some women at first felt comforted by the social support the saying seemed to imply:

> That's sort of comforting. . . . Not because I really believe that there is a God or anything but just because it's the fact that they care enough. . . . So, maybe on a bad day it would be nice to believe that there is somebody up there saying this woman is capable, she's the one that needs to be raising this child. That's a nice thought. (Mother of a girl with muscular dystrophy)

> I was talking to my cousin and she says, "You know, only certain people are blessed with certain kinds of kids and certain people can deal with it and certain people can't, but my own belief is He chose you because He knew you could do it." And that made me kind of happy to hear from just a relative of mine saying that. (Mother of a boy with mental retardation and cerebral palsy)

Yet after a year of mothering a child with a disability, few mothers interviewed accepted the validity of the saying in its entirety. "Someone cut that out for me and gave it to me. . . . I'd rather be the person it didn't happen—I'd rather have it happen to the other person," commented the mother of a child with cerebral palsy in the second interview.

> You do get sick of people saying to you, because I've had quite a few people come up and say, "Oh, you know, God gives special children to special people." Shut up! It's just like some of the dumber things people say. It's not really that bad, maybe because I never had another one before him. I've just adjusted. He's really not that bad. He's really kind of cute. He's got lots of personality. He's not, you know, this thing. (Mother of a boy with mental retardation and seizure disorder)

The old adage of, you know, like with, you know, God chooses the people that can handle the things to do it. I don't believe in that at all because I would have—am the first one to say that I would not be able to do it so He would not choose me to do it. (Mother of a boy with cerebral palsy)

I hear that, but that's a crock of bull, okay? They say, well, you know you have to—God—because you have patience or whatever. You have no choice. This is it. You know, either you give them up, send them away to a home or you deal with it. It's not in between. I choose to deal with it. (Mother of a girl with Down syndrome)

I've heard that a lot. . . . and I just say, I think you just handle what is given to you. You know, it's either that or crumble, and some can do it, some can't because obviously, there are people who can't handle it, and they either lose it or get rid of their child. I mean, it's just—luckily, we're able to handle it. I don't think that we are special parents, any specialer than any other parent because we were given one. We're lucky parents, really. I mean, we ran into a couple, an older couple in the mall one time with her, and they didn't say anything but "she will love you more than any child ever could," and I mean, you can see that they're probably right. (Mother of a girl with Down syndrome and heart defect)

In rejecting the statement "God gives special kids to special parents," mothers respond to (1) the diminishing of their child's personhood inherent in the concept, (2) the romantic glossing over of the pain and hardship involved in parenting a child with disabilities, and (3) the notion that prior to the child's birth they were somehow very different from normal people. That they are *now* different from other parents is clear to most mothers. Ironically, however, one major difference is that unlike mothers of normal children, these mothers of children with disabilities recognize how very much *like* everyone else they once were. They have come both to reject the notion that they were abnormal (special) *and* to see the experience of mothering a child with disabilities as transformative.

You know that whole idea of . . . this only happens to special people. . . . I find it annoying actually when people say that. I think it certainly *makes* you different, you know. . . . We're not special parents, we're average normal people who had this crazy thing happen to us. And we're doing the best we can, and maybe in the end we might turn out to be special parents, but we're just normal people struggling with, you know, making the best out of the situation we've got. (Mother of premature twins, one of whom has cerebral palsy)

Like many of the women in the study, this mother reflects that prior to having a child with disabilities, she also would have assumed that only special, different people could do this. This is the case even though as part of her job she had earlier taught swimming to children with disabilities.

It could never happen to me. It only happens to wonderful special people. . . . I mean, at the time I said to Steve, I know I'm not special, I know I can't do this. And that's what bothered me. It's almost condescending to feel as though . . . only special people can handle this sort of thing. No, it's like average normal people who have to deal with it. . . . I mean, you just do what—you become a parent, I mean.

A mother of a son with a chromosomal abnormality that has resulted in multiple disabilities similarly describes her resentment of the statement:

Those sorts of, again, platitudes don't really make me feel any better. . . . Because it negates or diminishes or belittles. Again, it's like a euphemism, labels that are not really accurate. It just diminishes the quality of—not the quality but the *adversity*. It belittles it. It undermines what you've been through. It's one thing to say, boy, he's lucky to have you as parents. That's true, I think. But to say that you were specially chosen, I just—it tries to candy-coat the fact of the situation. I'd have to think about why I resent that. It just leaves a bad taste in my mouth because it's usually people who haven't gone through it.

In expressing resentment of statements made by those who "haven't gone through it," mothers of children with disabilities link what they see as their fundamental difference from mothers of normal children with their inherent similarity to them. In this model normal women are transformed into special mothers by special children. These mothers often complain about pregnant friends or strangers talking with confidence about expecting "perfect" babies. "She had the amnio done. She came back in, she kept telling me how she was going to have this perfect, healthy little boy, and she was going on and on, and finally, after I heard it for about the thousandth time, I said, you know, the amnio only checks for three different genetic things. There is no guarantee that this child is healthy," one mother angrily recalls telling a friend. Women who give birth to children with disabilities were once no different from those who have "perfect" babies, they contend.

The interviews thus reveal mothers struggling to describe the ambiguity of knowing both their child's profound difference from other children and its full personhood, a woman's own "specialness" born of her experience of raising a child with disabilities and her equally held conviction that she's also just an ordinary person in extraordinary circumstances. Appreciating the "special" qualities being attributed to them, most mothers of children with disabilities argue that these traits were not innate, but rather acquired. It is to what was acquired and how that we now turn.

The Child as Giver

Despite their widespread rejection of having been chosen, many mothers experienced in raising a child with disabilities do utilize the language of the gift. The term appears throughout the narratives, across all classes and educational levels represented in the study. While those using the old saying that "God gives special children to special parents" assume a prior uniqueness that causes the gift to be given, mothers of disabled children themselves describe a personal transformation. The transformation is such that they too no longer see themselves as *producers or purchasers* of defective merchandise, but rather as *recipients* of a gift.

But what is the gift and from whom does it come? The image of mothers as chosen represents the child itself as the gift, with God as the giver. Mothers of children with disabilities, however, describe the gift as a lesson or enlightenment of a sort (a point I will elaborate later); rather than God, it is the *child* who is portrayed as the giver. The newsletter of the national support group Mothers United for Moral Support, for instance, publishes in each issue a section entitled

"The Greatest Gift This Child Has Brought to Our Lives." Parents' responses in this section, as in my interviews with mothers, most commonly refer to knowledge of unconditional love, and it is on this gift that I will later focus. The point for our purposes now, however, is that the child is the one who brings the gift to its mother. In the words of one mother, "Megan has brought us the true meaning of patience and love. She has brought us so much joy. It isn't a perfect world and sometimes we don't like what's handed down to us, but we learn through patience, time, and love" (Meister 1996).

The child with disabilities as the giver of gifts is epitomized in an essay entitled "I Am the Child" reprinted anonymously in numerous support group newsletters. The essay is written first in the voice of the child who cannot talk, and proceeds through the voices of the child who cannot walk and the mentally impaired child. An excerpt follows:

> You cannot conceive my isolation, so complete it is at times. I do not gift you with clever conversation, cute remarks to be laughed over and repeated. I do not give you answers to your everyday questions, responses over my well-being, sharing my needs, or comments about the world around me. I do not give you rewards as defined by the world's standards, great strides in development that you can credit yourself; I do not give you understanding as you know it. What I give is so much more valuable. I give you instead opportunities. Opportunities to discover the depth of your character, not mine; the depth of your love, your commitment, your patience, your abilities; the opportunity to explore your spirit more deeply than you imagined possible. . . . If you allow me, I will teach you what is really important in life. I will give you and teach you unconditional love. I gift you with my innocent trust, my dependency upon you.

In the cases of both open adoption and surrogacy (Modell, this volume; Ragoné, this volume), a woman obtains something of acknowledged value, a wished-for child. The rhetoric of the gift in such contexts becomes a means of masking the interconnections of the adoption or surrogacy process with the domain of commodity relations, which the financial transactions involved might otherwise seem to foreground. This formulation as gift represents more than a simple rejection of baby selling; it establishes social relationships. By freely giving the child as a "gift" to the adoptive parents, Modell (this volume) points out, a birth mother in an open adoption establishes a personal and enduring bond and creates a relationship of equality between herself and the new parents. This is compared with a closed adoption in which a mother gives up her child in exchange for redemption and thereby in "some fancy discursive footwork" becomes a receiver; as Mauss (1967) established, givers are generally considered superior to receivers.

A mother of a child with disabilities, however, does not receive something of acknowledged value. Her child is labeled "defective," its personhood diminished. As we have seen, most women in the study did make sacrifices in order to obtain what they thought would be a "perfect" baby; particularly by comparison with the "bad" mothers of crack babies, such mothers can be seen as analogous to what Carrier (1990) calls "Wise Shoppers." According to Carrier, Wise Shoppers actively exercise choice; they invest effort prior to and during the act of shopping itself and thereby stamp their commodities with personal identity (1990:586–88). This is not to say that all babies in the study were actively planned, but rather that once a pregnancy was known, all but one mother attempted to consciously exert control through her choice of dietary intake and her consumption of and compliance with biomedical prenatal care in order to ensure the birth of a "perfect" child. Counter to their expectations, these women did not get what they bargained for; for all their attempts at being Wise Shoppers, the product they got was defective. However, by later redefining her child neither as a product nor as a gift from God, but as a *giver* of gifts, a mother of a child with disabilities raises the value of her child beyond that of the "perfect" child she had once expected to acquire.

Interpretation of the child as giver is particularly ironic and subversive, in that the personhood of those with disabilities is diminished in American culture in large part because such individuals have been viewed not only as incapable of giving but as needing the gifts of others. The presumed neediness of people with disabilities is prominently displayed in appeals by a vast array of charitable organizations.[7] The historian Paul Longmore has described how the rhetoric of telethons in particular symbolically defines three categories of persons—givers, takers, and the recipients of giving. "Takers" in American society are those who turn away from the duty to aid the helpless, while the compassion of givers toward the "less fortunate" publicly validates givers' superior moral standing; the third category, people with disabilities, necessarily fits into this model as those ritually defined as dependent on the moral fitness of nondisabled people (Longmore 1997:136).

Through telethons, Longmore argues, people with disabilities are ceremonially defined as the natural objects of charity. The consequences are serious in that physical and economic self-sufficiency serves as a prerequisite to being moral agents in North American culture. The devaluation of recipients of charity is consistent with a liberal political theory that assumes an opposition of autonomy and dependency; the act of giving to the "less fortunate" serves as a display of superiority ironically made possible by acquisition unfettered by the demands of others. Both moral moves in North American culture—giving and boundless acquisition[8]—are assumed to be thwarted by dependency. For theorists such as Rousseau and Smith, "to become dependent is to learn how to act on behalf of others, not on behalf of the self. Dependent people lose the ability to make judgements for themselves, and end up at the mercy of others on whom they are dependent" (Tronto 1993:163).

Indeed it is because of the cultural opposition of autonomy and dependence, Adrienne Asch and Michelle Fine suggest, that the feminist movement, whose agenda involves portraying women's strengths and competence, so long ignored women with disabilities. Women with disabilities were seen to "reinforce traditional stereotypes of women being dependent, passive, and needy" (Asch and Fine 1988:4), and thus to work against the feminist notion of women as moral agents. Dependency and full personhood are conceptualized as incompatible. In short, the moral standing of "authentic" Americans is intertwined with both the act of giving and the attribution of less than full personhood to those with disabilities.

Putatively independent Americans thus have employed those they label "dependent" as a negative reference group against which to define themselves. Giving proves that the allegedly self-sufficient belong on the upper side of a great social divide that separates those designated autonomous from those branded dependent. Anyone resorting to public welfare or private charity is regarded as neither fully a person nor legitimately a citizen. The price of such societal aid in America is social invalidation (Longmore 1997:151).

Thus to define the child with disabilities as a giver of gifts is to place the child on the "upper side" of the great American social divide, the very place from which its label of disability would seem to exclude it. As the quote from "I Am the Child" makes explicit, mothers of children with disabilities may reverse the negative value of dependency: the child gifts the mother with its dependency on her.[9] To recategorize as a "giver" an infant previously interpreted as either the just consequences of a mother's morally inferior life or a tragedy she was chosen by God as strong enough to bear is to reestablish the full personhood of the child.

The Gift

If the child is cast as the giver in mothers' narratives, the gift most often cited is knowledge of unconditional love. There are two basic scenarios in which the ability to love unconditionally is given by the child to its mother. The child may itself be a *model* of unconditional love, as in this statement of a mother describing her daughter's hospital stay:

> She impresses me. I mean, I see what she goes through, and then turn around and be happy. When we were in Boston in June . . . (they were) putting her IV in, and they're having a really hard time, and I didn't go into the room. . . . and I could hear her screaming. Well, John . . . heard her screaming and went in. . . . He came out, and he said, it's so hard because here they're hurting her, and they finally get it in, and he says, "we're all done, so we're going back to the room, say bye." She turned around with these tears falling down her cheeks and smiles and says, "bye bye." I mean, she waves to them! And I'm like—like these people just hurt me, but it's okay, and I'm not holding a grudge. You just— that kind of stuff just amazes me.

Alternatively, the child may, by not meeting the normal developmental milestones by which American women commonly compare their children and mark their own successes as mothers, give these mothers the opportunity to learn unconditional love.[10] A mother of a young son diagnosed with mental retardation reflects,

> years ago, this you may or may not relate to it, but I had asked the Lord to teach me unconditional love, and I think I wanted him to diffuse it into my brain, not have to go through any fiery experience and to burn it into me, but I just wanted to know what it was like to love people without putting expectations on them of performance and other things, and it really wasn't until six months later that we found out about Ryan . . . so this situation is invaluable in that way. I mean, certainly nothing I would have ever chosen. No way . . . A lot of expectations for our own kids that he wasn't meeting, you know what I mean, and even that rejecting our own child feeling, which almost every parent I've ever talked to who had a child with disabilities has struggled with. . . . This is a lesson for everyone else to watch us. . . . I learned about my own conditional love . . . and there never would have been a spotlight on it if it hadn't been for Ryan.

The development of unconditional love is portrayed as a consequence of the experience of having a child with disabilities;[11] it emerges in the practice of mothering and is assumed to be shared by most others who have had such an experience. It was a quality repeatedly attributed to *me* by women I interviewed by virtue of my raising a child with a disability. For instance, the same woman commented later in the interview, "I'm sure you've seen changes in yourself after having DJ and valuing all children and not just the elite award winners and those who are A+ students from nursery school on." By the same logic, the gift of unconditional love is assumed to be withheld from, or at least more difficult to attain by, those whose experiences have not included a special child in the family.

This is not to imply, however, that unconditional love is a universal response to the experience of raising a child with a disability.[12] American mothers of children with disabilities themselves recognize, and sometimes lament the fact, that some mothers do not come to accept their children. They often offer commentary on women who feel they must institutionalize their children or give them up for adoption. Such mothers are not necessarily judged as bad people, but they are often viewed as commodifying their children, as still understanding them as alienable or returnable objects, rather than as givers of gifts from which mothers themselves will benefit.

The pain inherent in accepting the gift is that it comes at the expense of an innocent child. "I mean, it's like look at all the things he's taught me, patience, unconditional love. . . . I just hope that he doesn't have to suffer the rest of his life to teach me lessons," comments a mother whose son has pervasive developmental disorder, sometimes known as "high-functioning autism." Similarly, the mother of premature twins, one of whom has cerebral palsy, points out that "having these guys and having all the experiences that we've had, have made us far better people." But, she claims, "I worry that he's suffering and that some of us are getting better, being better people, but he's still suffering. . . . it's nice that other good things are coming from this. But I didn't want this at the cost of my child, you know."

As giver the child is established as morally superior to others, but a mother knows that the price of the gift she receives is all too often her child's own suffering.[13] A mother can therefore simultaneously see that she is (morally) better off for having the gift and still wish for, and work toward, her child's cure; she can, and does, often wish she never received the gift. Recognizing the child as a giver of precious gifts to the mother in no way negates the emotional, physical, and/or financial hardship of raising a child with disabilities; the gift rhetoric is not a simple or romantic denial of pain. Rather, the rhetoric of the child as giver of the gift of unconditional love helps account for and unify the "apparently conflicting stories of sorrow and hope, of pain and enrichment" told by mothers of children with disabilities (Landsman 1998).

Disability and Self

A gift, according to Carrier, bears the identity of the giver (1993:56). And as we have seen, the gift could not have been given by the child were it not for the disability. The question is therefore raised of whether the child and the disability are understood as existing apart from each other. How do those who raise children with disabilities understand the relation of the body, mind, and self? While a full elaboration of these relationships is beyond the scope of this chapter, two quite different approaches taken by mothers in the study will be briefly outlined.[14]

Some mothers present their children in the model of the child trapped in a disabled body. This is commonly the case for mothers of cognitively intact children whose physical disabilities limit mobility, fine motor skills, and/or the intelligibility of the child's speech. When these mothers represent their children in public it becomes important for them to distinguish the physical markers of disability from the child's intellectual capabilities. For instance, many mothers say they choose not to use the term "cerebral palsy" because they recognize that just as they themselves did before knowing better, the general public assumes that cerebral palsy implies mental retardation, when in fact it does not.

Even genetically based syndromes, which physicians see as part of the "blueprint" for the child's development, may also be presented by parents in terms of a disabled body or physical appearance trapping the child's mind. A mother of a child with Down syndrome sought information regarding a new vitamin therapy, not because she believed it would cure her daughter, but because she had heard it could change the child's physical appearance such that the child would no longer be immediately judged as mentally inferior.

> It's more important for outward appearance because people judge you on the outside first, nothing inside. . . . Hopefully she can make a difference, and maybe people will look at her and say, gee, she has Down's, but she's intelligent. You know, gee, she doesn't have to sweep floors, she doesn't have to bag groceries. That's not good enough for me and I won't accept that for her. You know, I wait tables because I choose to, not because I'm not intelligent enough.

Another mother, whose child has De Morsier syndrome, involving vision, hearing, and speech impairment as well as "mental retardation," compares her child to the classic image of a child's self hidden in a disabled body, Helen Keller. In so doing, she offers a theory for redefining features that physicians label cognitive impairment.

> She [Helen Keller] never learned how to talk. She never learned how to speak. Her parents didn't know how, but until Annie Sullivan taught

her how to speak, who taught her how to read, and communicate with her world, she was this—she had a brilliant mind, but when she was that little girl, nobody knew that. She would have been [called] mentally retarded, because she couldn't communicate with her world, but now that she's learned how to, she's a normal person. . . . It's just that until you learn how to communicate with your world, your cognition cannot be fully recognized.

A model of the child trapped in a disabled body does not necessarily imply a simple mind/body dualism, however. In many instances, including those of pervasive developmental disorder and autism, the disability may be seen as incorporating the mind, although not the child's true self or identity. In such cases the disability, though unmarked on the body, is understood as causing the child's patterns of thinking and behavior, and also as hiding the *real* child or self (who is distinct from these patterns). Therefore a mother may talk about "pulling her child out of" autism through practicing particular and sometimes controversial therapies.

> I spoke with Jane, and she gave me so much hope—the outcome that I could expect if he did continue with this program. . . . They worked through the crying, they worked through whatever tantrum he was going through. . . . I didn't realize how much he had going on up there that wasn't coming out. I mean talking, he said in the first six months, "I love you Mommy." I nearly died. . . . Whatever they were doing at the trials, brought everything out.

For the woman who sees her child as trapped in a disabled body, or in a body that others judge negatively (thereby trapping the child in other ways), her task may well become to work towards bringing forth the real child. This belief brings both hope and burdens. Here a mother of a child diagnosed with autism explains the dilemma.

> I've read books on kids that have totally pulled out of it when they were diagnosed as severely autistic. . . . Sometimes I wonder if I'm doing enough to try—I keep saying, "pulling her out of it," I don't know, for lack of other words or what to say. Sometimes I feel guilty that I'm not on the floor with her more and spending twenty-four hours a day educating her.

As these excerpts illustrate, the model of the "real" child as trapped or hidden in the disability may or may not present the disability as permanent. For some, as in the case of autism described above, making visible the child's true self would be the equivalent of elimination or cure of the disability; for others, it would create the opportunity for the child's personhood to be recognized by others despite the disability. In all these cases, the assumption is that elimination of the child's disability, were it to be possible, would theoretically reveal the child's true self. These mothers thus conceptualize their child's self as existing apart from the disabled body within which the self is housed.

Yet some mothers understand the relation of the child's personhood to its disabled body in different terms. This is so even for mothers of children with some of the very same diagnoses as those listed above: autism, pervasive developmental disorder, and Down syndrome. In this second model, mothers present their children and the gifts they bring as conceptually inseparable from the child's disability. In this sense, elimination of the disability, were it to be possible (as most mothers wish it were), would also result in a different child. As a mother of a boy missing the part of the brain connecting left and right hemispheres (agenesis of the corpus collosum) reflects, "You often wonder what they'd be like or who they'd be; they'd be a different child. . . . You have this little child that you love so much and if they didn't have that who would he be?" Other mothers similarly ponder the question of whether their child's self can be distinguished from the disability:

She's just been love, love, love, and I have heard that about Down's kids, that they're just so affectionate, and lovable, and loving, and she certainly is, and I don't know if it's Down's, or that's just her. But in that sense, I think we're the lucky ones, and not her. (Mother of a girl with Down syndrome)

Rather than think about what would he be like if he didn't have this, I just accept that, well, he does have it and this is the way he is, and this is—and it's not as if he has a disorder that could be magically lifted away to reveal some different boy because that's not—that's a part of his personality. This isn't something like your hair is dyed green, but it will grow out and your own self will be revealed again. This is him. I mean, his hair is green already. Not really, but anyway. (Mother of a boy with autism)

Mothers of children with disabilities who see a self that is integrated with a disabled body may also direct efforts toward "curing" or reducing disability or improving their child's ability to communicate with others as means of making their child's life easier. But the task is not conceptualized as pulling the child's self out from the disabled body, for the child's impairment, a feature of its body, is in this view also inextricably a part of the child's self. A conflation of self and body has long characterized the Western view of people with disabilities, generally with physical impairment taken as an outward marker of a tainted inner self.[15] Mothers who see their child's body and self as part of an integrated whole depart from this view in how they link the integrated body/self to personhood, that is, to social value. Loving their child's self, and in a move that from an ableist perspective appears to be one of resignation or denial, these mothers see value in the disability. "So, I honestly don't know that I'd want him any different than he is," reflects a mother of a boy with mental retardation. "Maybe I'd like his life to be easier for him, but he just is—almost all the time, just makes us happy."

The Gift of Unconditional Love and the Critique of Consumer Culture

"At first, they were like, 'I'm sorry to hear about Mac.' There ain't nothing to be sorry for. . . . It's like if it wasn't for him, maybe I wouldn't be that way," comments a mother of a boy with pervasive developmental disorder. Whether they understand their child's self as trapped inside a disabled body or as integrated with it, all mothers in the study attribute full personhood to their child. They directly credit their doing so to the experience of mothering, which they define as involving love.[16] A mother of a multiply handicapped girl confesses that she never really thought of disabled children as human beings before having one of her own. "I guess it isn't unless they're *in love* with a handicapped person, do you ever really sense that," she concludes. Similarly, a woman whose son was born missing a part of his brain talked to me of making her peace with it. "As you look back," I asked her, "what is it that helped you make that peace?" She responded,

> Falling in love with him. I remember when he was born wishing that I didn't love him, wishing I could just give him away and that we didn't have to bring him home. But . . . we were in the hospital for five days and had to stay a little longer because he was having feeding problems. I remember just wishing "I wish I didn't love him." But it was too late, I was already in love with him.

When a child is not imagined as being on a track of progress, a process of healing in which hard work and struggle lead to eventual independence, both child and mother may be conceptualized as failures.[17] But as we have seen, many mothers recast a child's dependency as a valuable opportunity to receive the gift of knowledge of unconditional love. Layne (this volume) suggests that for women who have experienced pregnancy loss, rhetoric of the gift becomes a means to reestablish a would-have-been mother as independent and thus as a moral person while simultaneously justifying her being a receiver. The dilemma such women face is how to nurture, *to give*, in the absence of a child. For mothers of children with disabilities, however, the dilemma is that one is *always* giving—love, nurturance, time, money, energy, and so forth. It is the disabled child, not its mother, who is analogous to the would-have-been mother of Layne's work. In a society of consumerist values, mothers' investments in "defective" children are constantly questioned; mothers report being openly advised not to "throw their lives away" in nurturance of a child with disabilities. As do bereaved mothers (Layne, this volume), mothers of children with disabilities utilize gift rhetoric to make it acceptable to be a receiver, but they do so by transforming the child with disabilities from a perpetual receiver into a giver; their *child's* projected dependency, not their own, is morally elevated. The mother in turn redefines her sometimes painful and often exhausting giving into an act of receiving. "I used to sit and think about this stuff and cry," reflects a mother of a child with Down syndrome, "but now, I mean, look at what I have got from it." While not what she originally "shopped" for, what she receives is now defined as more valuable. This enables a mother of a child with mental retardation to claim, "I really have been blessed with this mess, if you want to call it that. The *world* would say you have a mess."

Mothers often suggest that if others could receive the lesson of unconditional love they have received from a child with disabilities, the world would be a better place.

> I said to my mom the other day, it might sound cold, but I'm not meaning it to be cold; if everyone in the world had one person in their family that had a problem, that had Down's syndrome or, you know, cerebral palsy, or whatever, people wouldn't be so quick, the world wouldn't be such a mean place. . . . And I guess even, I was never really a prejudiced person, but I never really looked at how black people felt or whatever. You really think about it today and it's all along the same lines. People judge how a black person is and that's not fair. I guess it's really opened up another world for a lot of people. (Mother of a boy with Down syndrome and autism)[18]

Outside the norm, dependent, and permanently imperfect in a society in which perfection is deemed attainable, the child with disabilities is less than a full person. In an era in which mothers' social worth resides in their association with valued children (McMahon 1995:190), the woman who gives birth to a disabled child is therefore less than a full mother. However, redefining the child as a giver of valued gifts, rather than as the negative consequence of poor choices or a gift/burden that God chose her to bear, mothers of children with disabilities reinstate the personhood of their children and the full value of their own motherhood.

In faulting the social model of disability for its exile of the concept of the body, Hughes and Paterson (1997) argue that

> the extent to which impairment can be re-represented (displaced from its association with the grotesque and its role as the other relative to aesthetic ideals of the body) and reconstructed (in terms of pride and positivity as opposed to a site for the existential fears of the non-disabled community) could be a matter of considerable importance for the development of a cultural politics of identity. (1997:332)

Mothers who come to revalue the self as it exists with disability may be participating in such a cultural politics both for their children and for themselves. They offer a critique of consumer culture with an admission of their own past participation in it.

> I mean, of course, I always think, you know, when we had had those discussions earlier on in the pregnancy, what if the child had Down syndrome. . . . I mean, I wouldn't say punishment, but this is the answer that you wanted the perfect child. How selfish of you for wanting perfect children, you know. Children come in all different ways and I would have to say, if anyone asked, that I would say I have the perfect children. You know, in a very weird way I would say, they're not physically perfect, but they're perfect children. They're perfectly mine.

Mothers of children with disabilities talk about reassessing values, realizing true priorities, putting things in perspective, and above all, being less judgmental of others. The child's gift of knowledge of unconditional love provides mothers a vocabulary with which to develop a critique of consumer culture as it has entered the domain of reproduction. In portraying their child as giver of a gift, not for which they were specially chosen but which they learned, through any normal mother's love, to receive, mothers place recognition of their child's full personhood in opposition to the consumerist values of a society that would devalue their children and their own motherhood.

Notes

The research on which this chapter is based was primarily funded by the National Endowment for the Humanities, Humanities Studies of Science and Technology Program; additional support was received through a grant from the Faculty Research Awards Program of the State University of New York at Albany and the Small Grants Program of the Institute for Research on Women, State University of New York at Albany. I am grateful to the staff of the Newborn Followup Program of the Children's Hospital of Albany Medical Center, and particularly to Anthony Malone, M.D., for providing a supportive environment in which to carry out the research and for the many useful discussions that sharpened and expanded my understanding of the issues addressed here. Linda Layne's vision and energy in putting together a panel on gift rhetoric and transformative mothering at the AAA meetings helped bring this paper into being in the first place; her insightful comments, as well as those of discussant Rayna Rapp and other panelists, helped further my thinking on these issues. To the mothers of children with disabilities who shared their stories with me—you have given me a gift the value and meaning of which you, above all others, understand; thank you.

1. This accounts for the silence of the feminist movement on the issue of pregnancy loss. Layne (1997) argues convincingly that feminist fears of acknowledging the validity of something worth grieving is responsible for the absence of scholarly attention to the experiences of women who experience stillbirth or pregnancy loss, and for the feminist community's failure to develop rituals to mark the experience.

2. See Landsman 1999 on the impact, or lack thereof, of socioeconomic class.

3. Of the women interviewed, none identified themselves as Jewish, Buddhist, or Muslim; a range of Christian denominations was represented, as well as atheists, and those claiming no religion affiliation. Racially, the sample was predominantly white. Ages of women interviewed ranged from the teens to the late thirties, with educational levels ranging from high school dropout to graduate degree; 17 percent were single mothers. For a fuller description of the demographic characteristics of women in the sample, see Landsman, in preparation. There brief biographical sketches of all interviewees are provided. In this chapter, however, women are identified by the disability of their child.

4. This is consistent with the findings of Markens, Browner, and Press (1997); in their study they found no difference in attitudes toward prenatal diet based on social class or ethnicity.

5. Scheer and Groce (1988) provide many examples from the historical and ethnographic record in which birth defects are linked to parental misconduct; among the Dogon, women who have copulated with a bush spirit are believed to give birth to disabled infants, while among the Bantu, incestuous sexual unions are considered the cause of disability. And as Hillyer points out, the professional literature in Euro-American societies has until only recently considered mothers, through their overrigid perfectionism or extreme rage, the cause of their children's infantile autism (1993:88–89).

6. Prenatal screening for disability has been publicly portrayed as a means of preventing birth defects themselves. The primary way that prenatal screening currently does so, however, is through abortion of the fetus identified with the defect. Thus disability rights activists remind us that what are being prevented are not defects but the birth of people with disabilities. The issue is far more than one of semantics; in an article entitled "The Bad Baby Blues:

Reproductive Technology and the Threat to Diversity," Blumberg argues that among the questions prenatal screening should force us to ask is whether "we can view all people as equal and still feel that it is important to identify some traits prenatally" (1998:13).

7. The disability rights movement has actively challenged the presumption that people with disabilities are necessarily dependent, and have worked to transform the public stance toward disability from one of "helping" to one of guaranteeing civil rights. This is exemplified in a slogan that makes a less than subtle reference to a major charity appeal, the March of Dimes: "You gave us your dimes. Now we want our rights." Disability rights activists argue, for instance, that were discrimination against people with disabilities in employment eliminated, people with disabilities would more likely have the same chances as nondisabled people to be self-sufficient.

8. See Layne (this volume) for discussion of a similar paradoxical aspect of gift giving in Christian theology.

9. All infants, of course, are dependent. At issue here is the projected long-term or permanent dependency associated with disability in North American culture.

10. See Landsman 1997 on the notion of developmental delay.

11. That the gift of unconditional love is understood to be a *consequence* of, rather than a reason for, mothering a "special child" is one way that mothers of children with disabilities differ from the foster mothers in Wozniak's study (this volume). Both raise children who are not of acknowledged value in mainstream American society. However, as described by Wozniak (this volume), foster mothers see themselves as having inherent qualities that make them good mothers and that cause them to choose to receive the gift of a special child, whereas mothers of children with disabilities generally claim to have been normal women who have changed as a consequence of receiving a gift they did *not* originally choose.

12. In the case of Israel, for instance, Weiss reports a high rate both of abandonment of disfigured children at birth (Weiss 1994) and territorial isolation of such children within the home (Weiss 1997).

13. This is not to suggest that mothers see the physical or mental impairment itself as necessarily causing suffering. When they were asked what their greatest concern for the future was, by far the most common response was how the child would be treated by others. This concern is consistent with what has become known as the social model of disability developed in disability studies; it represents a rejection of the medical model of disability. The latter places the "problem" within the disabled individual rather than in society's discrimination and oppression of persons with disabilities.

14. See Landsman, forthcoming, for more detail.

15. Robert Murphy argues that people with disabilities in the United States suffer a "contamination of identity" (1995:145). In the words of Mitchell and Snyder, the "equation of physical disability with social identity creates a tautological link between biology and self (imagined or real) that cannot be unmoored—the physical world provides the material evidence of an inner life (corrupt or virtuous) that is secured by the mark of visible difference" (1997:3).

16. "Love" is here used as a native term, and no attempt is made to analyze its meaning. The significance of the distinction mothers make between unconditional love and other types of love is discussed in Landsman, in preparation.

17. Hillyer suggests that it is on this point that not only a competitive patriarchal society, but feminism itself, currently fails mothers of children with disabilities, for feminism too devalues dependency.

18. As the above quote from a white high school dropout reveals, recognition of the full personhood of their own child may lead mothers to extend full personhood to other groups whose personhood has been diminished in North American society. See Landsman 1999.

References Cited

Asch, Adrienne, and Michelle Fine
1988   Introduction: Beyond Pedestals. *In* Women with Disabilities: Essays in Psychology, Culture, and Politics. Michelle Fine and Adrienne Asch, eds. Pp. 1–37. Philadelphia: Temple University Press.

Blumberg, Lisa
1998   The Bad Baby Blues: Reproductive Technology and the Threat to Diversity. Ragged Edge 19(4):12–16.

Bombeck, Erma
1993   Perfect Moms Best for Disabled Kids. Albany Times Union, May 22. P. C2.

Carrier, James
1990   Reconciling Commodities and Personal Relations in Industrial Society. Theory and Society 19:579–98.
1993   The Rituals of Christmas Giving. *In* Unwrapping Christmas. Daniel Miller, ed. Pp. 55–74. Oxford: Clarendon.

Davis, Lennard J.
1995 Enforcing Normalcy: Disability, Deafness, and the Body. London: Verso.

Ginsburg, Faye, and Rayna Rapp
1995 Introduction: Conceiving the New World Order. *In* Conceiving the New World Order: The Global Politics of Reproduction. Faye Ginsburg and Rayna Rapp, eds. Pp. 1–17. Berkeley: University of California Press.

Hillyer, Barbara
1993 Feminism and Disability. Norman: University of Oklahoma Press.

Holzman, Claudia, and Nigel Paneth
1998 Preterm Birth: From Prediction to Prevention. American Journal of Public Health 88(2):183–84.

Hughes, Bill, and Kevin Paterson
1997 The Social Model of Disability and the Disappearing Body: Towards a Sociology of Impairment. Disability and Society 12(9):325–40.

Landsman, Gail
1997 Medical Technologies and Mothers of Infants with Disabilities. Paper presented at the annual meeting of the Committee on the Anthropology of Science, Technology, and Computing, Rennselaer Polytechnic Institute, Troy, NY.
1998 Reconstructing Motherhood in the Age of "Perfect": Babies: Mothers of Infants and Toddlers with Disabilities. Signs 24(1):69–99.
1999 "Real" Motherhood, Class, and Children with Disabilities. *In* Technologies and Ideologies of Motherhood. Heléna Ragoné and France Winddance Twine, eds. New York: Routledge.
forthcoming Redefining "Perfect" Babies: Motherhood, Personhood, and Children with Disabilities. New York: Routledge.

Layne, Linda L.
1996 "How's the Baby Doing?" Struggling with Narratives of Progress in a Neonatal Intensive Care Unit. Medical Anthropology Quarterly 10(4):624–56.
1997 Breaking the Silence: An Agenda for a Feminist Discourse of Pregnancy Loss. Feminist Studies 23(2):289–315.
1999 "I Remember the Day I Shopped for Your Layette": Goods, Fetuses, and Feminism in the Context of Pregnancy Loss. *In* The Fetal Imperative/Feminist Practices. L. Morgan and M. Michaels, eds. Pp. 251–78. Philadelphia: University of Pennsylvania Press.

Longmore, Paul
1997   Conspicuous Contribution and American Cultural Dilemmas: Tele-
       thon Rituals of Cleansing and Renewal. *In* The Body and Physical Differ-
       ence: Discourses of Disability. David Mitchell and Sharon Snyder, eds. Pp.
       134–58. Ann Arbor: University of Michigan Press.

Lorenz, John, Diane Wooliever, James Jetton, and Nigel Paneth
1998   A Quantitative Review of Mortality and Developmental Disability in
       Extremely Premature Newborns. Archives of Pediatric and Adolescent Med-
       icine 152:425–35.

Markens, Susan, C. H. Browner, and Nancy Press
1997   Feeding the Fetus: On Interrogating the Notion of Maternal-Fetal
       Conflict. Feminist Studies 23(2):351–72.

Mauss, Marcel
1967   The Gift: Forms and Functions of Exchange in Archaic Societies. New
       York: Norton.

McMahon, Martha
1995   Engendering Motherhood: Identity and Self-Transformation in Wo-
       men's Lives. New York: Guilford.

Meister, Renee
1996   Letter. Matchmaker: MUMS National Parent-to-Parent Network News-
       letter 66:12.

Mitchell, David, and Sharon Snyder
1997   Introduction: Disability Studies and the Double Bind of Representation.
       In The Body and Physical Difference: Discourses of Disability. David Mitchell
       and Sharon Snyder, eds. Pp. 1–31. Ann Arbor: University of Michigan Press.

Morgan, Lynn
1996   Fetal Relationality in Feminist Philosophy: An Anthropological Cri-
       tique. Hypatia 11(3):47–70.

Murphy, Robert
1995   Encounters: The Body Silent in America. *In* Disability and Culture.
       Benedicte Ingstad and Susan Reynolds Whyte, eds. Pp. 140–58. Berkeley:
       University of California Press.

Press, Nancy, Carole Browner, Diem Tran, Christine Morton, and Barbara
LeMaster
1998   Provisional Normalcy and "Perfect Babies": Pregnant Women's Atti-

tudes toward Disability in the Context of Prenatal Testing. *In* Reproducing Reproduction: Kinship, Power, and Technological Innovation. Sarah Franklin and Helena Ragoné, eds. Pp. 46–65. New York: Routledge.

Rapp, Rayna
1997   Real-Time Fetus: The Role of the Sonogram in the Age of Monitored Reproduction. *In* Cyborgs and Citadels: Anthropological Interventions in Emerging Sciences and Technologies. Gary Downey and Joseph Dumit, eds. Pp. 31–48. Santa Fe: School of American Research Press.

Scheer, Jessica, and Nora Groce
1988   Impairment as a Human Constant: Cross-Cultural and Historical Perspectives on Variation. Journal of Social Issues 44(1):23–37.

Tronto, Joan
1993   Moral Boundaries: A Political Argument for an Ethic of Care. New York: Routledge.

Weiss, Meira
1994   Conditional Love: Parents' Attitudes toward Handicapped Children. Westport, CT: Bergin and Garvey.
1997   Territorial Isolation and Physical Deformity: Israeli Parents' Reaction to Disabled Children. Disability and Society 12(2):259–71.

"True Gifts from God"

Motherhood, Sacrifice, and Enrichment in the Case of Pregnancy Loss

Linda L. Layne

To an even greater extent than pregnancy, pregnancy loss is largely beyond the control of individuals. Yet a number of things in our culture serve to disguise this fact. The ethic of individual self-control and responsibility runs deep throughout North American culture. In this chapter I describe the moral problem that pregnancy loss poses for individuals in a culture that often understands pregnancy in terms of capitalist production and deems moral stature and worldly success to be the result of purposeful, individual effort. I show how the rhetoric of the gift enables bereaved parents to articulate and negotiate several tensions arising from pregnancy loss in our culture: that between the out-of-controlness of most fetal and early infant deaths and the cultural mandate to be in control of one's body/self; and that between the patent sadness of these events and the North American compulsion to be happy.

Classical anthropological theories of the gift as well as more contemporary theories of consumption have focused primarily on the giving and consuming of things (see introduction, this volume). Much of this literature has focused on how the exchange of material objects forges and maintains social relationships. I have explored this dimension of gift exchange in two of my earlier essays. In "'I Remember the Day I Shopped for Your Layette': Goods, Fetuses and Feminism in the Context of Pregnancy Loss" (1999) and "'He Was a Real Baby with

Baby Things': A Material Culture Analysis of Personhood, Parent-hood and Pregnancy Loss" (in press b), I examine the ways that the buying and giving of consumer goods, during a pregnancy and after its demise, contribute to the cultural construction of fetal personhood by middle-class North Americans. In "Layette" I focus on the iterative practices by which women and their social networks construct fetal personhood through gifts, and discuss the implications of these prac-tices for a feminist response to pregnancy loss. In "Real Baby" I dis-cuss how the liminal qualities of fetuses, corpses, and the physically de-formed threaten the "personhood"—or "realness," to use a native term—of embryos, fetuses, and newborns who die. Using a material culture approach, I show how the tangibility of the "baby things" women and their social networks buy, give, and preserve helps them to deal with the "realness problem" of their loss.

In comparison with goods, much less attention has been given to other types of gifts (see introduction, this volume). In this essay, as in the other essays of this volume, the focus is on non–consumer good gifts, the most important of these being the child. Whereas in the case of surrogacy (Ragoné, this volume, Narayan 1995), adoption (Mod-ell, this volume), and fosterage (Wozniak, this volume), the rhetoric of the gift marks a discomfort with payments being made in exchange for the child or childbearing/rearing services, in the case of pregnancy loss, much like that of children with disabilities (Landsman, this vol-ume), the "gift" helps counteract the fact that dead children do not meet the standards set by consumer culture.

As discussed in the introduction to this volume, the meaning of "gift" in contemporary Euro-American culture is colored by a Christ-ian understanding of this notion. The Christian inflection of the gift is most evident in cases, like the one examined here, that deal with life and death issues. Recasting a devastating "loss" as a blessed "gift" is the most dramatic of a whole series of paradoxical reversals found in narratives of pregnancy loss—reversals that are implicitly, and some-times explicitly, intertextually related to the classical paradoxes of New Testament Christianity.

An important theme found in studies of gift exchange is the relative status of givers and receivers. It is this aspect of gifting that is exam-ined most closely here. Through their use of the rhetoric of the gift, bereaved parents reinforce the status quo by confirming the privileged position of the giver as a moral agent. This view resonates with the masculinist ideology of the Protestant ethic. At the same time, they undermine this ideology by asserting the Christian alternative that the ideal Christian is a "receiver," dependent on and receptive to the grace and blessings of God.

Pregnancy Loss as a Moral Problem

Newman (1988) has described how the "culture of meritocracy" functions to exacerbate the experience of unemployment and downward mobility in the United States. In this secular version of the Calvinist ethic, success in business is "viewed as a test of commitment, and the product of hard work and self-sacrifice" and therefore "a measure of one's moral worth" (1988:76). A lack of success is also evaluated in moral terms (especially by those who are accustomed to success). "If individuals are responsible for their own destinies, there is no one else to blame in case of failure" (Newman 1988:77).

This doctrine of individual responsibility is also evident in biomedical and popular understandings of health and illness. For example, in Martin's (1994) study of North American understandings of the immune system, she described an emerging form of social Darwinism. She observed that the immune system is coming to be used as "a scale measuring people and groups" and that this "allow[s] some people to feel especially potent" (1994:236) (and, one might extrapolate, others to feel especially impotent). Although Martin does not explicitly link her analysis to the protestant ethic, there are clear connections. People are thought to vary in the "quality of their immune systems." The "elect," those with strong systems, will have lasting, if not everlasting, life, while those with inferior systems will perish. The relative strength of immune systems is sometimes understood in terms of an individual's or group's genetics, but it is also frequently understood to be the result of an individual's conscious effort for self-improvement (Martin 1994:237). Thus, if one is slothful, one will not achieve success/health; if one is well-disciplined and gives one's system enough practice and training, one will be rewarded in the "currency of health" (Martin 1994:237).

Even in public health, there has been an increasing emphasis on individual "lifestyle" choices as the most important factor for improving (or diminishing) health. For example, Balshem describes how residents of a neighborhood with an elevated cancer rate in Philadelphia believed that their illnesses were caused by toxic exposure from the chemical factories clustered in their neighborhood and other sources of pollution. Representatives of the Fox Chase Cancer Center "sought to deflect this concern" and focused their efforts instead on getting individuals to "quit smoking, improve their diets, and schedule cancer screening tests at regular intervals" to reduce cancer risk (Balshem 1993:3).

The ethic of meritocracy is also conspicuous with regard to pregnancy and birth. In her study of abortion activists in the United States, Ginsburg (1989) argues that with the advent of legal abortion, motherhood shifted from being a status that was ascribed to one that was achieved. Once women could safely choose not to become mothers, even after they were pregnant, the choice to keep a pregnancy and mother a child came to be seen as a moral achievement. Many other dimensions of contemporary North American culture contribute to this understanding of pregnancy and childbirth as being the result of purposeful, moral-laden activity.[1] Many feminist authors have observed the ways production metaphors inform our understandings of pregnancy and birth.[2] Martin notes that "since the fifteenth century the same English word, 'labor,' has been used to describe what women do in bearing forth children and what men and women do in producing things for use and exchange in the home and market" (1987:66). While in earlier times this notion of reproductive labor referred to preindustrial forms of production, it now has specific, if somewhat outdated, references to industrial production. For example, writing in 1971, Mitchell observed that "the child is seen as an object created by the mother, in the same way as a commodity is created by a worker" (Mitchell quoted in Martin 1987:67). The Calvinist ethic and its more recent secular versions see productive labor as both a sign of, and avenue for, achieving moral stature.[3]

To the extent that pregnancy and birth are understood in terms of production, pregnancy loss is, by extension, an instance of failed production. Like success in business, reproductive success may be "viewed as a test of commitment, and the product of hard work and self-sacrifice," and thus "a measure of one's moral worth" (Newman 1988:76). Like failure in business, reproductive failure may be read as the result of a lack "of willingness and ability to drive beyond the limitations of self indulgence and sloth" (Newman 1988:76).[4]

It is not surprising, since the "successful production" of a baby may be credited as a moral achievement, the result of self-discipline and labor, that the inability to bear children is often attributed to a moral failing on the part of the woman. As Sandelowski has observed, "In a cultural milieu characterized by the expectation that conception can be prevented, terminated, and initiated at will, and in which individual habits and life-styles have been persistently implicated in the onset of disease, not being able to have a child . . . is still often viewed as a kind of failure of will" (1993:22).[5] She delineates the (selfish and immoral) "life style choices" of women that are commonly blamed for infertility: the (selfish) postponement of childbearing, which brings with it, in addition to age-associated risks, additional risks from prolonged exposure to contraceptive, occupational, and environmental hazards; sexually transmitted disease, associated with (immoral) early and frequent sexual contact and multiple sexual partners; and (selfish and immoral) personal habits such as overeating (the sin of gluttony) or undereating (the sin of vanity) and intensive exercise (1993:23).

Other reproductive experiences that do not measure up also tend to be blamed on women's moral failings. For example, Landsman (1998:80, this volume, in press) explains, mothers of children with disabilities often "either struggle to determine what they might have done wrong to bring about a disability or . . . [are] wrongfully judged by others as having done something improper such as using drugs or smoking cigarettes." Similarly, the current debate about fetal abuse focuses almost exclusively on maternal behaviors, particularly maternal substance abuse, rather than on the social and environmental hazards like poverty, malnutrition, and inadequate medical care that have long been associated with poor birth outcomes, or on the adverse birth outcomes caused by male behaviors (Schroedel and Peretz 1995:86).

When one looks specifically at obstetrical understandings of pregnancy loss one finds contradictory messages. For instance, in their

discussion of the causes of spontaneous abortion, Bourne and Danforth (1975) begin with a long paragraph designed to reassure the
would-have-been mother that it was not her fault: "It is certain that
there is virtually nothing a woman could possibly do herself to produce a miscarriage, . . . in almost all miscarriages the fetus dies . . . for
causes that are beyond anyone's voluntary control" (Bourne and Danforth 1975:261). This absolution is revoked, however, in a later chapter on perinatal death, where the authors argue that "the decline in
the perinatal death rate over the years has been due directly or indirectly to improvement in prenatal care." They conclude by revealing
that their reason for writing the book was to get "pregnant women
. . . to . . . accept more stringent supervision during their pregnancy."
According to the authors, in order for this to happen, women

> must understand the reasons for any inconvenience which they may un-
> dergo and they must realize that everything they are asked to do is for
> their own and for their babies' benefits. Above all, the mother and all
> the members of her family must realize that they must accept the final
> responsibility for her welfare and that of the unborn child. (Bourne and
> Danforth 1975:522)[6]

Regardless of patent reassurances that they were not responsible for a
miscarriage, and in fact are incapable of producing a miscarriage if
they wanted to, ultimately, "the final responsibility" for the health of
the mother and her fetus is placed squarely on the mother. Thus, while
women are assured *post facto* that there was nothing that they could
have done to have caused the loss, this message contradicts all the
messages they received from their doctors and popular culture
throughout the pregnancy on the importance of their agency in "producing" a healthy baby by maintaining self-discipline and submitting
to the authority of experts.[7]

Paradoxically, the women's health movement has contributed to
this ethic of individual achievement and in so doing has made the experience of pregnancy loss (or any other less than ideal birth) more
problematic for women (see Landsman, this volume, 1998). The fundamental premise of the movement that women must wrest back control of their bodies from physicians (especially during pregnancy and
birth) reinforces the ethic of individual control and responsibility.[8]

Childbirth educators who encourage pregnant couples to make a "birth plan" obscure the extent to which pregnancy and birth are unpredictable, largely uncontrollable processes. For example, throughout *The Bradley Method Student Workbook* (Hathaway et al. 1989), the emphasis is on women's control over their pregnancies and births. Even in the chapter on "variations and unexpected situations," the message is not that these things sometimes happen, but rather that if one is only diligent and hardworking enough (which one can determine by filling out a checklist of forty-four items that women should do on a daily basis throughout their pregnancies), such problems can be avoided (Hathaway et al. 1989:64–65).[9] It is clear that a "culture of meritocracy" applies as much here as it does in the business realm. Like those who suffer economic downward mobility, individual women may "fall from grace" and slip from "low risk" to "high risk" if they are not morally vigilant.[10] If the pregnancy ends with a less than desired birth experience or birth outcome (e.g., a healthy baby), it is hard to imagine a woman who could not go back over that daunting list and find at least some areas in which she should have done more, could have tried harder.

This ethic of individual achievement found in orthodox and alternative obstetrics and in popular culture exacerbates the experience of pregnancy loss. Among the middle classes, those who experience a loss may be cast (by themselves, at least) as failed achievers. One version of this focuses on the middle-class moral mandate to "finish what one starts." In the film *Some Babies Die*, a woman who had had three stillbirths in three years articulates these issues clearly: "You've failed, no matter how you look at it, you've failed, because if you set out to do something, I believe you've got to finish it, and here's something that you're trying to see through and you've got no control over, and that's one thing that is to me vitally important, control."

Donna Brunner (1992) vividly illustrates how the rhetoric of natural childbirth exacerbates the experience of pregnancy loss in a piece entitled "Me? Guilty?" She describes how after her first delivery, which was a c-section, she attempted a "natural" vaginal delivery and lost her baby. She explains that she "held off those unnatural drugs for as long as possible" (19.5 hours) and now worries that if only she had taken some pitocin sooner she might have saved her baby.

Guilty? Oh, I'm guilty all right. . . . How come the "childbirth educa-tion" didn't do any good? . . . of course, the classes tell you (or strongly imply) that *everyone* can handle the birth process if you just get in tune with your body and breathe, breathe, and breathe some more. But what about us who don't have easy births and who don't maintain the ability to "hout" during 26 hours of labor? . . .

Guilty? Oh I'm guilty all right. I didn't do it right. I didn't hear her cry; I didn't see her move; I didn't hold her while she lived (guess I failed the "nursing on the table" criteria too).

Oh well, I'm guilty either way. I took it [pitocin] and Demeral and had an epidural and it was still a complicated birth, so I failed in the eyes of the natural childbirth/no drugs crowd *and* in the eyes of the world because I couldn't produce a baby that lived. (Brunner 1992)

This creates for women who experience a loss a double bind. Either they accept responsibility for the pregnancy loss and therefore blame themselves for the death of their "baby," or they must admit that the loss was a bodily event over which they had no control. Despite the much discussed dominance of the Cartesian split between mind and body, this is still experienced as "I am/was out of control." This alter-native—acknowledging that one was not in control of oneself—is hardly more palatable than self-blame. Lack of control is the first item Donna Brunner (1992) includes in her list of things she feels guilty for—"Guilty? Oh, I'm guilty all right. Guilty for not being 'in con-trol.'" Sue Friedeck (1995), one of the coeditors of the SHARE newsletter, whose son had survived fetal surgery for congenital di-aphragmatic hernia but then was born prematurely and died thirteen days later, explains, "One of the hardest aspects of our loss of Michael was the feeling of helplessness and loss of control."

Nor is it easy to contemplate or accept the fact that the formidable forces of technoscience were not able to control nature when it really counted. Davis-Floyd has described "the need to create a sense of cul-tural control over birth, a natural process resistant to such control" (1992:63) and how the biomedical rituals of obstetrics "provide at least a sense of certainty and security to women that a natural process perceived as terrifying and uncontrollable can be controlled and ren-dered conceptually safe when its course is mechanistically channeled into predictable pathways" (1992:64).

Hence, it is not surprising that many North American women who experience pregnancy losses tell of feeling "out of control" and express an acute discomfort with this state of affairs. At the same time, nearly all women worry that they were in some way responsible.[11] Indeed, one of the most disturbing findings of my current research on the experience of pregnancy loss in toxically assaulted communities is how deeply ingrained and pervasive is this tendency to self-blame (Layne 1997c). Even in communities where there is a ready-made, highly plausible "it wasn't me, it was them" explanation, many of the women I have interviewed persist in blaming themselves. The most notable example comes from Alsea, Oregon, where eight women signed a letter that eventually led to the EPA's ban on federal use of 2,4,5-T. In their community, the National Forest Service and timber companies had been routinely spraying the local roadways and watersheds with the ingredients of Agent Orange; each time they did, statistically significant numbers of the local women miscarried. Nevertheless, one of the women who signed still believes, twenty years later, that her loss was due to a hike she took.

Newman identified two ways that downwardly mobile managers in the United States fend off the tendency to self-blame. Some use the concept of "categorical fate," that is, they see themselves as part of a group of victims whose plight is the result of large "social forces beyond their control" (1988:65). Others focus on their individual personalities, but rather than finding fault with themselves, they attribute their difficulty to "manly flaws" such as exceptional "aggressiveness, rationality, and principled commitment, . . . praiseworthy attributes in American business" (1988:72). Neither of these strategies seem to work very well for women who have had a pregnancy loss. For most women in the United States, pregnancy loss is experienced as a highly private, individual, usually hidden event.[12] There is no equivalent of "manly flaws" for women who experience pregnancy loss. One cannot argue that it was because one was too much of a woman that this unfortunate event took place. On the contrary, since pregnancy loss is so directly tied to their sexuality, many women feel that these events threaten their womanliness.

And while a woman's role in reproduction (and pregnancy loss) is much more extensive and direct, men also suffer these losses, and their sexual identity likewise may be significantly challenged. Men may question their ability as able reproducers and may feel a sense of powerlessness at not having been able to avert disaster, help their wives, and protect their children.

But members of pregnancy loss support groups have found other resources for dealing with the threat to their identities as able, moral individuals that comes with pregnancy loss. The rhetoric of the gift appears to be one of the most widely used and versatile such devices. It enables bereaved parents to articulate and negotiate several of the tensions that result from pregnancy loss in our culture. It enables would-be parents to reassert some sense of control over a devastating personal event without condemning themselves. It also bridges the tension between the parent's sorrow and what Aries has identified as the modern "need for happiness—the moral duty and the social obligation to contribute to the collective happiness by avoiding any cause for sadness or boredom, by appearing to be always happy, even if in the depths of despair" (1974:93–94). In other words, some of the most important redemptive resources for the "spoiled identity" (Goffman 1963) that pregnancy loss threatens are found not in the sphere of secular production and commodity exchange, but in the spiritually infused discourse of the gift.[13]

One of the most important features of the rhetoric of the gift in this context is the way the notion of the gift functions paradoxically.[14] The recasting of a devastating loss as a blessed gift is the most dramatic of a whole host of paradoxical reversals found in narratives of pregnancy loss. By situating their experience in the context of the paradoxical reversals of Christian dogma, many bereaved parents are able to reconcile the gap between their expectations and reality, and in so doing, reassert a sense of themselves as virtuous and able.

Pregnancy Loss Support Groups

This work is based on research with three pregnancy loss support groups in the New York/New Jersey area: Unite (not an acronym), a regional group with, as of 1995, ten support groups serving Pennsylvania and New Jersey; SHARE (Source of Help in Airing and Resolving Experiences), the nation's largest pregnancy loss support organization with, as of 1995, ninety-seven groups throughout the United States; and the New York Section of the National Council of Jewish Women's (NCJW) support group in New York City. Over nine hundred such groups were established throughout the country during the 1980s.

My research has involved attending support group meetings, participating first as a "parent" and later as a "professional" at Unite's annual conference, and attending other special seminars and events sponsored by these groups. I also completed Unite's training program for support counselors, participated in the New York Section of the National Council of Jewish Women's telephone counseling program, and interviewed some of the founding members of these and other groups. More recently, I have been engaged in a textual analysis of the quarterly newsletters of Unite (starting with its first issue in 1981 to the present) and the six annual issues of the SHARE newsletter (from 1984 to the present), which include contributions from members throughout the country.

The membership of these three organizations is predominantly white and middle-class. There is evidence that socioeconomic status influences the rate of pregnancy loss (MacFarlane and Mugford 1984),[15] and although white women have a larger total number of pregnancy losses nationwide, the estimated rate of pregnancy loss is nearly double for women of color than for non-hispanic white women.[16] Because of the profound impact that race and class have on the experience of pregnancy and motherhood in our country, one must not assume that the experience of members of pregnancy loss support groups is representative of the U.S. population.

Most support group meetings are attended by couples (this was strongly encouraged by the NCJW group), but some women and an occasional man attend on their own. Women, mostly bereaved mothers but also sometimes other female relatives, friends, and nurses, write the vast majority of the newsletter items. Men (again, mostly bereaved fathers but also occasionally would-have-been grandfathers or brothers) contribute more regularly to the SHARE newsletter (about 12 percent of the personal items) than they do to the Unite newsletter (about 4 percent).[17] There is a certain amount of interchange between the two newsletters; Unite and SHARE occasionally reprint pieces published in each other's newsletters. The editors of the SHARE newsletter routinely include information about the circumstances of the contributor's loss and their place of residence after a piece, in the Unite newsletter one must glean such information from the contributed piece itself. Members frequently contribute multiple selections and their contributions sometimes span a number of years. In these cases one can piece together a more detailed understanding of their loss and gain some understanding of how the loss is experienced over time.

All three groups are ecumenical and include Jewish, Catholic, and Protestant members.[18] Testimony of participants at pregnancy loss support group meetings and the personal narratives published in the newsletters indicate that many members of pregnancy loss support groups turn to religion in their search for answers. Judging from these sources, participants vary in the strength of their religious commitment. Some held deep religious convictions prior to the loss, and for many of these individuals their convictions provided an important source of solace, while for others these convictions were severely challenged by the loss. Other individuals who normally led relatively secular lives turned to religion in their efforts to deal with this life crisis. For some of these individuals the idea of an afterlife and/or a master plan proved to be of comfort, while others found such beliefs wanting.

Some founders of pregnancy loss groups are supporters of women's right to choose, while others clearly feel that their work in this area complements their anti-abortion stand.[19] This divisive issue has remained submerged in the pregnancy loss support movement as leaders work to champion their shared goals with the added strength of unity. It is not safe to assume that individuals who participate in groups share or even know the position of their group's leaders on abortion.

Miscarriages are by far the most frequent type of pregnancy loss. Most pregnancy losses occur during the first trimester, and it is estimated that only 3.1 percent of all intrauterine deaths take place after sixteen weeks gestation (Bongaarts and Potter 1983:39). Based on a survey of the Unite and SHARE newsletters and my observations at support group meetings, I have found that later losses are proportionately much more frequently represented. Of the 447 losses reported in the newsletters (Unite 1981–94/SHARE 1984–94), 56 percent refer to a loss that takes place after twenty-four weeks gestation (of which 25 percent were stillbirths; 18 percent were a newborn death following a full-term pregnancy, and 13 percent were a newborn death after premature birth). Only 44 percent (197) referred to a miscarriage.

In the medical and social scientific literature the term "stillbirth" is used to designate a loss that occurs after a point in the pregnancy at which the fetus had a chance of surviving ex utero. In the United States this is currently around twenty-four weeks, the same gestational age, not coincidentally, after which abortion is illegal. In other publications on the subject of pregnancy loss I have used a combination of terms to describe what was "lost"—for example, biomedical terms like "embryo," "fetus," "blighted ovum," "products of conception," and "native" terms like "baby," "child," "my little angel," as well as my own terms, for example, "would-have-been baby." Most of the narratives of loss on which I focus in this chapter describe losses that occurred during the third trimester of a pregnancy or shortly after birth, and so in this chapter I mostly use the "native" terms.

Of Gifts and Agency

Gifts play a prominent role in the personal narratives of miscarriage, stillbirth, and early infant death of members of pregnancy loss support groups. In this chapter I focus on the various types of spiritual gifts associated with pregnancy loss, the qualities most often described as inhering to them, and the trajectories of these gifts, paying special attention to the issue of agency in each case.

Spiritual gifts routinely appear in the narratives of pregnancy loss in the following ways: (1) the "baby" is interpreted as a gift from God; (2) the death of the child is interpreted, often in the language of sacrifice, as a gift from the parents to God; (3) the "baby's" life and death are experienced as a source of valuable spiritual and/or interpersonal gifts for the parents and others; these gifts are often understood to be gifts from God but are also frequently understood to be gifts from the child; (4) parents (especially mothers) are seen as givers of life and/or birth for which they may or may not receive credit; (5) others acknowledgment of the loss is defined as a gift to the parents; (6) the social support given to bereaved parents is understood to create an obligation to "pay back" what they received by helping others.

1. Baby as Gift from God

The "baby" is frequently interpreted as a gift. Sometimes the child is understood to be a gift of self from the child to the parents. For example, in a piece written one year after his daughter was born and died at twenty-three weeks gestation, a father from Canton, Massachusetts, writes, "It's been a year since you gave us the gift of your oh so short life" (Atwood 1990). Another father thanks his son for this gift: "Thank you, Jonathan, for giving us the time you had. We will always love you for it" (Nagele 1986).

More typically the baby is understood to be a gift from God. For example, in the poem from which I take my title, Jennifer Habercorn (1996) begins, "There are two more angels in heaven tonight" and goes on to describe her son and daughter as "true gifts from God." Patricia Shute writes of her granddaughter, "God sent to us for six short days, Jennifer Maria to hold and love. And with his gift sent from above, came stronger faith and richer love" (Shute 1988).

Others interpret the baby not as a "true gift" from God, but as only a loan.[20] In a poem entitled "My Little Angel" a man identified as Uncle Rick states, "Children come to this world on borrowed time" (Alvarado 1995).[21] This notion is also found in a poem entitled "God's Promise" by the nineteenth-century American poet John Greenleaf Whittier, reproduced in the Unite newsletter: "'I'll lend you for a little while a Child of mine,' He said. 'For you to love her while she lives and mourn for when she's dead. It may be six or seven years. Or twenty-two or three. But will you, til I call her back, Take care of her for me?'" (Whittier 1995–96).[22]

Whether the child is understood to be a gift or a loan, parents are required to give in return: to give the child love and care, and to give God gratitude for this privilege. Whittier ends his poem with God overhearing the parents agree to be grateful—"for the happiness we've known, forever grateful stay"; and the piece by the grandmother ends, "For now we know the privilege given in caring for his gift from heaven" (Shute 1988).

2. Sacrifice: The Baby as Gift to God

There is another way that construal of the baby as a gift from God may be understood to obligate the parents to reciprocate. The child's death may be understood as a return gift from the parents to God. One example is found in a poem by an uncle from Corpus Christi, Texas, written in the voice of a baby boy, Ray.[23] The poem begins by granting God agency, "born out of love by God's design, a light for all to see," but ends by reversing the roles and stressing the agency of the parents as givers to God: "I'm now God's Ray of joyous light—a gift from Mom and Dad" (Dunham 1986). In another piece, John Fuchs of Indianapolis, the father of a baby girl who was born with lung and heart problems and lived for two days, depicts a similar two-way exchange—from God to them, then back to Him. In his piece entitled "Our Littlest Angel," addressed to God, he writes, "We didn't know why you'd required this baby we had conceived. Or why her time on earth was short, this daughter we'd received. We dedicated her to You before we gave her up" (Fuchs 1987). Even in cases like this, when the parents acknowledge that the logic of such gifts challenges their comprehension, constructing the loss as a gift to God edifies the loss and attributes agency to the parents at this moment of extreme helplessness.

One of the most common ways this is accomplished is by analogy with Christ's sacrifice.[24] With the Crucifixion, God engages in what Kermode has called "the ultimate sacrificial excess" by allowing his only son to be killed for the salvation of sinners (Kermode 1987:393).[25] According to Miller (1998:115), in Christianity sacrifice serves as a "prevalent . . . model for appropriate religious behavior. The ideal of sacrifice and especially the abnegation of self-sacrifice remains close to the dominant ideals of Christian devotional love." God's gift of his only son provides a model by which some bereaved parents understand their loss.[26]

The thought that because of his own son's death God can empathize with their grief makes the grief more bearable for some. One father writes, "We feel that if God so loved the world that He was willing to give up His Son, that we, too, could bear the pain" (Herr 1984). Judy Ward also compares her loss with God's: "for He too lost

His precious Son before His earthly work was done. . . . so God understands our pain" (Ward 1987).

This analogy also helps bereaved parents transform/reverse the shame they may feel, as a result of what in another discourse would be defined as a "reproductive failure," into pride. By analogizing their child to Christ, they reverse the valuation process that deems dead babies to be of no value. Not only are their babies of equal worth to other people's, in fact, they are of even greater worth for they are, like Christ, no ordinary babies, but special, chosen ones (cf. Landsman, this volume).[27] For example, Ward makes explicit the analogy between Christ's death and that of her son by capitalizing "Son" in the final line of the poem: "Sweet little Tyler, God's chosen one. We are so proud you were our Son" (Ward 1987). Another mother (from Beaver, Pennsylvania) shares this view. Of her son who lived a few hours after his birth at twenty-four weeks gestation due to a uterine infection, she writes, "Our infant son was born today, He came and died to show the way. As Jesus died, upon the cross" (Yoder 1985).

This analogy to the archetypical Christian sacrifice is also made by means of the symbol of the Lamb (see Hyde 1979:19). Jesus is often referred to as the Lamb because of his sacrificial death, and bereaved parents sometimes refer to their dead children as lambs. One poem written in the voice of the child reassures the parents, "I'm resting now beside the Lamb" (Dunham 1986). Another poem written by a bereaved father (from Lexington, Nebraska) writes of his stillborn son, "Our little lamb has gone away"; later he makes explicit this analogy with Christ: "My son I know you are not an angel, But a son of God I see" (Cantrell 1987).

In poems written at Christmas and Easter time, some bereaved mothers compare themselves to Mary. At Christmas the focus is on Mary's relationship with "baby Jesus" and the pangs that bereaved mothers may feel when they "view the manger scene" (Ingle 1982–83). Like "every baby in a stroller," each "Christ Child in a manger may pull . . . at the core of [the] hearts and . . . souls" of bereaved mothers (Gana 1998). For example, a woman whose daughter was stillborn on December 15 and left the hospital empty-handed the next day describes how hard it was for her while waiting for her husband to bring the car, to see a woman with a new baby get into a car and to see the nativity scene set up in the lobby of the hospital (Amendolara 1997). In such cases, Mary may be an object of envy; just one more lucky woman who got the baby she desired.

At Easter time, the focus is on Jesus's death. Whereas God actively chose to sacrifice his son, poor Mother Mary wasn't consulted and her powerlessness to prevent his death is cause for empathy. For example, Mary Cushing Doherty, a lawyer and member of Unite's board of directors, published a piece entitled "At the Foot of the Cross" in an April issue of Unite's newsletter. She explains in a note preceding the poem that she "composed the following Easter remembrance . . . while thinking about the death of Jesus and about the death of my own son, Tommy [who died three days after his birth]. I began to understand the grief that Jesus's mother must have felt while watching the untimely death of her son." It begins,

> *She stood at the foot of His cross.*
> *She asked God if she could pray hard*
> *Enough for a miracle to keep Him alive.*
> *She received Him into her arms*
> *Bruised, cold limp*
> *She wished to hold the warmth of His life.*
> *She cried because she could not protect Him from an untimely death.*
> *She asked if she had done something wrong.* (Doherty 1988)[28]

Whereas in the earlier examples, parents were comforted by the thought that God could understand their pain, in this case, a bereaved mother offers compassionate understanding to Mary qua bereaved mother.

As this example makes clear, not everyone experiences their loss as a gift; for some it is quite the contrary. Other examples include a mother who writes of the stillbirth of her twins, "I feel like I have been robbed of the two most precious things in my life" (Hunn 1995).[29] Jody Kozak (1987) from Salt Lake City likens her stillbirth to having "Christmas treats . . . stolen in the night."[30] Kathy Rosso Gana likens grief to a number of socially mandated but onerous fiscal obligations—unwelcome solicitations for charity, the obligation to pay bills and dues. She writes, "Two autumns in a row a child died within me. When grief came knocking on my door the second time around, I tried to tell him 'I gave at the office' . . . whether I like it or not the dues must be paid—one year of pain and suffering per child. Well, my bill is almost paid up" (Gana 1985).

For still others, the emphasis is not on giving or sharing but on the pleasures of exclusive possession. Susan Erling (1984) of St. Paul, Minnesota, who miscarried at ten weeks, writes, "for just 10 weeks I had you to myself."

3. Baby Brings Gifts to Parents

Many members of pregnancy loss support groups report feeling that the experience of loss resulted in valuable changes in their lives; changes often described as gifts. Of all the types of gifts discussed in pregnancy loss support group newsletters and literature, the idea that the life/death experience is a source of spiritual/personal enrichment is the most common and most thoroughly developed. Sometimes these gifts are attributed to God, but more frequently they are attributed to the child. In other words, whereas in the earlier examples, God and parents were cast as givers, in this case, it is the child that has the active role as giver (cf. Landsman, this volume).

The most fundamental gift these children are thought to give is that of making their mothers "mothers." For example, Bonita Martin dedicates her poem "I'm Still a Mother" to the memory of her son, "who gave me the gift of being a mother" (1995).

In addition to this primary gift, the child is frequently construed to be the bearer of a whole host of other transformative gifts. For example, Diana Widell's daughter Kira died during labor two weeks before her due date. She had Down syndrome and a serious heart defect. In a piece reprinted in the 1995 holiday issue of the SHARE newsletter Diana writes, "The Holidays are a time to count our blessing and to thank God for all we have been given. For those of us who have lost a child, giving thanks can sometimes be difficult. . . . Yet even in our grief we have found good. And there are things to be thankful for" (Widell 1995). She itemizes the benefits:

> I became more certain of who I was and what I wanted as my faith and dependency on God became essential in just getting through each day.

. . . We found much we thought important before, no longer was. We also found things we took for granted before were suddenly very important. . . . Kira's death taught us . . . contentment. We try to live day to day and have learned there are no guarantees in life. We have learned just wishing for something does not make it true. (Widell 1995)

She ends with "While I am not happy about Kira's death, I am thankful for all she has given me."

Another example is found in a piece entitled "What I Learned from Baby Adam," written by Andrea D'Asaro, who describes how her amniotic water started leaking at twenty-three weeks gestation. After several days of hospitalization she developed a fever and the doctors induced labor. She gave birth to a "previable" son who stopped breathing once they cut the umbilical cord. As a result of "Adam's birth and death" she reports that she resolved "to give up complaining about my husband's faults, to throw out my lists of grievances I collect in a file by my bed waiting for a chance to read them to Ralph." She is still often annoyed by her husband's habits but she doesn't take them so seriously now, and instead, turns her focus outwards to others who are in distress: "my heart goes out to the homeless woman on the street, the stressed co-worker, the harried driver behind me" (D'Asaro 1996).

Most of the losses described in pregnancy loss support newsletters take place well after the first trimester, but the notion that the child is a source of enrichment is not restricted to later losses. For example, Marie Allen and Shelly Marks end their book *Miscarriage* with a chapter entitled "Gifts," which focuses on how "our babies' lives and the process of grieving our babies' deaths brought us emotional, psychological, and spiritual gifts that changed our lives," gifts "that touched not only our lives but also the lives of countless others" (Allen and Marks 1993:211). Susan Erling (1984), who miscarried at ten weeks, writes, "It seems you only needed 10 weeks to make my life so much richer, and give me a small glimpse of eternity." Perry-Lynn Moffitt, a SHARE contributor and coauthor of a book on pregnancy loss, describes how the two miscarriages she had before the birth of her two healthy children helped her cope with her four subsequent miscarriages. She writes, "although their lives had been

short, these miscarried babies had left an enduring legacy by aug-
menting my ability to order my priorities and cherish living loved
ones more. . . . It is these babies' lasting gift to us as we struggle to
integrate their absences into our lives" (1991:2).

This sense of gifts incurring from pregnancy loss is also a frequent
topic at collective memorial services (which commemorate the full
range of pregnancy losses from earliest to those that occur after birth).
For example, SHARE published a prayer written by its founder, Sister
Jane Marie Lamb, for a memorial service held in Akron in 1986:

> oh God, . . . we come to you with all that has been part of the special
> gift of our babies, the joyful anticipation, the mourning period, the
> memories and letting go–reaching out. We are grateful for all those
> times. . . . For the times of letting go, and for the times of reaching out,
> for each new day and each ray of hope, for the gifts our babies left us: in
> giving us new eyes with which to see, new ears to hear more, a new
> heart to love with, and new values in many areas of our lives. (Lamb
> 1986).[31]

For those who believe that their babies are still alive, now living in
heaven, often in the form of angels (see Layne 1992), their children
remain a source of ongoing gifts to their families on earth. Cathy
Hintz, a registered nurse and Unite member, hangs crystal snowflakes
in her kitchen window as a way of remembering her three dead children and her one survivor: "everyday as the sun kisses each snowflake,
our home is filled with rainbows—unexpected gifts from our children
in heaven" (Hintz 1988).[32]

Another example is found in a letter written in the name of a dead
baby, who explains, "I would like to share the full depth of love that
one can only experience in heaven. I would like to share that love with
you and ask that you use my gift well. I give you this gift." (Kevin
1985–86).[33]

After a loss, a number of parents describe their subsequent children
as a gift, not from God, but from their children now in heaven.[34] Laurie Holper (1991b) describes her subsequent daughter (who was born
prematurely but survived) as "a gift from Josh," her son who died two
hours after birth.[35] In a piece called "One Mother's Feelings on Subsequent Pregnancy," Linda Rabinowitz (1983) writes, "In essence,

she [her daughter who died after living two months] has given Joshua to us." During an anxious pregnancy following the death of a son who died at forty-two weeks gestation, Debbie Hein describes how her husband reassured her by telling her that their daughter "would be a gift of love from Timmy" (Hein 1984). Linda McCann (1985) expressed a similar thought in "A Love Letter to My Baby Girl," where she describes how when their subsequent child was born alive "I cried . . . tears of joy. And silently I thanked you over and over again. Joey is your gift to us."[36]

A few brave souls buck the mandate to find good in adversity. Pat McCann (1984) explains in her piece entitled "Growth through Pain" that while she considers the fact that she has been forced to "grow farther than my years" "a very special gift from a very very special baby," she also acknowledges that "the knowledge almost never has been worth the pain." Marion Cohen, a mathematician, author of numerous collections of poetry and essays on her many traumatic birth experiences, and Unite member, writes in a poem entitled "Bereavement and Growth," "It matures you they said. It matures you, they say. Wasn't I mature enough before? Was I really that bad? Was I one of the worst? How come God chose me?" (Cohen 1981a). Another example is found in the piece discussed above by Mary Doherty in which she compares her loss to that of Mother Mary; she concludes by saying of Mary, "She knew friends would say His death would teach people to value life. She asked why her son's life needed to serve as a lesson" (Doherty 1988).

4. Parents as Givers of Life and/or Birth For Which They May or May Not Receive Credit

Some bereaved parents construe themselves as "givers" by virtue of the fact that they created life and/or "gave" birth. There are a number of possible recipients of this "gift of life," including the child, the world, and oneself. For example, Gia Strozzieri writes of the birth of her daughter, who lived sixteen days, "Today I brought into this world. A gift of love, my little girl. My little girl so pure and sweet. A gift to make my life complete. . . . Consumed with love that all could see for this little girl, who came from me" (Strozzieri 1996).[37] In this piece the mother clearly takes credit for this gift and identifies two recipients: the world and herself. David Nagele (1986) casts his role as father as co–gift giver. In a piece given to his wife after the death of their son he writes, "we have lost a part of ourselves, a gift to each other, to mankind, to time. For children are a gift."

Cathi Lammert, one of the coeditors of the SHARE newsletter, describes how at the funeral for her stillborn son, "the priest told Chuck and I that we needed to be congratulated for being Christopher's parents, for giving him life, eternal life" (Lammert 1996). It is unclear whether this gift of eternal life is understood to come from the act of conceiving and bearing him or from the rituals of baptism and Christian burial that the parents arranged for him subsequently, but Lammert goes on to suggest that it is "the gift of love" that qualifies people as parents. She tells her readers that "you too need to be congratulated for being your child's parent; for loving and wanting them with all your heart and soul" (Lammert 1996).

Not all women are acknowledged in this way, and this lack of public recognition for their role as parent (i.e., as giver of birth, life, and love) creates an imbalance in the reciprocity required at gift-giving events like Mother's Day. Kelly Gonzalez, coordinator of the Pikes Peak SHARE group, writes, "You may not even have gotten 'credit' for giving birth at all. . . . It can . . . be painful as you purchase a card for your mother or father and realize that you should be receiving one, not just sending a card" (Gonzalez 1996).

Although women are the ones normally cast in this way, fathers are also occasionally thought of in these terms. For instance, Karen Burton wrote a piece for the Mother's and Father's Day issue of the SHARE newsletter, in which she contrasts the experience of parenting her three living sons with that of parenting her son Joey. Joey was born with a major heart defect. He underwent surgery but a few days later suffered a massive heart attack. The parents disconnected the life support and he died nine days after birth.

As most people celebrate Mother's/Father's Days, they will reflect on the gifts they have received from their own parents or on the gifts they have received in being a parent. I cannot help but reflect on the great cost many of us have paid to be a "Mom" or "Dad." . . . We are parents who have paid a great price and we deserve recognition on these special days whether we have surviving children or not. (Burton 1996)[38]

5. Acknowledgment of the Baby after Its Death— A Gift to the Bereaved Parents

The four trajectories of giving examined so far have primarily concerned exchanges between the principal triad of God, child, parents. The final two trajectories described in this chapter involve exchange between bereaved parents and members of their wider social networks, including other members of support groups. One is the acknowledgment of the loss, which is construed as a gift from others to the parents. Since our cultural norm is to ignore pregnancy loss—to avoid any reference to it, to act as if it never happened—the acknowledgment of the loss by family members, friends, the clergy, and others may be experienced as a valuable gift for which the parents are grateful. For example, during her editorship of the Unite newsletter, Janice Heil wrote a piece entitled "Your Gift to Me" for the holiday issue in 1982–83. "What can you give me this holiday season? Your greatest gift to me is your listening" (1982–83). Cathi Lammert, whose priest "congratulated" her and her husband "for being Christopher's parents and for giving him life," experienced this act as a precious gift—"I will treasure that compliment in my heart forever" (Lammert 1996). Another woman whose family gives a memorial gift in the name of their dead child every year at Christmas says, "We are grateful that they never forget" (Sariego 1996). It is the fact that such acknowledgment is so rare and so much desired that qualifies it as a "gift."

6. The Need to "Pay Back" Others for Their Support

Members of pregnancy loss support groups often remark upon their need to "pay back" the help and support they received when they were going through the "early stages" of grief. Hannah Campbell (1993) explains in a piece entitled "Going Back and Giving Back to Group Meetings" that she still attends group meetings five years after the stillbirth of her son because "part of my remembering Marc is to give to others what I have gotten from others." In 1986 Unite published a letter from Shelley Cocke thanking the organization for help in dealing with the stillbirth of her son. She describes how after a year, the grief felt less and she considered dropping out, but decided to continue with Unite. After the birth of her daughter, she "felt ready to try to give back some of the encouragement, the knowledge of the grief process, and the support [she] had received from other members."[39] Her piece is followed by a note from the editors of the Unite newsletter thanking her for her return gifts: "Thank you Shelley, for your gift to UNITE—your time, your caring, yourself."

Despite the fact that this type of exchange is described in terms of "paying" or "giving back," in fact, such exchanges do not usually involve reciprocity within a dyad. More typically such gifts move from A to B to C and so on. For example, Tami Leather credits a friend for enabling her to engage in this type of exchange. She thanks a friend for "loving support" and observes, "You have given me the courage to pass on to others the love and support that you have given to me" (Leather 1995). Sue Friedeck, while serving as editor of the SHARE newsletter, tells how helping others can help restore the feeling of efficacy and control that is so challenged by a pregnancy loss. She refers to "A Hindu Proverb [which] says, 'Help they brother's boat across, and lo! thine own has reached the shore'" (Friedeck 1995). While in this proverb the message is that one helps oneself by helping others, that is, that the two things can happen simultaneously, in her next sentence she stresses the more common temporal script of sequential role shifting from helpee to helper. "At first, we may be the ones to be helped. In time, we can help others" (Friedeck 1995). Another female contributor worries about this time lag: "I know one can receive without giving for only so long, but I have not yet had enough energy to return the attention I've received" (Whipple 1995:5).

Hyde (1979) describes such exchanges as a common feature of transformative gifts and notes that spiritual conversions have the same structure.[40] "With gifts that are agents of change . . . passing the gift along is the act of gratitude that finishes the labor." This rhetoric may be a common feature of self-help groups in the United States. For example, in the twelfth step of the Alcoholics Anonymous twelve steps to recovery program, "the gift is passed along" as "recovered alcoholics help other alcoholics" (Hyde 1979:46).

This form of gift giving is especially important for bereaved parents in terms of reasserting their ability to act as able, moral agents. The experience of pregnancy loss creates "children" of the would-be parents to the extent that the experience incapacitates them and this type of gift giving reinstates the normative structure of dependency wherein parents hold the primary role as helpers.[41]

The Qualities of the Gifts

We have examined six gift-giving trajectories involving God, dead babies, bereaved parents, and their social networks. Let us now focus on the gifts themselves. A number of qualities characterize the gifts involved in the gift-giving trajectories discussed above, including preciousness/specialness and durability/inalienability.

By far the most common adjective used to describe these gifts is "precious." The most frequent use of this term is in the context of the child as gift. Take, for example, the summer 1995 issue of the Unite newsletter. The first item is a thought from the director, Janice Heil, on the occasion of the twentieth anniversary of the organization where she asserts, "grief is a natural response to the loss of a loved and cherished person. Our babies are precious beyond words." The next item is a poem describing the stillbirth of twins who the author describes as "the two most precious things in my life" (Hunn 1995). On the following pages appear a piece that ends with the line "I thank you, my precious son"; another written "for my precious boy" (Warren 1995); and a birthday message "to our precious little girl" (Mommy and Daddy 1995).[42]

The term "precious" means "of great price or value; costly, of great desirability, held in high esteem, beloved; dear" (Guralnik 1970b).[43] Like "precious," the adjectives "valuable," "priceless," and "cherished," which are also frequently assigned to these gifts, also highlight the great worth of these gifts/lives and in so doing reverse the social hierarchy of worth normally associated with such deaths.[44]

Although the quality of preciousness is most frequently assigned to the baby, it is also sometimes used to describe the other types of gifts associated with pregnancy loss. In 1987 SHARE reproduced the philosophy of a support group called Precious Parents (a not-for-profit organization of parents offering support to parents who have experienced the death of a baby in Cuyahoga Falls, Ohio), which delineates the many other ways the quality of "preciousness" may be considered applicable to the gifts that result from a pregnancy loss. In addition to asserting the preciousness of their dead babies, they define the relationship they had with the baby and the memories and keepsakes of the baby as "precious." The lessons they learned as a result of the loss (for example, to value life and relationships) are likewise defined as "precious," and of value not only to themselves but to other bereaved parents and professionals as well. They also use the concept of "preciousness" to critique the way the experience of loss is handled in our culture—singling out the lack of "precious recognition" that they deserve as parents, how "precious-little-time" they are given to mourn, and how "people make our baby. . . . less precious by believing babies can be replaced" (Precious Parents 1987).

"Specialness" is another related quality often attributed to the gifts of loss. Like "precious," "special" means "highly regarded" or "valued," but it also stresses the exceptionality of that described. Pregnancy losses are not the statistical norm; most pregnancies that are not voluntarily terminated do result in the live birth of a healthy baby. Even miscarriages, which are relatively common, occur in only about 15 to 20 percent of all pregnancies (if one does not include those losses that take place during the first two weeks after conception), and the second- and third-trimester losses and early infant deaths that feature so prominently in pregnancy loss support group newsletters represent only a tiny minority of pregnancies. As I have discussed elsewhere (Layne 1997b, 1996), the infrequent occurrence of such events combined with a cultural taboo regarding discussion of these deaths leads some members of pregnancy loss support groups to liken themselves or their loss to a "freak of nature." For example, Janis Heil, one of the founders of Unite, tells how following the stillbirth of her daughter she "felt like a freak" (1981); another woman describes the freakish "birth on Halloween night" of her daughter, who had a "deformed face, caused by a condition called Trisomy 13" (Brown 1988) and the "freak snowstorm" that occurred the day of her funeral. According to Fiedler, in our not too distant history, all fetuses were considered freakish—"travesties of the human form even the normal among us are at two, three, or four months after conception" (1978:18). Throughout Europe during the sixteenth and seventeenth centuries the collections of "curiosities of nature" popular among the aristocracy, natural scientists, doctors, lawyers, and educators often included "bottled embryos" (Duden 1991:41) or illustrations of human malformations, including those of miscarried or stillborn fetuses (Hood 1991). What in an earlier era might have been prized as an example of what Francis Bacon called "nature erring[s]" (Hood 1991:3) are now sometimes prized as "my precious baby" especially chosen by God.

Much like mothers of children with disabilities who respond to the cultural devaluation of their children by asserting their specialness (Landsman in press), bereaved parents also use the rhetoric of "specialness" to counter the rhetoric of reproductive failure and to transform a statistical abnormality into something meaningful. The rhetoric of the gift transforms "a mistake" or "random error" into a "special child," "precious gift," "part of a special plan."

In a piece written for her grandson who died during delivery and who is now pictured as "our precious angel up in the sky," Judy Ward of Willington, Colorado, writes, "you are gone from us, we don't know why" but then immediately provides an explanation—the baby was special and was chosen for this reason by God. "You were so perfect in form and face that He took you to His heavenly place. . . . He knew you were a special boy and He needed you to spread His joy" (Ward 1987). Another woman describes how, following the stillbirth of her son, she asked, "God, why my son? Then I remembered, the verse: I go to prepare a place for you. . . . Maybe my son has a special mission or job to attend to. Maybe he is helping in the preparations and getting everything ready for me" (Rodgers 1987).[45]

The notion of "special parent" is also found, though to a lesser extent than that of "special children." The reason that the quality of specialness is not as frequently used to describe bereaved parents may be that unlike their babies, these parents are not in themselves considered gifts. In addition, unlike the foster mothers described by Wozniak (this volume), they do not typically portray themselves as especially gifted parents. And whereas parents of foster children or children with disabilities face the day in/day out problems of caring and providing

LINDA L. LAYNE

for the "special needs" of their children (Wozniak, this volume; Landsman, this volume), parents of children who die at birth or shortly thereafter do not face these special challenges and, in fact, are spared/denied the normal demands of parenting. In fact, the extra needs of foster children and the extended dependency of children with disabilities on their parents contrast sharply with the experience of bereaved parents, whose children no longer need them at all.[46] Nevertheless, as the givers and/or recipients of "special gifts," the parents are sometimes also construed as "special." For example, the "precious parent" group philosophy described above ends with the assertion, "We are precious parents." This quality is derived from their role as both giver and receiver of "precious" gifts.[47] In addition, the typological thinking whereby the specialness of Christ is extended by analogy to the dead babies is sometimes, though much less frequently, found with regards to parents. For example, in a piece entitled "I Was Chosen," Kathy Casey, group leader of a support group, tells of the eleven weeks that she carried her baby, "Jesse."[48] She writes, "It still amazes me how I was chosen—It was as if I was favored, blessed among women to carry him on his brief journey" (Casey 1995).

The other qualities most frequently attributed to the gifts of loss are durability and inalienability, and these qualities speak to an implicit and sometimes explicit contrast between material and spiritual gifts. A number of bereaved parents use the term "lasting" to describe the gifts they received from their babies. For example, Perry-Lynn Moffitt describes her "babies' lasting gift to us" (Moffitt 1991:2); and Andrea D'Asaro concludes her piece "What I Learned from Baby Adam" with the assertion that "This landscape, where the people in my life come first, is my lasting gift from Adam" (D'Asaro 1996). Cathi Lammert wrote in the 1995 holiday issue about her experience during the first holiday season after the loss of their son on December 4. "We didn't get caught up with the hoopla of the season that year because our priorities changed. Perhaps this is the gift we experienced from little Christopher that season. Hold on to the love; this gift no one can take from you" (Lammert 1995). Whereas the embodied baby as gift can and indeed was taken away, these spiritual lessons are lasting and inalienable.

| 194 |

Others describe how their pregnancy loss prompted a revaluation of their preoccupation with worldly goods in favor of things of more enduring value. For instance, in a Christmas poem in which she mourns the fact that she cannot buy gifts for her daughter who died at thirty-three weeks gestation, Kristen Ingle writes, "But I know in my heart you have the best Christmas gift, for you are with Him and no better gift could I give" (Ingle 1981–82). Similarly, in a poem entitled "Chanukah Is Here," a mother describes buying Chanukah gifts for others, and although she mourns the fact that her son is not there to enjoy the pretty Chanukah candles, she casts the fact that she need not buy for him in a positive light: "This year, again, once more, I won't be in a quandary of what to buy. I give you my love . . . for that is eternal" (Kravet 1994). The notion of "true" gifts, after which I title this chapter, also points to the contrast between the glittery seduction of this-worldly consumer goods, which are soon outdated or broken, and the gifts of the world hereafter, which are eternal. Janis Heil, in a piece called "A Gift of Meaning" written for the winter issue of the Unite newsletter, writes, "This is a season of gifts. Too easily it becomes plastic, artificial time of hurried irritation, looking for a gift that will fit, that will be the right color, or that will not break" (Heil 1985–86). She contrasts these superficial preoccupations of the Christmas season with four "realizations" that are "gifts"—"gifts from a child to its parents, and gifts we can, in turn, share with others." They are "(1) that people are important, no matter how small or how short they live, (2) that love exists in ways previously unknown, (3) life is delicate and precious and must be handled with loving care, and (4) as other were there to help us in our need, we want to be there to help others in their need" (Heil 1985–86).

Conclusions: The Paradox of the Gift

I began this chapter with a description of the moral problem that pregnancy loss often poses for individuals in our culture. We have seen how members of pregnancy loss support groups use the rhetoric of the gift to negotiate the double bind of either blaming themselves for the loss or admitting that they were not in control of themselves. Like the classic elegists analyzed by the literary critic W. David Shaw, these popular elegists turn "the wounds [death inflicts] on our conscious- ness. . . . into performances that are self-therapeutic and cathartic" (Shaw 1994:8), and they do so by playing with and elaborating on the paradoxical nature of the gift.[49]

The rhetoric of the gift is a morally laden one, and in the United States, especially when applied to life and death issues, it is colored by a Christian understanding of the gift. Through the use of paradox, the rhetoric of the gift effects a series of transformative reversals, reversals that are intertextually related to the classical paradoxes of New Testa- ment Christianity. As Kermode explains in his literary analysis of the book of Matthew, "the new world is to be a world of paradox. . . . Under this new authority the world is turned upside down." Probably the best known of such paradoxes are those presented in the Beati- tudes in the Sermon on the Mount: blessed are the poor, the mourn- ers, the meek, the persecuted, the reviled (Kermode 1987:391), but the Gospels are teeming with them. Other examples include the para- ble of the laborers in the vineyard told by both Mark and Matthew, "so the last shall be first, and the first last." Another passage from Matthew reads, "But he that is greatest among you shall be your ser- vant. And whosoever shall exalt himself shall be abased; and he that shall humble himself shall be exalted" (Matt 23:11–12, quoted in Booth 1974:237). All these paradoxes lead up to, and are transfig- ured, by the greatest New Testament paradox of all—that death is not what it seems.

As Shaw has observed, paradox has been a key trope in Anglo- American elegies historically. Paradox is defined as a "statement which seems false but is true" (Shaw 1994:2). In the case of pregnancy loss, the principal example is that a "loss" is really a "gain." But as Shaw points out, paradox is a contradiction that "invites a solution," and the way it accomplishes this is by inviting "the thinker to remove the contradiction to [another] plane of consciousness," to cause "the mind to expand" (Shaw 1994:2, 3). The paradoxical nature of the gift permits the "transcendence of the antinomies" by "allow[ing] one term to preserve its identity in a wider context" (Shaw 1994:3). This is what Shaw means by the "'both-and' of a genuine paradox" (Shaw 1994:3). Thus, pregnancy loss can be, and indeed is, frequently understood to be simultaneously a great loss and a source of significant gain. "Paradox" is defined as "a statement contrary to common belief," a statement that seems contradictory but may actually be true (Guralnik 1970a), and members of pregnancy loss support groups, like "the righteous" described by Kermode, "must defy common sense" if they are to find some good in the death of a wished-for child.

From this principal paradox stem other paradoxes. As we have seen, the rhetoric of the gift addresses the problem of control by reasserting parents' agency as givers. When parents construe the death of their baby as a sacrifice to God, or when they describe their newfound wisdom as gifts they have to offer other bereaved parents and the professionals who care for them, they are reinscribing the conventional status hierarchy that privileges givers. But at the same time, in narratives of loss that construe the baby as a gift from God and the purveyor of valuable spiritual lessons for the parents,[50] they are, paradoxically, casting themselves as receivers and doing so in a manner that challenges the moral superiority of giving. In these cases, being the recipient of such gifts is understood as both an indicator of moral worth and a pathway for enhanced spiritual/personal growth.

This paradoxical aspect of gift giving is also found in Christian teachings. Despite the biblical instruction that it is "better to give than to receive," Christianity hinges on the fact that believers must accept Christ's gift of salvation. Christians are fundamentally receivers. It is God the Father who gives his children blessings and peace, and grants eternal life.

This paradoxical status of gift giving is also evident in secular arenas of contemporary capitalist culture. In tribal societies, social status is both marked and made via the exchange of gifts, with status accruing to the giver.[51] But in Anglo-American culture, the status ramifications of gift giving are not so clear. It is well understood that more is better and getting more by means of gifts (e.g., inheritance) remains one of the more morally acceptable routes for acquisition. Furthermore, what one has, one is not morally required to give to others. For instance, as Hayden has observed, the Queen of England very rarely gives anything away.[52] Given the mandate for capital accumulation, the "collections" of rich people, especially if they are men, are often respected and admired (Goldstein 1987).

The rhetoric of the gift also addresses the problem of self-blame, and it does so in a way that does not jeopardize the treasured notion of control. If one understands the baby's birth and death to be a part of a master plan, one is no longer accountable for the event. The loss is still not understood to be a random statistical event, but it is controlled by God rather than the self. Unlike the unemployed male managers and air traffic controllers Newman studied, who fended off the impulse to self-blame with the notion of categorical fate, these bereaved parents are achieving similar results by turning to a form of hyperindividuality via the notion of a special, precious, chosen child.

In sum, narratives of pregnancy loss published in support group newsletters highlight the paradoxical nature of the gift in our consumer culture. They also show how we may marshal poetic forms and paradoxes to help us in moments of anguish and crisis.

Notes

This essay was first delivered on the panel "The Child as Gift: Transformative Mothering in a Consumer Culture" at the American Anthropological Association's annual meeting, Washington, D.C., organized by Layne and Wozniak. In thinking through the use of the rhetoric of the gift in the case of pregnancy loss I have been greatly influenced by Mary Huber's work (1988, 1996, in prep.) on the uses of irony and paradox among missionaries in New Guinea. I thank her for sharing her ideas so generously with me. I am also deeply grateful to Francis Bronet, Susanne Hand, and Gail Landsman for talking me through my own impulses to self-blame and in the process helping me to better define the problem that frames this essay.

Liz Wright at RPI, Roxanne Mountford and her colleagues and students at the University of Arizona, and Alan Nadel from RPI graciously shared their thoughts on rhetoric, irony, and paradox.

1. Feminist critics of obstetrics have sometimes overstated the extent to which obstetrical knowledge and practice cast pregnant women as passive and pregnancy as an involuntary process to which the woman has little to actively contribute. For example, according to Davis-Floyd, the fetus is understood to be "a being separate from its mother . . . [that] can grow and develop without the mother's will or involvement" (1992:58); and Martin depicted the obstet-

rical understanding of women's role during the first stage of labor as "a passive host for the contracting uterus" (1987:61). This is only half the story.

2. Feminist scholars have frequently decried the "commodification of children and the proletarianization of mothers" (Katz Rothman 1989:66). For example, both Martin and Katz Rothman have been concerned not only with the application of the values and images of capitalist production to pregnancy and birth, but also with women's relatively low status "as laborers" in this system. But when the alternative is not to produce, to be outside the realm of production, one can see that the role of producer, even such a lowly one, is a morally more desirable one; for in our system production is understood to be active, willful, and moral.

3. This language of production is not only found in obstetrical discourse (and its feminist critiques), but is also used by women to describe their experience. For example, Peggy Morton, who recently completed a dissertation in Social Welfare on the topic of subsequent children following pregnancy loss, explains that her choice of topic was prompted by her personal experience of suffering from posttraumatic stress syndrome after having a successful but difficult pregnancy following five years of pregnancy losses. Others could not understand why she wasn't finally happy, after having "attain[ed] the goal, producing a child" (1996:xi). She also uses this terminology in her acknowledgments section, where she thanks her therapist, who made it possible for her "to produce both: a child and a dissertation" (1996:ix).

4. Martin (1987) described the way gynecological textbooks portray menstruation in these terms and noted the horror that the "lack of production" evokes in our culture. She cites Winner's (1977) depiction of "the stopping and breakdown of technological systems in modern society" as "the ultimate horror" (quoted in Martin 1987:45). She also quotes a nineteenth-century inventor who understood the world to be a factory that God designed (1987:45). "In this great workshop, human's role is to produce: 'God employs no idlers'" (Ewbank quoted in Martin 1987:46).

See Taussig (1997) for a description of the way Calvinism informs understandings of genetic abnormalities and pregnancy loss in the Netherlands.

5. Sandelowski (1993:32–37) also discusses the Freudian understanding that infertility is caused by "a true lack of desire for children."

6. Similarly, in *Williams Obstetrics* (1956), a "there is nothing to be done" explanation is quickly countered with the prescription of numerous things for would-be mothers to do "for their own good and their babies' benefit," such as "a good schedule of diet, exercise, and rest with limitations of alcohol, tobacco and drugs and [avoidance of] excessive fatigue, insufficient sleep, nervousness, and tension due to overwork or social activities" (Eastman

1956:533). The primary responsibility incumbent on would-be mothers, however, is clearly to trust their doctors and follow their orders.

7. The extent to which physicians and popular books on pregnancy loss feel the need to reassure women that there is nothing they did that could have caused their loss attests to the strength of this problematic tendency to self-blame (cf. Simonds and Katz Rothman 1992). In nearly every interview I have done with women who have had a pregnancy loss, women have spontaneously produced a litany of the culturally defined list of prescribed and prohibited activities, which they scrupulously abided by during their pregnancies. See also Landsman (in press) on this phenomenon among mothers of infants and toddlers with disabilities.

8. Another example can be found in a brochure put out by the birthing center that I went to during my first pregnancy. It begins, "You've nourished a credo of 'yes, I can!'" (Familyborn 1985). The implication is that if one believes in oneself and tries hard enough, just like the little engine that could, one can achieve one's goal, in this case, having a healthy baby and a drug-free labor.

9. Items on the list include doing six types of exercises, drinking eight to ten glasses of water, and avoiding pesticides and stress. It is doubtful that any woman would not find at least some areas in which she could/should have tried harder to achieve excellence. Indeed, the workbook leaves space for the woman to self-criticize and suggest ways for doing better regarding each of the suggested activities (Hathaway et al. 1989:64–65).

10. The worst birth outcome mentioned is Cesarean birth (as opposed to, say, a stillbirth or the birth of a child with disabilities). The authors assure those who must settle for this dreaded outcome that they "should be just as proud of themselves as other couples, since they *worked* just as hard (perhaps harder)" than other couples (Hathaway et al. 1989:61; emphasis added).

11. Even Mother Mary is imagined by one contributor to the Unite newsletter to be vulnerable to self-blame for the untimely death of her son: "She asked if she had done something wrong" (Doherty 1988).

12. I am currently investigating the extent to which pregnancy loss is experienced as a matter of "categorical fate" among members of toxically assaulted communities in the United States (Layne 1997c).

13. Another important resource for both physicians and bereaved parents is an equally spiritually infused idea of "nature" (Layne 1997b).

14. Paradox is in many ways similar to "stable" and "overt" ironies (Booth 1974). Unlike "covert ironies," which require an act of ironic reconstruction (the reader must figure out what the author *really* meant), the ironies of preg-

nancy loss described in support group newsletters "require no special act of reconstitution or translation. They simply assert an irony in things or events that the speaker has observed and wants to share" (Booth 1974:236). See Huber (1996, in prep.) for a discussion of the differences between irony and paradox in the context of missionary experience.

15. Like other pregnancy outcomes, the frequency of pregnancy loss varies dramatically from country to country and appears to be linked to socioeconomic factors (MacFarlane and Mugford 1984:103). In the United Kingdom, regional variations in perinatal and infant mortality "have a broadly similar pattern to regional variations in mortality in adults both of which are statistically associated with measures . . . such as the state of the housing stock and consumption of food, alcohol and tobacco" (MacFarlane and Mugford 1984:113–14).

16. The estimated rate per 1,000 women in the United States in 1991 is 12.9 percent for non-Hispanic white, 21.3 percent for black, and 23.2 percent for Hispanic (Ventura et al. 1995:18).

17. Of 387 personal items from the SHARE newsletters published from 1984 to 1994, women authored 294, girls 1, men 45, boys 2; in 23 cases the gender of the author is unknown. Twenty-two items were signed by both a man and a woman, and it is impossible to know the extent to which the items were in fact coauthored or simply written by one person, presumably the woman, and attributed to both. In addition, these issues contained 31 professional advice articles.

Of 372 personal items published in the Unite newsletter between 1981 and 1993, 330 were written by women, 7 by girls, 11 by men, 3 by boys; 12 were coauthored, and 9 authors were unknown. Forty-nine professional articles also appeared.

18. Shelley Cocke describes her experience of attending Unite support group meetings:

> We didn't talk that much about God during our meetings, except to say we felt angry or betrayed by the cruelty of our loss. I believe the group leaders brought a spirituality to the meetings that was probably unintentional. It is irrelevant that they are Christians and I am Jewish. They preached, and I use that word purposefully, that we should join our souls in grief and find comfort in each other's caring. We should forgive ourselves for our human imperfections and for our powerlessness to prevent the loss of our children. (Cocke 1986)

19. See Layne (1997a) for a fuller discussion of this.

20. "True gift" also has a legal definition in the United States: a gift for which a tax deduction may be taken. An important aspect of this definition, as

made clear in the case of the dialysis center discussed by Fox and Swazey, is that the gifts need not be returned, even if, for instance, they were designated for a specific patient and the patient dies before the funds are used up (1974:234).

21. His nephew was born at thirty-three weeks gestation and died one day later. The cause of death was oxygen deficiency from placenta abruption.

22. This poem also appears in the September–October 1985 issue of the SHARE newsletter as "Understanding," "author unknown," and in the December 1989 Unite newsletter as "God's Lent Child," "author unknown."

Some women also bargain with God for their children—"If you only give me a child (or let my next baby live) I'll . . ." For example, in a piece entitled "My Second Pregnancy," Kelly Gonzalez (1988) tells of how she "prayed and begged God to let me become pregnant" after the stillbirth of her daughter at twenty-two weeks gestation. When she became pregnant she felt she should not ask for more, for example, help with labor. "During 16 hours of labor I refused to ask God for any help. To show Him that I could do this, no matter how bad it was. It all paid off."

23. This child died due to a rare genetic disease after living for twenty-one months. Most losses mourned at pregnancy loss support groups involve babies who, if they lived at all after birth, survived only a matter of days.

24. See Harding's (1987, 1992) account of the way an evangelical preacher used New Testament resources to enact the story of his accidental killing of his son. I have not found similar use of the Old Testament story of Abraham, who proves his devotion to God by his willingness to sacrifice his son. Hyde discusses the Old Testament Scriptures regarding the sacrifice of first fruits, including the firstborn son. "In the pentateuch the first fruits always belong to the Lord. The Lord gives the tribe its wealth, and the germ of that wealth is then given back to the Lord" (Hyde 1979:19). Miller offers a possible explanation for this in that Jewish religion turned away from human sacrifice and used a symbolic substitution in place of Isaac, whereas Christianity distinguished itself from Judaism by the actual sacrifice of the son (1998:115–16).

Also see Miller's (1998) discussion of theories of sacrifice and how they relate to shopping as transcendent giving.

25. I am indebted to Mary Huber (1996) for this reference.

26. Sometimes Christ's sacrifice appears without the analogy between Christ and their child being made. For example, an anonymous woman explains that God's sacrifice of Jesus provided comfort for her. Because "He gave his son's life," both she and her deceased son were assured salvation (Anonymous 1995).

In this case, self-blame prevents the author from construing her loss as a gift to God. In the first stanza she construes herself as the agent in the conception, in the second, as agent of the wrongful death of her child "because I didn't take care of myself." In the third and final stanza she and her son are receivers of salvation (thanks to God's sacrifice) despite their status as sinners.

27. The notion of the baby as specially chosen sometimes appears without a direct analogy between Christ and the baby. For example, in a piece written the day his daughter was stillborn Michael Stagoski writes, God "said to her, 'I have chosen you little one to share My kingdom and be part of My Special Flock" (1995). He goes on to explain, "I have chosen you for a reason. You will be your family's guardian angel." Another author writes of "Souls so perfect that God up above called them back home" (Phillips 1995).

28. She also attributes to Mary doubt as to whether she will be reunited with her son in heaven and acknowledges that, even if she were certain, that would not negate the fact that she was deprived of his company in the present. "She wanted to believe in heaven, another existence with her son. But she knew that time would come later. And she wanted Him to be with her now" (Doherty 1988).

29. One woman who lost twins reassures herself that she can bear the pain: "But God never gives out an impossible sacrifice" (Clancy 1995). This is a variation on the saying that "God never gives burdens greater than one can bear," but in this case what God is giving is the obligation to give (cf. Landsman, this volume).

30. She develops the theme that it doesn't matter if the items taken "are imperfect to some eyes . . . or incomplete" (Kozak 1987). Because they were theirs, they are loved and cannot be replaced.

31. Another example is found in a 1995 SHARE issue where the editors printed a piece they planned to use at their upcoming "day of remembrance." One of the refrains is "Let us treasure the gifts you left us as you have etched your mark on our hearts."

32. The wonders of nature, like rainbows, have long been understood as reflections of God's glory. In the Judeo-Christian tradition, rainbows are further understood to be a special sign from God, his covenant never again to flood the earth. Here the dead child has replaced God as the giver of rainbows.

33. In one case, a mother imagines her child as giver within a heavenly family instead. In a poem entitled "Miscarried Joy" Teresa Page (1986) of Rockford, Illinois, whose baby "Sammy D. Page" was miscarried at ten and a half weeks gestation, wonders "What gifts and talents do you share in heaven, with God's family there?"

34. Rabinowitz (1983) likens her children born after a loss to a "sweepstakes prize": unlikely, unexpected, unearned, based solely on chance.

35. She also lists a number of less tangible gifts: "Why am I so grateful to you? For making me appreciate more than ever the good in people—the giving, caring, comforting, and sharing. For forcing me to *really* feel—sorrow, hurt, anger, and love. For teaching me the immeasurable value of life, the importance of health, the beauty of true friendship, and the priceless gift of love" (Holper 1991a).

36. The substitution of the child for God as giver of children is part of the move toward the sacralization of children (Zelizer 1985). I have described elsewhere how dead babies sometimes replace God as an immanence in nature (Layne 1997b, forthcoming). This fits with Miller's observation that God was replaced first by husbands and more recently by children as the object of devotion (1998, 1997).

37. Cindy Lee Foster of Venice, Florida, whose baby girl was born on Christmas Eve and died the day after Christmas due to meconium pneumonia and hyaline membrane disease, wrote, "You were with me for the holiday. A gift I'll always love" (Foster 1985).

38. It is unclear from these pieces written about Mother's Day and Father's Day the extent to which this notion is meant to apply to and/or is embraced by women who have first-trimester losses.

39. She ends, "I treasure the lessons of love and caring, listening and sharing, that I received from the members of the group."

40. According to Hyde, "the Word is received, the soul suffers a change (or is released or born again), and the convert feels moved to testify, to give the Word away again. . . . The transformation is not accomplished until we have the power to give the gift on our own terms" (Hyde 1979:46–47).

41. See Layne (1999a, forthcoming) on the unequal flow of material gifts between generations.

42. This little girl died seven days after her birth.

43. I use *Webster's* instead of the *Oxford English Dictionary* as it is likely to reflect popular American understanding of the term more accurately.

44. These qualities are also sometimes used to describe subsequent children. For example, Jean Schwabe (1984) of Kansas City, Missouri, writes of her son Nathan, who was born after a loss, "he is truly a 'gift given of God' which is the meaning of his name. We have found through this waiting time that the gift is more valuable, more priceless and cherished when one has waited for God's perfect timing."

45. This woman uses a Christian paradox to reverse the view that it is better to live than to die. In this poem heaven is portrayed as the more desirable

place to be. Therefore her son is lucky and those remaining in this world are to be pitied. "Through my soul searching I have come to believe: we live in a fallen world, and pain and suffering from this fallen world touches our lives. It doesn't seem fair, but nothing will until we reach Heaven" (Rodgers 1987).

46. Many narratives of loss include a list of missed opportunities to care for their babies. Such lists often include the less desirable child-rearing tasks like caring for a sick child or night feedings. In an unusual piece by Sarai Rodgers of Lake Charles, Louisiana, written a year after the stillbirth of her son she construes these missed moments as a gift. "I was never hurt by my child's rebellion, was never embarrassed by my child's actions, and I never had to discipline him. This was a gift only God could give" (Rodgers 1987). She gave this as her personal testimony in her church on the one-year anniversary of her son's stillbirth due to renal vein thrombosis (Rodgers 1987).

47. In the Whittier poem we learn that the parents were chosen because they were gifted teachers. "I cannot promise you she will stay since all from Earth return; But there are lessons taught down there I want this child to learn. I've looked the wide world over. In search of teachers true, And from the throngs that crowd life's land I have selected you" (Whittier 1995–96). This is more in keeping with the "special parents" notion described by Landsman. It is the only such instance I have found in the pregnancy loss support group newsletters.

48. This piece was read at the dedication of the Littlest Angels Memorial in Baton Rouge, Louisiana.

49. I am indebted to Mary Huber for this reference.

50. This also applies, though to a lesser extent, when bereaved parents define acknowledgment of their loss by others as a valuable gift.

51. See Layne (1994) for a discussion of gift giving as a hierarchical identity-making practice in the Hashemite Kingdom of Jordan.

52. See also Carrier (1993:65) on year-end giving in England where historically gifts flowed from subordinates to their superiors.

References Cited

Allen, Marie, and Shelly Marks
1993   Miscarriage: Women Sharing from the Heart. New York: John Wiley.

Alvarado, Uncle Rick
1995   My Little Angel. SHARE Newsletter 4(6):11.

Amendolara, Phyllis
1997   Marissa's Story. Unite Notes 15(3):1.

LINDA L. LAYNE

Anonymous (M. for Mommy)
1995   Because. Unite Notes 14(4):5.

Aries, Philippe
1974   Western Attitudes toward Death from the Middle Ages to the Present. Baltimore: Johns Hopkins University Press.

Atwood, Richard
1990   Finding the Way. SHARE Newsletter 13(5):1.

Balshem, Martha
1993   Cancer in the Community: Class and Medical Authority. Washington, D.C.: Smithsonian Institution Press.

Bongaarts, John, and Robert G. Potter
1983   Fertility, Biology, and Behavior: An Analysis of the Proximate Determinants. New York: Academic Press.

Booth, Wayne C.
1974   A Rhetoric of Irony. Chicago: University of Chicago Press.

Bourne, Gordon, M.D., and David N. Danforth, M.D.
1975   Pregnancy. New York: Harper and Row.

Brown, Dotti
1988   Photographs of a Funeral. Unite Notes 7(4):1.

Brunner, Donna L.
1992   Me? Guilty? Unite Notes 11(2):3.

Burton, Karen
1996   On Being a Mother This Mother's Day. SHARE Newsletter 5(3):10.

Campbell, Hannah
1993   Going Back and Giving Back to Group Meetings. Unite Notes 11(4):3.

Cantrell, Keith
1987   To Justin. SHARE Newsletter 10(6):1.

Carrier, James
1993   The Rituals of Christmas Giving. *In* Unwrapping Christmas. Daniel Miller, ed. Pp. 55–74. Oxford: Clarendon.

Casey, Kathy
1995   I Was Chosen. SHARE Newsletter 4(4):6.

Clancy, Lisa A.
1995   Angels Always Come Early. Unite Notes 14(1):6.

Cocke, Shelley
1986   Closure. Unite Notes 6(1):5.

Cohen, Marion
1981a   Bereavement and Growth. Unite Notes 1(1):2.
1981b   Funeral Poem #1. Unite Notes 1(1):1.

D'Asaro, Andrea
1996   What I Learned from Baby Adam. Unite Notes 15(2):3.

Davis-Floyd, Robbie E.
1992   Birth as an American Rite of Passage. Berkeley: University of California Press.

Doherty, Mary Cushing
1988   At the Foot of the Cross. Unite Notes 7(3):1.

Duden, Barbara
1991   The Woman beneath the Skin: A Doctor's Patients in Eighteenth-Century Germany. Trans. Thomas Dunlop. Cambridge: Harvard University Press.

Dunham, Charles
1986   From Ray with Love. SHARE Newsletter 9(4):1.

Eastman, Nicholson J.
1956   Williams Obstetrics. Eleventh edition. New York: D. Appleton-Century-Crofts.

Erling, Susan
1984   Just 10 Weeks. SHARE Newsletter 7(2):1.

Familyborn
1985   Familyborn . . . An Idea Whose Time Has Come. Brochure.

Fiedler, Leslie A.
1978   Freaks: Myths and Images of the Secret Self. New York: Simon and Schuster.

Foster, Cindy Lee
1985   Christmas Angel. SHARE Newsletter 8(6):1.

Fox, Renee C., and Judith P. Swazey
1974   The Courage to Fail: A Social View of Organ Transplants and Dialysis. Chicago: University of Chicago Press.

Friedeck, Sue
1995   Milestone or Millstone. SHARE Newsletter 4(5):5.

Fuchs, John
1987   Our Littlest Angel. SHARE Newsletter 10(3):1.

Gana, Kathleen Rosso
1985   As the Wounds Heal. Unite Notes 5(1):2–3.
1998   Sleep in Heavenly Peace. Unite Notes 16(3):7.

Ginsburg, Faye D.
1989   Contested Lives: The Abortion Debate in an American Community.
Berkeley: University of California Press.

Goffman, Erving
1963   Stigma. New York: Simon and Schuster.

Goldstein, Judith L.
1987   Lifestyles of the Rich and Tyrannical. American Scholar, spring, pp.
235–47.

Gonzalez, Kelly
1988   My Second Pregnancy. Unite Notes 7(4):7–8.
1996   Am I Really a Parent? SHARE Newsletter 5(3):11. Reprinted from
Pikes Peak SHARE Newsletter (1995) 3(5).

Guralnik, David B., editor in chief
1970a   Paradox. *In* Webster's New World Dictionary of the American Language. P. 1029. New York: World Publishing Company.
1970b   Precious. *In* Webster's New World Dictionary of the American Language. P. 1120. New York: World Publishing Company.

Habercorn, Jennifer
1996   Two More Angels. SHARE Newsletter 5(3):2.

Harding, Susan
1987   Convicted by the Holy Spirit: The Rhetoric of Fundamental Baptist
Conversion. American Ethnologist 14(1):167–81.
1992   The Afterlife of Stories: Genesis of a Man of God. *In* Storied Lives:
The Cultural Politics of Self-Understanding. George Rosenwald and Richard Ochberg, eds. Pp. 60–75. New Haven: Yale University Press.

Hathaway, Marjie, Jay Hathaway, Susan Hathaway Bek, and James Hathaway, eds.
1989   The Bradley Method Student Workbook. Sherman Oaks, CA: American Academy of Husband-Coached Childbirth.

Heil, Janice
1981   Jessica. Unite Notes 1(1):5.
1982–83   Your Gift to Me. Unite Notes 2(2):2.
1985–86   A Gift of Meaning. Unite Notes 5(2):3.

Hein, Debbie
1984   A Special Dad. Unite Notes 3(4):1–2.

Herr, Ron
1984   A Letter to My Son. SHARE Newsletter 7(3):2.

Hintz, Cathy, R.N.
1988   Rainbows. Unite Notes 7(3):3.

Holper, Laurie
1991a   Marni. Unite Notes 10(4):5.
1991b   Josh. Unite Notes 10(4):3.

Hood Museum of Art
1991   The Age of the Marvelous. Exhibition catalog. Dartmouth College.

Huber, Mary
1988   The Bishop's Progress: A Historical Ethnography of Catholic Missionary Experience on the Sepik Frontier. Washington, D.C.: Smithsonian Institution Press.
1996   Irony and Paradox among Catholic Missionaries in Colonial Papua New Guinea. Paper presented at the annual meeting of the American Anthropological Association, San Francisco.
In prep.   Irony and Paradox in the "Contact Zone": Missionary Discourse in Northern New Guinea. *In* Irony, Practice, and the Moral Imagination. James Fernandez and Mary Taylor Huber, eds. Manuscript under review.

Hunn, Cindy
1995   Forever Gone. Unite Notes 14(1):1.

Hyde, Lewis
1979   The Gift: Imagination and the Erotic Life of Property. New York: Random House.

Ingle, Kristen
1981–82   For Elizabeth at Christmas. Unite Notes 1(2):1.

1982–83   Christmas Thoughts. Unite Notes 2(2):1, reprinted in SHARE Newsletter (1987) 10(6):1.

Katz Rothman, Barbara
1989   Recreating Motherhood: Ideology and Technology in a Patriarchal Society. New York: Norton.

Kermode, Frank
1987   Matthew. *In* The Literary Guide to the Bible. Robert Alter and Frank Kermode, eds. Pp. 387–401. Cambridge: Harvard University Press.

Kevin
1985–86   A Baby's Gift. Unite Notes 5(2):6.

Kozak, Jody
1987   Stillbirth in Winter. SHARE Newsletter 10(4):3.

Kravet, Ginette
1994   Chanukah is Here. SHARE 3(6):7.

Lamb, Sister Jane Marie
1986   A New Year's Message from Sister Jane Marie. SHARE Newsletter 9(1):4.

Lammert, Cathi A.
1995   Dear Friends. SHARE Newsletter 4(6):3.
1996   Letter from the Editor. SHARE Newsletter 5(3):3.

Landsman, Gail
1998   Reconstructing Motherhood in the Age of "Perfect" Babies: Mothers of Infants and Toddlers with Disabilities. Signs 24(1):69–99.
in press   "Real" Motherhood, Class, and Children with Disabilities. *In* Ideologies and Technologies of Motherhood. Helena Ragoné and France Winddance Twine, eds. New York: Routledge.

Layne, Linda L.
1992   Of Fetuses and Angels: Fragmentation and Integration in Narratives of Pregnancy Loss. Knowledge and Society. Hess and Layne, eds. 9:29–58.
1994   Home and Homeland: The Dialogics of Tribal and National Identities in Jordan. Princeton: Princeton University Press.
1996   "Never Such Innocence Again": Irony, Nature and Technoscience in Narratives of Pregnancy Loss. *In* Comparative Studies in Pregnancy Loss. Rosanne Cecil, ed. Oxford: Berg.

1997a   Breaking the Silence: An Agenda for a Feminist Discourse of Pregnancy Loss. Invited submission to a special issue of Feminist Studies
23(2):289–315.

1997b   Mother Nature/Freaks of Nature. Paper presented at the electronic
conference "Cultures and Environments: On Cultural Environmental
Studies," Washington State University American Studies Web site.

1997c   "In Search of Community": Tales of Pregnancy Loss in Three Toxi-
cally-Assaulted Communities in the U.S. Paper presented at the annual
meeting of the Society for Social Studies of Science, Tucson.

1999   "I Remember the Day I Shopped for Your Layette": Goods, Fetuses
and Feminism in the Context of Pregnancy Loss. *In* The Fetal Impera-
tive/Feminist Practices. Lynn Morgan and Meridith Michaels, eds. Pp.
251–78. Philadelphia: University of Pennsylvania Press.

forthcoming   Motherhood Lost: The Cultural Construction of Pregnancy
Loss in the United States. New York: Routledge.

in press a   Fertility, Gender, and Healing: Contributions toward a Comparative Anthropology of Reproduction. Reviews in Anthropology 28:33–52.

in press b   "He Was a Real Baby with Baby Things": A Material Culture
Analysis of Personhood, Parenthood and Pregnancy Loss. *In* Ideologies
and Technologies of Motherhood. Heléna Ragoné and France Winddance
Twine, eds. New York: Routledge.

Leather, Tami
1995   A Loving Support. Unite Notes 14(1):7.

MacFarlane, Alison, and Miranda Mugford
1984   Birth Counts: Statistics of Pregnancy and Childbirth. National Perinatal Epidemiology Unit (in collaboration with Office of Population Cen-
suses and Surveys). London: Her Majesty's Stationery Office.

Martin, Bonita
1995   I'm Still a Mother. Unite Notes 14(1):2. Reprinted in SHARE
Newsletter (1996) 5(3):8.

Martin, Emily
1987   The Woman in the Body: A Cultural Analysis of Reproduction. Boston: Beacon Press.

1994   Flexible Bodies: Tracking Immunity in American Culture From the
Days of Polio to the Age of AIDS. Boston: Beacon Press.

McCann, Linda
1985   A Love Letter to My Baby Girl. Unite Notes 4(4):7.

McCann, Pat
1984   Growth through Pain. Unite Notes 3(3):5.

Miller, Daniel
1997   How Infants Grow Mothers in North London. Theory, Culture & Society 14(4):67–88.
1998   A Theory of Shopping. Ithaca: Cornell University Press.

Moffitt, Perry-Lynn
1991   Miscarriage: The Most Silent of Sorrows. SHARE Newsletter 3(7):1.

Mommy and Daddy
1995   Happy 2nd Birthday Sherri Maria Porter. Unite Notes 14(1):3.

Morton, Peggy A.
1996   Perinatal Loss and the Replacement Child: The Emotional Limits of Reproductive Technology. Unpublished dissertation, Social Welfare, City University of New York.

Nagele, David F.
1986   For Jonathan. Unite Notes 6(1):3.

Narayan, Uma
1995   The "Gift" of a Child: Commercial Surrogacy, Gift Surrogacy, and Motherhood. *In* Expecting Trouble: Surrogacy, Fetal Abuse and New Reproductive Technologies. Patricia Boling, ed. Pp. 177–20. Boulder: Westview.

Newman, Katherine S.
1988   Falling from Grace: The Experience of Downward Mobility in the American Middle Class. New York: Random House.

Page, Teresa
1986   Miscarried Joy. SHARE Newsletter 9(3):4.

Phillips, Laura
1995   Angel Children. SHARE Newsletter 4(3):7.

Precious Parents
1987   Precious Parents Philosophy. SHARE Newsletter 10(6):2.

Rabinowitz, Linda
1983   One Mother's Feelings on Subsequent Pregnancy. Unite Notes 3(1):4.

Rodgers, Sarai
1987   A Letter to SHARE. SHARE Newsletter 10(2):4.

Sandelowski, Margarete
1993   With Child in Mind: Studies of the Personal Encounter with Infertility. Philadelphia: University of Pennsylvania Press.

Sariego, Lauren
1996   They Never Forget. Unite Notes 14(4):2.

Schroedel, Jean Reith, and Paul Peretz
1995   A Gender Analysis of Policy Formation: The Case of Fetal Abuse. *In*
Expecting Trouble: Surrogacy, Fetal Abuse & New Reproductive Technologies. Patricia Boling, ed. Pp. 85–198. Boulder: Westview.

Schwabe, Jean
1984   Joyful Subsequent Child. SHARE Newsletter 7(5):3.

Shaw, W. David
1994   Elegy and Paradox: Testing the Conventions. Baltimore: Johns Hopkins University Press.

Shute, Patricia
1988   Six Days. Unite Notes 7(3):5.

Simonds, Wendy, and Barbara Katz Rothman
1992   Centuries of Solace: Expressions of Maternal Grief in Popular Literature. Philadelphia: Temple University Press.

Stagoski, Michael
1995   Open Arms. SHARE Newsletter 4(3):7.

Strozzieri, Gia Kathleen
1996   My Little Girl. Unite Notes 15(2):1.

Taussig, Karen-Sue
1997   Calvinism and Chromosomes: Religion, the Geographical Imaginary,
and Medical Genetics in the Netherlands. Science as Culture
6(4):495–524.

Ventura, Stephanie J., et al.
1995   Trends in Pregnancies and Pregnancy Rates: Estimates for the United
States, 1980–92. Monthly Vital Statistics Report 43(11) May 25. Centers
for Disease Control and Prevention/National Center for Health Statistics.

Ward, Judy
1987   Our Angel. SHARE Newsletter 10(6):2.

Warren, Bambina
1995   Peace. Unite Notes 14(1):3.

Whipple, D. Loren
1995   Please Understand: A Letter to Friends. Unite Notes 14(1):5. Reprinted with permission from Bereavement Magazine June 1993.

Whittier, John Greenleaf
1995–96   God's Promise. Unite Notes 14(3):7.

Widell, Diana
1995   Holiday Greetings. SHARE Newsletter 4(6):4.

Winner, Langdon
1977   Autonomous Technology: Technics Out of Control as a Theme in Political Thought. Cambridge: MIT Press.

Yoder, Pam
1985   Untitled. SHARE Newsletter 8(2):1.

Zelizer, Viviana A.
1985   Pricing the Priceless Child: The Changing Social Value of Children. New York: Basic Books.

CONTRIBUTORS

GAIL LANDSMAN is an associate professor of anthropology at the State University of New York at Albany. In addition to *Sovereignty and Symbol: Indian-White Conflict at Ganienkeh*, she has published research on images of Indians in the woman suffrage movement; efforts to pass family and medical leave legislation; and issues of disability, nurturance, and reproduction. Her recent article "Reconstructing Motherhood in the Age of 'Perfect' Babies" appeared in *Signs* (1998). She edits a newsletter for parents of children who receive early intervention services, and serves on the New York State Early Intervention Coordinating Council Parent Involvement Committee. She is currently writing a book based on her three-year research project on mothers of infants and young children with disabilities.

LINDA L. LAYNE is Hale Professor in the Department of Science and Technology Studies at Rensselaer Polytechnic Institute in Troy, New York. She is the author of *Home and Homeland: The Dialogics of Tribal and National Identities in Jordan* and *Motherhood Lost: The Cultural Construction of Pregnancy Loss in the United States* and the editor of two collections on anthropological approaches in science and technology studies. Her current research projects focus on the experience of pregnancy loss in toxically assaulted communities and the medicalization of pregnancy loss.

JUDITH S. MODELL is a professor of anthropology, history, and art at Carnegie Mellon University, where she has been teaching since 1984. Her publications include *Ruth Benedict, Kinship with Strangers,* and *A Town without Steel: Views of Change in Homestead,* as well as numerous articles exploring the significance of adoption, foster care, and child placement in the United States. Her current research includes a study of open adoption and work on aspects of American family policy as these impinge upon Hawaiian-Polynesian families in the state of Hawaii. A monograph on American adoption policy and its implications for kinship is in its final stages. Her ongoing research interests are in kinship, family, and the links between interpretations of those concepts and the policies imposed by national and state institutions.

HELÉNA RAGONÉ is the author of *Surrogate Motherhood: Conception in the Heart,* the first ethnographic study of surrogate motherhood. In this work she documents the experiences of surrogate mothers, commissioning couples, and surrogate mother program staff. She is also the coeditor of three collections—*Situated Lives: Gender and Culture in Everyday Life, Reproducing Reproduction: Kinship, Power, and Technological Innovation,* and *Ideologies and Technologies of Motherhood: Race, Class, Sexuality and Nationalism.* She is currently completing *Distant Kin: Gestational Surrogacy and Gamete Donation* and *Riding Danger: Women in Horse Culture.*

RAYNA RAPP teaches in the Department of Anthropology, New School for Social Research, where she chairs the Master's Program in Gender Studies and Feminist Theory. She is the editor of *Toward an Anthropology of Women* and coeditor of *Promissory Notes: Women in the Transition to Socialism, Articulating Hidden Histories,* and *Conceiving the New World Order: The Global Politics of Reproduction.* Her book *Testing Women, Testing the Fetus: the Social Impact of Amniocentesis in the USA* analyzes the cultural meaning of prenatal diagnosis in the United States.

DANIELLE F. WOZNIAK is an assistant professor at Western Michigan University with joint appointments to the social work and anthropology departments. Dr. Wozniak explores the subject of foster mothering in greater depth in a forthcoming book entitled *They Are All My Children: Foster Mothering in America.* She is currently working (with Janelle Taylor and Linda Layne) on an edited collection on motherhood in a consumer culture and is planning a research project with elderly women in the West Indies on their family identities in the context of dramatic economic and demographic change.

INDEX

Rituals of giving, 5, 8, 21. *See also*
  Chanukah; Christmas; Easter; Father's
  Day; Mother's Day; Thanksgiving
Rousseau, xii
Rubin, Gayle, xii

Sacrifice, xii, 8, 18, 20n. 19, 104, 108,
  202nn. 24, 26; self, 49, 71, 90, 104,
  126n. 6, 169, 171, 181–84, 187, 197.
  See also Altruism
Sandelowski, Margarete, 11, 171, 199
Schmidt, Leigh Eric, 5, 6, 19n. 11,
  20n. 19
Schneider, David, xvi, 72–73
Schrift, Alan D., 2, 17n. 2
Schroedel, Jen Reith, and Paul Peretz,
  171
Scott, Russell, 55, 56
Search movement, 32–34
Self improvement, xiii, 3–4, 134, 136,
  143–45, 150–58, 169, 184–91, 194,
  196, 204nn. 35, 39, 40
Selfishness, 30, 41, 42, 50, 171
Self-sufficiency, 149. *See also* Indepen-
  dence
Sharing, 6–7, 36, 57, 79, 186, 204nn.
  35, 39
Shaw, W. David, 196
Shopping, xvii, 2, 3, 5, 8, 55, 102, 110,
  126n. 6, 167, 168, 194–95
Simmel, Georg, 71
Social solidarity, xi–xviii, 12, 13, 29–61,
  71, 147; vs. kinship, 57; kinship as,
  99; support groups as mechanism for,
  xiv, 31
Social workers, xvii, xiv, 31, 33, 35, 45,
  48, 56, 103, 106, 115, 116, 127n. 12
Special: children, xiii, 14, 92, 97, 99,
  104–9, 133–59, 192–94, 203n. 27;
  gifts, 192–94; needs, 10, 97–99, 104,
  106, 107, 109, 141–46, 193; parents,
  xiii, 14, 21n. 28, 104–9, 133–59,
  193–94, 205n. 47; plan, God's, 193,
  203n. 27

Sperm donation, 8, 67, 70, 77
Spoiled identity, 11, 135, 176, 149, 162n.
  15. *See also* Personhood, diminished;
  Stigma
Stack, Carol, 126
State, the, xvi–xvii, 14, 56, 57, 90–93,
  107, 111–21
Stigma, 38, 45
Stillbirth. *See* Pregnancy loss
Strathern, Marilyn, 2, 4, 8, 17n. 3, 72,
  124; and Sarah Franklin, 73
Success, 55, 92, 101, 109, 135, 150, 169;
  rates of IVF, 76; of search movement,
  32–34
Support groups, xiv, 31, 146, 176–79, 190
Surrender, 49, 55, 62n. 12
Surrogate motherhood, xv, 1, 3, 8, 9–12,
  45, 65–88, 91, 112–13, 123, 147, 168
Swartz, Barry, 71–72

Taussig, Karen-Sue, 199
Taylor, Janelle, 2
Technology: belief in, 82, 141–42, 146,
  174. *See also* New reproductive tech-
  nologies
Thanksgiving, 7
Thank-you notes, 45, 62n. 10. *See also*
  Gratitude
Titmuss, Richard, 3, 56, 83n. 1
Tocqueville, xii
Tronto, Joan, 149

Ultrasound, 139

Victims, 49, 68

Weiner, Annette B., 2
Weiss, Meira, 161n. 12
Women's health movement, 141, 172–73
Wozniak, Danielle, xvii, 2, 3, 5, 6, 10, 11,
  12, 13, 21, 22, 30, 51, 73, 161n. 11,
  168, 192, 194

Zelizer, Viviana, 69, 101, 123